INDUS WATER TREATY

Conflict between India and Pakistan

INDUS WATER TREATY
Conflict between India and Pakistan

Col. C.R. Vashishth (Retd.)

GAURAV Book Centre
Private Limited

Publisher
GAURAV BOOK CENTRE PVT LTD
4832/24,Prahlad Lane,S-207 Ansari
Road, Daryaganj, Delhi-110002
Ph.: 43570976, 23278261
Email: gauravbookcentre@gmail.com

Edition: 2026

ISBN: 978-93-83316-52-6

Laser Typesetting
JEE-VEE Graphics # 09911902109

Price: 1295/-

Printed
Neeta Press, Delhi

Preface

In India, competition for water has a history of provoking conflict between communities. In Pakistan, water shortages have triggered food and energy crises that ignited riots and protests in some cities. Most troubling, Islamabad's diversions of water to upstream communities with ties to the government are inflaming sectarian loyalties and stoking unrest in the lower downstream region of Sindh.

Some growth models predict that by 2025, India's population will grow to triple what it was—and Pakistan's population to six times what it was—when the Indus treaty was signed. Lurking in the background are fears that climate change is speeding up the melting of the glaciers that feed the river.

The treaty has been widely hailed as a success, having survived three post-independence wars between the hostile nuclear neighbors. But its resilience is increasingly being tested by challenges thrown up by the 21st century. For one, Pakistan is on the brink of water scarcity. Its once-lush agricultural fields, which employ half of all Pakistanis and account for a quarter of its GDP, are now frequently parched. This predicament, experts say, is attributable in large part to the country's haphazard water management policies, unproductive agricultural practices, dilapidated infrastructure and grossly inadequate water storage facilities. Climate change, too, has begun to have an impact. A recent Dutch study found that by 2050, shrinking glaciers are predicted to reduce the flows of the Indus by 8%. But in Pakistan, which is deeply distrustful of its larger and more powerful neighbor, the country's crippling water shortage is seen as a direct result of India's upstream dams and water projects.

The book will be very helpful for the researchers, veterinarians, students and persons involved in this subject.

—Author

Contents

1

Introduction

The Indus Waters Treaty is a water-sharing treaty between India and Pakistan, brokered by the World Bank (then the International Bank for Reconstruction and Development). The treaty was signed in Karachi on September 19, 1960 by Indian Prime Minister Jawaharlal Nehru and President of Pakistan Ayub Khan. The treaty was a result of Pakistani fear that since the source rivers of the Indus basin were in India, it could potentially create droughts and famines in Pakistan, especially at times of war. However, India did not revoke the treaty during any of three later Indo-Pakistani Wars. Since the ratification of the treaty in 1960, India and Pakistan have not engaged in any water wars. Disagreements and disputes have been settled via legal procedures, provided for within the framework of the treaty. The treaty is considered to be one of the most successful watersharing endeavours in the world today even though analysts acknowledge the need to update certain technical specifications and expand the scope of the document to include climate change.

Provisions

The Indus System of Rivers comprises three western rivers the Indus, the Jhelum and Chenab and three eastern rivers - the Sutlej, the Beas and the Ravi. The treaty, envisages the sharing of waters of the rivers Ravi, Beas, Sutlej, Jhelum and Chenab which join the Indus River on its left bank (eastern side) in Pakistan. According to this treaty, Ravi, Beas and Sutlej, which constitute the eastern rivers, are allocated for exclusive use by

India before they enter Pakistan. However, a transition period of 10 years was permitted in which India was bound to supply water to Pakistan from these rivers until Pakistan was able to build the canal system for utilization of waters of Jhelum, Chenab and the Indus itself, allocated to it under the treaty. Similarly, Pakistan has exclusive use of the western rivers Jhelum, Chenab and Indus but with some stipulations for development of projects on these rivers in India. Pakistan also received one-time financial compensation for the loss of water from the eastern rivers. Since March 31, 1970, after the 10-year moratorium, India has secured full rights for use of the waters of the three rivers allocated to it. The treaty resulted in partitioning of the rivers rather than sharing of their waters.

The countries agree to exchange data and co-operate in matters related to the treaty. For this purpose, treaty creates the Permanent Indus Commission, with a commissioner appointed by each country.

HISTORY AND BACKGROUND

The waters of the Indus basin begin in Tibet and the Himalayan mountains in the state of Jammu and Kashmir. They flow from the hills through the arid states of Punjab and Sindh, converging in Pakistan and emptying into the Arabian Sea south of Karachi. Where once there was only a narrow strip of irrigated land along these rivers, developments over the last century have created a large network of canals and storage facilities that provide water for more than 26 million acres (110,000 km^2) - the largest irrigated area of any one river system in the world.

The partition of British India created a conflict over the plentiful waters of the Indus basin. The newly formed states were at odds over how to share and manage what was essentially a cohesive and unitary network of irrigation. Furthermore, the geography of partition was such that the source rivers of the Indus basin were in India. Pakistan felt its livelihood threatened by the prospect of Indian control over the tributaries that fed water into the Pakistani portion of the basin. Where India certainly had its own ambitions for the profitable development of the basin, Pakistan felt acutely threatened by a conflict over the main source of water for its cultivable land.

During the first years of partition the waters of the Indus were apportioned by the Inter-Dominion Accord of May 4, 1948. This accord required India to release sufficient waters to the Pakistani regions of the basin in return for annual payments from the government of Pakistan. The accord was meant to meet immediate requirements and was followed by negotiations for a more permanent solution. Neither side, however, was willing to compromise their respective positions and negotiations reached a stalemate. From the Indian point of view, there was nothing that Pakistan could do to prevent India from any of the schemes to divert the flow of water in the rivers. Pakistan's position was dismal and India could do whatever it wanted. Pakistan wanted to take the matter to the International Court of Justice but India refused, arguing that the conflict required a bilateral resolution.

WORLD BANK INVOLVEMENT

In this same year, David Lilienthal, formerly the chairman of the Tennessee Valley Authority and of the U.S. Atomic Energy Commission, visited the region to write a series of articles for Colliers magazine. Lilienthal had a keen interest in the subcontinent and was welcomed by the highest levels of both Indian and Pakistani governments. Although his visit was sponsored by Colliers, Lilienthal was briefed by state department and executive branch officials, who hoped that Lilienthal could help bridge the gap between India and Pakistan and also gauge hostilities on the subcontinent. During the course of his visit, it became clear to Lilienthal that tensions between India and Pakistan were acute, but also unable to be erased with one sweeping gesture. In his journal he wrote:

"India and Pakistan were on the verge of war over Kashmir. There seemed to be no possibility of negotiating this issue until tensions abated. One way to reduce hostility... would be to concentrate on other important issues where cooperation was possible. Progress in these areas would promote a sense of community between the two nations which might, in time, lead to a Kashmir settlement. Accordingly, I

proposed that India and Pakistan work out a program jointly to develop and jointly to operate the Indus Basin river system, upon which both nations were dependent for irrigation water. With new dams and irrigation canals, the Indus and its tributaries could be made to yield the additional water each country needed for increased food production. In the article I had suggested that the World Bank might use its good offices to bring the parties to agreement, and help in the financing of an Indus Development program. "

Lilienthal's idea was well received by officials at the World Bank, and, subsequently, by the Indian and Pakistani governments. Eugene R. Black, then president of the World Bank told Lilienthal that his proposal "makes good sense all round". Black wrote that the Bank was interested in the economic progress of the two countries and had been concerned that the Indus dispute could only be a serious handicap to this development. India's previous objections to third party arbitration were remedied by the Bank's insistence that it would not adjudicate the conflict, but, instead, work as a conduit for agreement.

Black also made a distinction between the "functional" and "political" aspects of the Indus dispute. In his correspondence with Indian and Pakistan leaders, Black asserted that the Indus dispute could most realistically be solved if the functional aspects of disagreement were negotiated apart from political considerations. He envisioned a group that tackled the question of how best to utilize the waters of the Indus Basin - leaving aside questions of historic rights or allocations.

Black proposed a Working Party made up of Indian, Pakistani and World Bank engineers. The World Bank delegation would act as a consultative group, charged with offering suggestions and speeding dialogue. In his opening statement to the Working Party, Black spoke of why he was optimistic about the group's success:

One aspect of Mr. Lilienthal's proposal appealed to me from the first. I mean his insistence that the Indus problem is an engineering problem and should be dealt with by engineers. One of the strengths of the engineering profession is that, all over the world, engineers speak the same language and approach problems with common standards of judgment. Black's hopes for a quick resolution to the Indus dispute were premature. While the Bank had expected that the two sides would come to an agreement on the allocation of waters, neither India nor Pakistan seemed willing to compromise their positions. While Pakistan insisted on its historical right to waters of all the Indus tributaries, and that half of West Punjab was under threat of desertification the Indian side argued that the previous distribution of waters should not set future allocation. Instead, the Indian side set up a new basis of distribution, with the waters of the Western tributaries going to Pakistan and the Eastern tributaries to India. The substantive technical discussions that Black had hoped for were stymied by the political considerations he had expected to avoid.

The World Bank soon became frustrated with this lack of progress. What had originally been envisioned as a technical dispute that would quickly untangle itself became an intractable mess. India and Pakistan were unable to agree on the technical aspects of allocation, let alone the implementation of any agreed upon distribution of waters. Finally, in 1954, after nearly two years of negotiation, the World bank offered its own proposal, stepping beyond the limited role it had apportioned for itself and forcing the two sides to consider concrete plans for the future of the basin. The proposal offered India the three eastern tributaries of the basin and Pakistan the three western tributaries. Canals and storage dams were to be constructed to divert waters from the western rivers and replace the eastern river supply lost by Pakistan.

While the Indian side was amenable to the World Bank proposal, Pakistan found it unacceptable. The World Bank allocated the eastern rivers to India and the western rivers to Pakistan. This new distribution did not account for the historical usage of the Indus basin, or the fact that West Punjab's Eastern districts could turn into desert, and repudiated Pakistan's negotiating position. Where India had stood for a new system of allocation, Pakistan felt that its share of waters should be based on pre-partition distribution. The World Bank proposal was more in line with the Indian plan and this angered the

Pakistani delegation. They threatened to withdraw from the Working Party and negotiations verged on collapse.

But neither side could afford the dissolution of talks. The Pakistani press met rumors of an end to negotiation with talk of increased hostilities; the government was ill-prepared to forego talks for a violent conflict with India and was forced to reconsider its position.

India was also eager to settle the Indus issue; large development projects were put on hold by negotiations and Indian leaders were eager to divert water for irrigation.

In December 1954, the two sides returned to the negotiating table. The World Bank proposal was transformed from a basis of settlement to a basis for negotiation and the talks continued, stop and go, for the next six years.

One of the last stumbling blocks to an agreement concerned financing for the construction of canals and storage facilities that would transfer water from the western rivers to Pakistan. This transfer was necessary to make up for the water Pakistan was giving up by ceding its rights to the eastern rivers. The World Bank initially planned for India to pay for these works, but India refused. The Bank responded with a plan for external financing supplied mainly by the United States and the United Kingdom. This solution cleared the remaining stumbling blocks to agreement and the Treaty was signed by the Prime Ministers of both countries in 1960.

TREATY PROVISIONS

The agreement set up a commission to adjudicate any future disputes arising over the allocation of waters. The Permanent Indus Commission has survived three wars and provides an ongoing mechanism for consultation and conflict resolution through inspection, exchange of data and visits. The Commission is required to meet regularly to discuss potential disputes as well as cooperative arrangements for the development of the basin. Either party must notify the other of plans to construct any engineering works which would affect the other party and to provide data about such works. In cases of disagreement, a neutral expert is called in for mediation and arbitration. While neither side has initiated projects that could cause the kind of conflict that the Commission was created to resolve, the annual inspections and exchange of data continue, unperturbed by tensions on the subcontinent.

BACKGROUND

Irrigation in the Indus River basin dates back centuries; by the late 1940s the irrigation works along the river were the most extensive in the world. These irrigation projects had been developed over the years under one political authority, that of British India, and any water conflict could be resolved by executive order. The Government of India Act of 1935, however, put water under provincial jurisdiction, and some disputes did begin to crop up at the sites of the more-extensive works, notably between the provinces of Punjab and Sind.

In 1942, a judicial commission was appointed by the British government to study Sind's concern over planned Punjabi development. The Commission recognized the claims of Sind, and called for the integrated management of the basin as a whole. The Commission's report was found unacceptable by both sides, and the chief engineers of the two sides met informally between 1943 and 1945 to try to reconcile their differences. Although a draft agreement was produced, neither of the two provinces accepted the terms and the dispute was referred to London for a final decision in 1947.

Before a decision could be reached, however, the Indian Independence Act of August 15, 1947 internationalized the dispute between the new states of India and Pakistan. Partition was to be carried out in 73 days, and the full implications of dividing the Indus basin seem not to have been fully considered, although Sir Cyril Radcliffe, who was responsible for the boundary delineation, did express his hope that, "some joint control and management of the irrigation system may be found". Heightened political tensions, population displacements, and unresolved territorial issues, all served to exacerbate hostilities over the water dispute.

As the monsoon flows receded in the fall of 1947, the chief engineers of Pakistan and India met and agreed to a "Standstill Agreement," which froze water allocations at two points on the river until March 31, 1948, allowing discharges from headworks in India to continue to flow into Pakistan.

On April 1, 1948, the day that the "Standstill Agreement" expired, in the absence of a new agreement, India discontinued the delivery of water to the Dipalpur Canal and the main branches of the Upper Bari Daab Canal. Several motives have been suggested for India's actions. The first is legalistic-that of an upper riparian establishing its sovereign water rights. Others include an Indian maneuver to pressure Pakistan on the volatile Kashmir issue, to demonstrate Pakistan 's dependence on India in the hope of forcing reconciliation, or to retaliate against a Pakistani levy of an export duty on raw jute leaving East Bengal. Another interpretation is that the action was taken by the provincial government of East Punjab, without the approval of the central government.

THE PROBLEM

Even before the partition of India and Pakistan, the Indus posed problems between the states of British India. The problem became international only after partition, though, and the attendant increased hostility and lack of supra-legal authority only exacerbated the issue. Pakistani territory, which had relied on Indus water for centuries, now found the water sources originating in another country, one with whom geopolitical relations were increasing in hostility.

The question over the flow of the Indus is a classic case of the conflicting claims of up- and down-stream riparians. The conflict can be exemplified in the terms for the resumption of water delivery to Pakistan from the Indian headworks, worked out at an Inter-Dominican conference held in Delhi on 3-4 May 1948. India agreed to the resumption of flow, but maintained that Pakistan could not claim any share of those waters as a matter of right. This position was reinforced by the Indian claim that, since Pakistan had agreed to pay for water under the Standstill

Agreement of 1947, Pakistan had recognized India 's water rights. Pakistan countered that they had the rights of prior appropriation, and that payments to India were only to cover operation and maintenance costs.

While these conflicting claims were not resolved, an agreement was signed, later referred to as the Delhi Agreement, in which India assured Pakistan that India would not withdraw water delivery without allowing time for Pakistan to develop alternate sources. Pakistan later expressed its displeasure with the agreement in a note dated 16 June 1949, calling for the "equitable apportionment of all common waters," and suggesting turning jurisdiction of the case over to the World Court. India suggested rather that a commission of judges from each side try to resolve their differences before turning the problem over to a third party. This stalemate lasted through 1950.

ATTEMPTS AT CONFLICT MANAGEMENT

In 1951, Indian Prime Minister Nehru, whose interest in integrated river management along the lines of the Tennessee Valley Authority had been piqued, invited David Lilienthal, former chairman of the TVA, to visit India. Lilienthal also visited Pakistan and, on his return to the US, wrote an article outlining his impressions and recommendations (the trip had been commissioned by Collier's Magazine-international water was not the initial aim of the visit). These included steps from the psychological-a call to allay Pakistani suspicions of Indian intentions for the Indus headwaters, to the practical-a proposal for greater storage facilities and cooperative management. Lilienthal also suggests that international FINANCING be arranged, perhaps by the World Bank, to fund the workings and findings of an "Indus Engineering Corporation," to include representatives from both states, as well as from the World Bank.

The article was read by Lilienthal's friend, David Black, president of the World Bank, who contacted Lilienthal for recommendations on helping to resolve the dispute. As a result, Black contacted the prime ministers of Pakistan and India, inviting both countries to accept the Bank's good offices. In a subsequent letter, Black outlined "essential principles" that might be followed for conflict resolution. These principles included the following: that water resources of the Indus basin should be managed cooperatively; and that problems of the basin should be solved on a functional and not on a political plane, without relation to past negotiations and past claims. Black suggested that India and Pakistan each appoint a senior engineer to work on a plan for development of the Indus basin. A Bank engineer would be made available as an ongoing consultant.

Both sides accepted Black's initiative. The first meeting of the Working Party included Indian and Pakistani engineers, along with a team from the Bank, as envisioned by Black, and met for the first time in Washington in May 1952. The stated agenda was to prepare an outline for a program, including a list of possible technical measures to increase the available supplies of Indus water for economic development. After three weeks of discussions, an outline was agreed to, whose points included

- determination of total water supplies, divided by catchment and use;
- determination of the water requirements of cultivable irrigable areas in each country;
- calculation of data and surveys necessary, as requested by either side;
- preparation of cost estimates and a construction schedule of new engineering works which might be included in a comprehensive plan.

In a creative avoidance of a potential and common conflict, the parties agreed that any data requested by either side would be collected and verified when possible, but that the acceptance of the data, or the inclusion of any topic for study, would not commit either side to its "relevance or materiality."

When the two sides were unable to agree on a common development plan for the basin in subsequent meetings in Karachi, November 1952, and Delhi, January 1953, the Bank suggested that each side submit its own plan. Both sides did submit plans on October 6, 1953, each of which mostly agreed on the supplies available for irrigation, but varied extremely on how these supplies should be allocated. The Indian proposal allocated 29 million acre-feet (MAF) per year to India and 90 MAF to Pakistan, totaling 119 MAF (MAF = 1233.48 million cubic meters; since all negotiations were in English units, that is what is reported here). The Pakistani proposal, in contrast, allocated India 15.5 MAF and Pakistan 102.5 MAF, for a total of 118 MAF.

The two sides were persuaded to adjust somewhat their initial proposals, but the modified proposals of each side still left too much difference to overcome. The modified Indian plan called for all of the eastern rivers (Ravi, Beas, and Sutlej) and 7% of the western rivers (Indus, Jhelum and Chenab) to be allocated to India, while Pakistan would be allocated the remainder, or 93% of the western rivers. The modified Pakistani plan called for 30% of the eastern rivers to be allocated to India, while 70% of the eastern rivers and all of the western rivers would go to Pakistan.

The Bank concluded that not only was the stalemate likely to continue, but that the ideal goal of integrated watershed development for the benefit of both riparians was probably too elusive a goal at this stage of political relations. On February 5, 1954, the Bank issued its own proposal, abandoning the strategy of integrated development in favor of one of separation. The Bank proposal called for the entire flow of the eastern rivers to be allocated to India, and all of the western rivers, with the exception of a small amount from the Jhelum, to be allocated to Pakistan. According to the proposal, the two sides would agree to a transition period while Pakistan would complete link canals dividing the watershed, during which India would continue to allow Pakistan's historic use to continue to flow from the eastern rivers.

The Bank proposal was given to both parties simultaneously. On March 25, 1954, India accepted the proposal as the basis for agreement. Pakistan viewed the proposal with more trepidation, and gave only qualified acceptance on July 28, 1954; they considered the flow of the western rivers to be insufficient to replace their existing supplies from the eastern rivers, particularly given limited available storage capacity. To help facilitate an agreement, the Bank issued an aide memoir, calling for more storage on the western rivers, and suggesting India 's financial liability for "replacement facilities"-increased storage facilities and enlarged link canals in Pakistan which could be recognized as the cost replacement of pre-partition canals.

Little progress was made until representatives from the two countries met in May 1958. Main points in contention included whether the main replacement storage facility ought to be on the Jhelum or Indus rivers-Pakistan preferred the latter but the Bank argued that the former was more cost-effective; and what the total cost of new development would be and who would pay for it-India's position was that it would only pay for "replacement" and not "development" facilities.

In 1958, Pakistan proposed a plan including two major storage facilities: one each on the Jhelum and the Indus; three smaller dams on both tributaries; and expanded link canals. India, objecting both to the extent and the cost of the Pakistani proposal, approximately $1.12 billion, proposed an alternative plan which was smaller in scale, but which Pakistan rejected because it necessitated continued reliance on Indian water deliveries.

By 1959, the Bank evaluated the principal issue to be resolved as follows: which works would be considered "replacement" and which "development," in other words, for which works would India be financially responsible. To circumvent the question, Black suggested an alternative approach in a visit to India and Pakistan in May. Perhaps one might settle on a specific amount for which India is responsible, rather than arguing over individual works.

The Bank might then help raise additional funds among the international community development for watershed development. India was offered help with construction of its Beas Dam, and Pakistan 's plan, including both the proposed dams would be looked at favourably. With these conditions, both sides agreed to a fixed payment settlement, and to a ten-year transition period during which India would continue to provide Pakistan 's historic flows to continue.

In August 1959, Black organized a consortium of donors to support development in the Indus basin, which raised close to $900 million, in addition to India 's commitment of $174 million. The Indus Water Treaty was signed in Karachi on September 19, 1960 and government ratifications were exchanged in Delhi in January 1961.

Outcome

The Indus Water Treaty addressed both the technical and financial concerns of each side, and included a timeline for transition. The main points of the treaty included :

- an agreement that Pakistan would receive unrestricted use of the western rivers, which India would allow to flow unimpeded, with minor exceptions
- provisions for three dams, eight link canals, three barrages, and 2500 tube wells to be built in Pakistan
- a ten-year transition period, from April 1, 1960 to March 31, 1970, during which water would continue to be supplied to Pakistan according to a detailed schedule
- a schedule for India to provide its fixed financial contribution of $62 million, in ten annual installments during the transition period
- additional provisions for data exchange and future cooperation

The treaty also established the Permanent Indus Commission, made up of one Commissioner of Indus Waters from each country. The two Commissioners would meet annually in order to establish and promote cooperative arrangements for the treaty implementation; promote cooperation between the Parties in the development of the waters of the Indus system; examine and resolve by agreement any question that may arise between the Parties concerning interpretation or implementation of the Treaty; submit an annual report to the two governments.

In case of a dispute, provisions were made to appoint a "neutral expert." If the neutral expert fails to resolve the dispute, negotiators can be appointed by each side to meet with one or more mutually agreed-upon mediators. If either side (or the mediator) views mediated agreement as unlikely, provisions are included for the convening of a Court of Arbitration. In addition, the treaty calls for either party, if it undertakes any engineering works on any of the tributaries, to notify the other of its plans and to provide any data which may be requested.

Since 1960, no projects have been submitted under the provisions for "future cooperation," nor have any issues of water quality been submitted at all. Other disputes have arisen, and been handled in a variety of ways. The first issues arose from Indian non-delivery of some waters during 1965-66, but became instead a question of procedure and the legality of commission decisions. Negotiators resolved that each commissioner acted as government representatives and that their decisions were legally binding.

One controversy surrounding the design and construction of the Salal Dam was resolved through bilateral negotiations between the two governments. Other disputes, over new hydroelectric projects and the Wuller Barrage on the Jhelum tributary and the Baglihar dam on the Chenab River in Kashmir, have yet to be resolved.

Shifting political boundaries can turn intra-national disputes into international conflicts, exacerbating tensions over existing issues. Shifting borders and partition exacerbated what was, initially, an intra-national Indian issue. After partition, political tensions, particularly over Kashmir territory, contributed to tensions of this newly international conflict.

Power inequities may delay the pace of negotiations. Power inequities may have delayed pace of negotiations. India had both a superior riparian position, as well as a relatively stronger central government, than Pakistan. The combination may have acted as disincentive to reach agreement.

Positive, active, and continuous involvement of a third party is vital in helping to overcome conflict. The active participation of Eugene Black and the World Bank were crucial to the success of the Indus Water Treaty. The Bank offered not only their good offices, but a strong leadership role as well. The Bank provided support staff, funding, and, perhaps most important, its own proposals when negotiations reached a stalemate.

· *Coming to the table with financial assistance can provide sufficient incentive for a breakthrough in agreement.* The Bank helped raise almost $900 million from the international community, allowing for Pakistan 's final objections to be addressed.

Some points may be agreed to more quickly, if it is explicitly agreed that a precedent is not being set. In the 1948 agreement, Pakistan agreed to pay India for water deliveries. This point was later used by India to argue that, by paying for the water, Pakistan recognized India 's water rights. Pakistan, in contrast, argued that they were paying only for operation and maintenance. In an early meeting, both sides agreed that any data may be used *without* committing either side to its "relevance or materiality," thereby precluding delays over data discrepancies.

Sensitivity to each party's particular hydrologic concerns is crucial in determining the bargaining mix. Early negotiations focused on quantity allocations, while one of Pakistan 's main concerns was storage-the timing of the delivery was seen to be as crucial as the amount.

In particularly hot conflicts, when political concerns override, a sub-optimal solution may be the best one can achieve. The plan pointedly disregards the principle of integrated water management, recognizing that between these particular riparians, the most important issue was control by each state of its own resource. Structural division of the basin, while crucial for political reasons, effectively precludes the possibility of increased integrated management.

CREATIVE OUTCOMES RESULTING FROM RESOLUTION PROCESS

In a creative avoidance of a potential and common conflict, the parties agreed that any data requested by either side would be collected and verified when possible, but that the acceptance of the data, or the inclusion of any topic for study, would not commit either side to its "relevance or materiality."

Water was separated out from other contentious issues between India and Pakistan. This allowed negotiations to continue, even in light of tensions over other topics. Water problems were to be viewed as "functional" rather than political.

When both sides were unable to agree on a common development plan in 1953, the Bank suggested that each prepare its own plan, which the Bank would then inspect for commonalities. This active strategy to breaking impasses is currently being attempted with the riparians of the Jordan River watershed in conjunction with the multilateral working group on water.

Timeline

Pre-1935: British India has authority to resolve interstate water conflicts by executive order.

1935: Government of India Act makes water a subject of provincial jurisdiction, unless asked to intervene by states.

Oct 1939: Province of Sind formally requests Governor-General to review new Punjabi irrigation project and potential detriment to Sind

Sep 1941: Indus Commission established.

July 1942: Commission submits its report suggesting that withdrawals by Punjab would cause "material injury" to inundation canals in Sind, particularly during the month of September. Incidentally called for management of the river system as a whole. Report found unacceptable to both sides.

1943-5: Chief engineers of both states meet informally, finally producing a draft agreement-provinces refuse to sign. Dispute referred to secretary of state for India in London early 1947.

15 Aug 1947: Independent states of India and Pakistan established. Eastern Punjab becomes part of India, western Punjab and Sind become part of Pakistan. Conflict becomes international, British role now irrelevant. Chair of Punjab Boundary Commission suggests that Punjab water system be run as joint venture-declined by both sides.

10 Dec 1947: "Standstill Agreement" negotiated by chief engineers of west and east Punjab, freezing allocations at two points until 31 Mar 1948.

1 Apr 1948: Without new agreement, India discontinues delivery of water to Dipalpur Canal and main branches of Upper Bari Daab Canal.

30 Apr 1948: India resumes water delivery as negotiations undertaken.

3-4 May 1948: Inter-Dominion conference, and an agreement is signed. India assures Pakistan that India will not withdraw water delivery without allowing time for Pakistan to develop alternate sources. Other issues remain unresolved.

16 June 1949: Pakistan sends a note to India expressing displeasure with agreement. The note calls for a conference to resolve the "equitable apportionment of all common waters," and suggesting giving the World Court jurisdiction on the application of either party. India objects to third party involvement, suggests judges from each side might narrow dispute first. Stalemate results through 1950.

1951: David Lilienthal, past chairman of the Tennessee Valley Authority, invited to India as Prime Minister Nehru's guest. He later publishes an article with his suggestions, which captures the attention of Eugene Black, president of the World Bank.

Aug 1951: Aug 1951

Jan-Feb 1952: Meetings continue, Black finds "common understanding," at least that neither side will diminish supplies for existing uses.

May 1952: First meeting of working party in Washington of engineers from India, Pakistan, and Bank engineers. Agreement to: determine future supply and demand; calculate available and desired data; prepare cost estimates and construction schedule of necessary infrastructure.

Nov 1952 & Jan 1953: Meetings continue in Karachi and Delhi without agreement. Bank suggests each side submit its own plan.

6 Oct 1953: Plans submitted with proposed allocations and sources for each state. Agreement on available supplies, not on allocations.

5 Feb 1954: Bank puts forth own proposal, essentially suggesting dividing the western tributaries to Pakistan, and the eastern tributaries to India. The proposal also provided for continued deliveries to Pakistan during transition period.

25 Mar 1954: India accepts proposal. Pakistan is less enthusiastic-it would have to replace existing facilities.

28 July 1954: Pakistan delivers a qualified acceptance of proposal.

21 May 1956: Bank Aide Memoire suggests that replacement facilities be FINANCED by India.

May- Nov 1958: Disagreements over which storage facilities are "replacement," for which India would pay, and which are "development" for which Pakistan would be responsible.

May 1959: Black visits India and Pakistan. Suggests that India 's share be a fixed cost, rather than by facility, and that the Bank would arrange for additional FINANCING. India agrees, and accepts a 10-year transition period.

Sep 1960: Bank arranges an international Indus Basin Development Fund Agreement. Raises $893.5 million.

19 Sep 1960: Indus Water Treaty signed in Karachi. Provisions call for an Indian and Pakistani engineer to constitute the Permanent Indus Commission, which will meet at least once a year to: establish and promote cooperative arrangements.

29 Jul 2004: Talks about the Wuller barrage and Baglihar dam begin in Lahore. Pakistan indicates that it might seek World Bank arbitration if the matter is not sorted out through bilateral talks.

WATER CONFLICTS AND HYDROELECTRICITY IN SOUTH ASIA

Water and Power Nexus

Hydroelectricity is the prevalent most economic source of

white energy. There is little chance of inventing a genius innovatory energy source anytime soon that will not engage nations to water conflicts to produce electric power. Hydroelectricity is derived from gravitational force (potential energy) of the flowing or falling waters. A hydropower house may take the form of a run-of-river (flowing) or dam (falling). Hydroelectric power plants use water turbines instead of water wheel. The Water turbine has a swirling component for force to pass on kinetic energy to spinning rotor.

French engineer, Bernard Forest de Belidor, conceived the idea of water power in the 1770s. Different types of turbines such as Francis (1849), Pelton (1879) and Kaplan (1913) are considered suitable for10-350, 50-1300 and 2-40m heads whereas waterwheels are used for 0.2-4m falls. Typical capacities of pico, micro, small, medium and large dams are <5 kW, 5 to 100 kW, 100 to 10 MW, 10 to 10,000 MW and >10 GW. There only three large dams worldwide namely Three Gorges Dam (22.5 GW), Itaipu Dam (14 GW) and Guri Dam (10.2 GW). Global small scale hydropower capacity is 85 GW out of which 65 GW in China, 3.5 GW in Japan, 3 GW in USA and 2 GW in India. Norway, Brazil, Venezuela, Canada, and Sweden produce 98.25, 85.56, 67.17, 61.12 and 44.34% of their national power demands by hydro power plants. Hydropower is considered the cleanest white energy.

The World's first DC hydropower house, Cragside in Northumberland, was operated in England (UK) in 1878. Thomas Edison invented the first long life incandescent lamp in 1879 before which carbon filament based short lived lamps were available. The first US Niagara hydropower station started delivering DC electricity in 1881.

Nicolas Tesla invented the first three phase AC generator used in the Niagara Falls hydro station. Most European countries got hydropower stations from 1880 to 1890 simultaneously. The British brought this technology to India in the early 1900s. The Water and Power Development Authority (WAPDA) was established in Pakistan in 1959.

The British government had already developed large barrages and canals systems for irrigation. WAPDA engineers constructed

1000 MW Mangla dam in 1867, 3500 MW Tarbella dam in 1976 and 2000 run-of-river Chashma power house in 2004. World's largest hydropower producers are China, Canada, USA, Brazil, Russia, India, Norway and Japan which have total installed capacities of 196.79, 88.974, 79.511, 69.08, 45.00, 33.60, 27.528 and 27.229GW. Famous Chinese three gorges dam since 1994 produces 22,500 MW electricity and proposed Congo Grand Inga dam will produce 39,000 MW by 2014.

A 50,000 MW dam is under proposal on the Red Sea. China's installed hydropower capacity is more than the total combined hydropower capacities of USA, Canada and Japan. Chinese hydropower generation capacity is about six times more than that of India and 33 times more than Pakistan's hydropower generation.

India's hydropower generation capacity is about 5-6 times more than Pakistan's, yet it is building dozens of dams on rivers which were given to Pakistan under the Indus Water Treaty in 1960. India had 300 dams in 1947. This number increased to 4000 by 2000. About 70% of new dams were built during the 1971-1989 period.

TRANSBOUNDARY RIVERS CONFLICTS

In view of widespread water scarcity, due to climate change, it is time to fine tune the clauses of international rivers sharing laws. The United Nations adopted existing European and US agreements in light of Helsinki rules in 1997 as an international water law which has failed to protect downstream "riparian rights" (Pakistan) when the "upstream riparian" country (India) started building multiple dams on the Indus, Jhelum and Chenab without permission.

World Bank Vice president, Ismail Serageldin, said in 1995 that the next century wars would be fought over water and not over oil.

If there has not been any exclusive war on waters in past that does not mean it can not be in future. European countries share 4 river basins under 175 treaties, 4-5 African countries share 12 river basins under 34 treaties, 4-5 Asian countries share 5 river basins under 31 treaties. There are 48 joint river commissions in Europe, 23 in the Americas, 10 in Africa and 9 in Asia. European and American states had disagreements over water quality in Rhine and Colorado rivers but African, Middle East and Asian countries have water quantity disputes on Zambezi, Mekong, Nile, Euphrates, Tigris, Indus and Ganges. We love or hate each other we have to share the water, air and sun. Oil and water do not mix but can entangle to develop water, watts and war trinity. Some social scientists are covertly producing amphoteric solutions of oil and water in blood geopolitically.

Upper riparian India has started diverting and holding off shared rivers waters under its innovatory dam policies which is starving lower riparian Pakistan.

India has embarked on diverting western rivers waters through connecting canals from Jehlum to Chenab through an 80km long tunnel, Chenab to Ravi through the Marhu tunnel, interconnection of Beas to Sutlej and Sutlej to the Ganges through a proposed express link canal which is in blatant violation of the Indus Water Teaty.

IPCC experts believe that global warming caused the August 2010 flash flood in Pakistan which affected 20-25 million people. Climate change experts speculate that under rapidly rising global warming, water distribution conflicts could potentially lead to armed conflicts among nations in future. Transboundary river conflicts include water shortages as well as geopolitical issues.

Water conflict between Pakistan and India is building up due to the fast melting of the glaciers. Middle Eastern countries take water availability as a strategic weapon. Palestinians per capita water consumption is 60 liters per day in the West Bank whereas Israelis use 330 liters per day (5 times more).

Fair water distribution is one of the key issues in Israel-Palestinian agreement today. Arab-Israel conflict is getting aggravated by water conflicts. Israel is also trying to secure access to Nile, Euphrates and Ceyhan in Turkey. Global research observers blame Israel for stealing Arab waters. People have been occupying waters since antiquity but the water flows today and they have gone the same is going to happen with present and future generations.

Historic wrecks are often the source of conflict as well as consensus. Transboundary water conflicts cannot be resolved using game theory geopolitics bearing undercurrents. Fair rules must be developed by United Nations in the name of International Rivers Water Sharing Laws. Shared river waters conflicts are both of the inter and intra state types that require global laws to safeguard lower riparian. Without UN backed water laws, the long held agreements may break leading to political confrontations.

Water distribution experts have already proposed several models that facilitate the UN to formulate transboundary water sharing and conflict resolution laws. Mass migrations and water conflicts intensification has been noted in Tanzania since last one decade and Pakistan during August 2010 floods. The developed countries sustain dilemmas in developing countries that lead to talent migration causing serious blows to economies of developing countries.

The Water situation is getting worse in the USA and China. It is extremely critical in Brazil, and in India and Pakistan where the underground water table is falling at rate of 3-5cm per year.

India is building several dozen dams and diversion canals on shared rivers; Indian hydro tactics have caused droughts and flash floods horrors in Pakistan. India is constructing 24-25 dams on river Chenab that feeds to central Punjab housing 90-100 million people.

India relates it to her growing power needs but Pakistan takes it aqua bomb capable of causing droughts and flash floods. The Recent flash flood due to monsoons rains and timed injection of Indian dam waters has inflicted 25000 lives, 1-2 billion crops and 5-7 billion property losses.

The United Nations have no global law on transboundary water distribution. Due to natural scarcity of freshwaters, concerned experts have long been warning of water wars.

European and Americans water agreements under Helsinki Rules and the International Law Commission Convention on Law of the Non-Navigational Uses of International Water courses have been universalized for global water treaties which have no consensus across the board. Despite 2 dams on Beas, 4 on Sutlej, 6 on Ravi, 7 on Indus, 8 on Jhelum and 24 on Chenab India assumes full right on all six rivers falling down to Pakistan and blames colonial period water laws creating schism that locks the water sector into a developmental catharsis.

In response to a satellite research on ground water depletion in Punjab reporting underground water table declining rate of 3-5cm/yr, an Indian water expert tried to justify multiple dams policy on western Pakistani rivers as a sensible measure to mitigate their water depletion crisis. Pakistan, being downstream riparian, supports Radha's demand for international legislature on transboundary water sharing laws to avoid water conflicts but does not support Saumitra's innovatory policy to steal others waters to solve own problems. Pakistan proposes United Nations to frame laws governing distribution of international river waters including construction of dams in high hazards seismic areas. In view of multiple river basins shared by two or more countries it has become imperative to formulate global river water distribution laws acceptable to upper and lower riparian, déjà vu, water fracas and frays might escalate to dismal water wars in forthcoming decades. Several water experts have pointed out Indian ingenuity based maneuvers to hoodwink lower riparian.

BREACH OF INDUS WATER TREATY

India and Pakistan used to share the River Indus and its five contributories Jhelum, Chenab, Ravi, Beas and Sutlej under British rule. The Pakistani areas had no dam to store water, therefore 80% of the water from six rivers would eventually fall into the Arabian Sea. When water conflicts started intensifying after the division of British India in 1948, the World Bank's President Eugene Black acted in an arbitration procedure between Pakistan and India which resulted in 1960 in the Indus Water Treaty. Under this agreement three eastern rivers Ravi, Beas and Sutlej were given to India and three western rivers the Indus, Chenab and Jhelum were given to Pakistan. It was "water division" rather than 'water sharing". Pakistan also agreed to allow India to use some of western rivers' waters for local agriculture around rivers in India and produce run-of-river style hydroelectricity provided tyhe water flow did not fall below 55,000 cusecs at Marala and other interface barrages that went below 20,000 in 2009.

The Indus Water Treaty worked well up to the 1980s before the Indian Government decided to build dams in Shiwaliks (Himalchal, Punjab, Jammu & Kashmir) on the western rivers. Geotechnical studies were carried out in Ballowal, Takarla and Karoan areas from 1984 to 1995. Generally pre-monsoon, monsoon and post-monsoon rain fall in Kashmir valley (Handwara) used to be 305, 161.8 and 89mm from 1903 to 1982 which increased to 1117 to 1249mm in 1990s that prompted India to go for multiple dams on western rivers without seeking permission of lower river riparian.

Building dams on active faults in Zone-V was in violation of the Indus Water Treaty.

The Indian Government conducted several more studies on geotechnical and hydrological parameters for the design of small earth filled dams in the 1990s.

Initially, the small dams construction experience using local expertise led to micro-earthquakes around Thien Dam in Himalayas in 1980s which forced them to seek international assistance on dams. Feasibility studies on 400 MW Hasti Dul (400 MW) and other dams were carried out in Kashmir valley and the adjacent provinces of Himachal and Punjab in the 1990s.

Uri-I (240 MW) dam on river Jhelum and Nathpa (1650 MW) dam on river Sutlej were carried out to test geological and geotechnical responses which hardly complied. If the Indian dams were to fail for technical reasons or as a result of earthquakes the people who would suffer would be Kashmiri or Pakistanis.

Building tens of dams without consulting lower riparian renders the Indus Water Treaty virtually defunct. Under the

Indus Treaty of 1960, India is supposed to inform at least six months before launching any hydropower project. India did not comply in this regard.

India has several dam projects including water diversion tunnels and canals. India had allocated RS.33 billion for the 330 MW Krishanganga project and Rs. 18 billion for the 240 MW Uri-II hydropower dam on River Jhelum, Rs.51 billion for 1000 MW Pak Dul and 1200 MW Sawalkot dams projects on Chenab. The Sawalkot dam is 646-feet height which is more than the 485-feet height Tarbela and 453 feet height Mangla in Pakistan. These dams are 160 km away from Kangra where a 8.0 Richter scale earthquake occurred in 1905 on record.

India has already built 60 MW Madekheda dam on Indus river and is constructing 130 MW Chuttak, 600 MW Monpreet n Randeep, 44 MW Dumkhar and 60 MW Nimo Bazgo dams on river Indus. After completion of 330 MW Wular barrage and 240 MW Uri-I dam India is further constructing 330 MW Krishanganga and 240 MW Uri-II dams on the river Jhelum.

India completed 450 MW Baglihar, 345 MW Salal-I and 345 MW Salal-II on river Chenab on which Pakistan objected seriously. India has diverted Jhelum river water to Chenab through a 80km long tunnel which is clear breach of Indus Water Treaty. India is constructing another 1200 MW Bursar dam on this tunnel. Instead of respecting Indus Water Treaty India has started construction of 400 MW Hasti Dul, 460 MW Rattle, 400 MW Gyspa, 100 MW Pakdul, 800 MW Karthai, 180 MW Raoli, 725 MW Seli, 1200 MW Sawalkot, 90 MW Tangat, 50 MW Pattan, 50 MW Teling, 100 MW Tandi, 180 MW Sach Khas, 300 MW Dueli/ Dugli, 100 MW Rashal, 100 MW Myar, 190 MW Gondhala, 240 MW Dogar, 100 MW Shatru, 110 MW Dang, 20 MW Thai Rot and Chenai dams. After completion of so many dams all the western rivers will become dry. Bhutan has a hydropower potential of 23,000 MW out of which 4,484 MW is expected to be harnessed by constructing six dams by 2024. Pakistan has 50,000 MW hydro potential which is under threat due to 39,000 MW power Indian dams on western rivers. Pakistan is generating 71.9% thermal, 25.2% hydel and 2.9% nuclear power. Our energy mix consists of 43.5% oil, 41.5% gas, 0.3% LPG, 4.5% coal, 9.2% hydropower and 1.1% nuclear electricity. Pakistan has over 40,000 MW wind, 30,000 MW solar and 800 MW geothermal potential.

India has already contributed to the drying up of the eastern rivers Ravi, Sulej and Beas. Water only flows in these rivers when India has significant dam overflows. India is digging a Sulej-Ganges Link canal to divert waters to the southern Indian states on which Indian riparian have taken stay from the Indian court.

India has built 390 MW Pong, 360 MW Pandoh and 126 MW Larji dams on river Beas, 1000 MW Bhakra, 1650 MW Nathpa and 800 MW Kol, 1000 MW Karcham Wang and 77 MW Nangal dams on river Sutlej, 1200 MW Baira Siul, 540 MW Chamera and 600 MW Ranjeet Agar, 120 MW Sewa-II and 70 MW Budhil dams on river Ravi. Indian dam mania is causing drought to both eastern and western riparian farmers.

Pakistan has only two dams which usually stay partially filled throughout the year except monsoon months Wikipedia, 2010). Unfortunately, 95% Indian dams in Himachal, Jammu and Kashmir regions are located on dangerous earthquake faults zones.

Recently India has launched another dams construction drive in Himachal Pardesh to build 300 MW Baspa, 231 MW Holi, 70 MW Dhamwar, 2050 MW Parbati, 192 MW Allian, 162 MW Swara, 370 MW Sham Not, 560 MW Rattle, 430 MW Kiru, 320 MW Kawar and 35 MW Bichlari dams. United Nations water experts must formulate global water legislation to avoid water wars especially between India and Pakistan which may engulf many others.

When Pakistan came to know of water shortages in rivers India had completed 70% of 48 dams. Indus river system is spread over 944,473 km2 out of which 553,416 km^2 lies in Pakistan. Pakistan declared failure of Indus Commission in 2005 referring the case to neutral expert. India has 34 large dams out of which 10 are in Kashmir. Indian links between Neelum, Jhelum, Chenab through Tavi river uplift canal, Ravi, Beas, Sutlej and Yamana transfer western rivers water to Indian highlands.

There is no dam on Chenab, Ravi, Beas and Sutlej rivers on the Pakistani side. However, India is building over three dozens dams on Western rivers which are viewed as a matter of grave concern by Pakistan.

Science news and global warming observations conclude that the Himalaya region will be affected in the near future. Dams worth 150,000 MW have been proposed in India, Nepal, Bhutan and Pakistan. International Rivers point it out that these projects are environmentally determinental (ie from a global warming perspective). Melting glaciers, like Dig Tsho Glof in Nepal in 1985, may lead to glacial lake bursts causing flash floods. Bhutan noted 25 dangerous glacial lakes in 2009.

Over one billion people rely on Himalaya waters. Upstream countries should not store waters in dams to starve lower riparian. India must focus on other sources of energy instead of blocking the flow of water to Pakistan.

United Nations and Indian scientists and engineers must advise the Indian Government to curtail dam construction in fault zones on western rivers under 1960 Indus Treaty to discourage water war for long term regional security. We have long history of using waters amicably but energy crisis is driving the conflicts. Global irrigation potentials exists 68% in Asia, 17% in Americas, 9% in Europe and 1% in Oceania. Indus Basin western rivers contribute to 15-20% of Asian food cycle. Transboundary rivers are not local rather global assets which need due attention on merits. Indus water treaty went well for last 50 years but recent Indian dam drive is worsening the scenario.

Salaman's claim the lower riparian (Pakistan) can harm upper riparian (India) is not a valid argument as Pakistan and India have divided rivers instead of sharing them.

Eastern rivers Sutlej, Beas and Ravi were chosen by India and Western rivers Indus, Jhelum and Chenab were left for Pakistan due to geographical locations. Eastern rivers had annual water capacity of 41 billion cubic meters (33 MAF) whereas western rivers had capacity of 188 billion cubic meters (135 MAF). Uri dams have storage capacity of 3.07 MAF in 1999 which increased to 6.37 MAF in 2002. Sutlej-Yamana (SYL) can transfer 3.5MAF water. India is transferring this water from western rivers into eastern rivers through Tavi-Ravi 31 meter high uplift link canal. India stopped Neelum River to divert water to Wular Barrage through 27 km long tunnel which is further diverted from Jhelum to Chenab through 77 km long tunnel. Asia Times called it race to death over Kashmir waters.

WATER, POWER AND ENERGY CONFLUENCE

Population growth, industrial expansion and the consumer economy have increased electricity demand from 17PWh in 2000 to 20PWh in 2010. Demand is esitamted to increase to 24 PWH by 2020 and 30PWh by 2030.

About 2.5 billion people out of global 6.8 billion population lived with severe water conditions in 2005 which are likely to increase to 3.95 billions out of 8.5 billions population by 2030.

The IEEE believes trading water for watts is start of hard choices era. Hydroelectric, solar, nuclear and wind power plants consume 5.4, 2.5-2.8, 1.5 and 0 liters water per kWh but produce no carbon.

Coal and gas fired power plants consume 1.1-1.8 and 0.5-1.8 liters per kWh energy producing 0.43 to 0.96 kg/kWh carbon. P

hotovoltaic power generation uses 0.1 liter/kWh water producing 0.02 kg/kWh carbon. Wind power is the cleanest form energy which neither uses water nor produces carbon. Pakistan is among least coal burning countries but global warming is hitting hard on it since 1998. A recent temperature rise to 54°C in Mohenjo Daru followed by 1200,000 cusecs flash floods has affected over 2 to 2.5 million people across Pakistan. The climatologists say it makes no difference whether a single country increases or decreases greenhouse gases emissions at global scale. A country injecting thousands miles away can affect you through the common atmosphere. Recent industrialization in China and India has led to accumulation of green gases over Pakistan that has changed monsoon flow patterns from Bangladesh to India to Southern Punjab to northern mountains exacerbating glacier melting.

World power demand is 17 PWh whereas thousands of dams installed electric power capacity is 777 GWe that supplies just 2.9 PWh which is 18% of total demand. The remaining 82% demand is met with fossil fuels which are likely to be deplete after 2050.

DAMS HAZARDS & DRAWBACKS

A large dam may fail during earthquake and flash flood. Dam failures may lead to serious consequences. It causes flash flood causing catastrophes. The Chinese Banqiao dam failure killed 26,000 by drowning in flood water and 145,000 people by subsequent epidemics in addition to billions dollars property losses.

Vajont Dam failure by geological reasons killed 2000 people in Italy in 1963.

Kelly Barnes Dam failed due to flash flood killing 27 people in 1957.

It is very dangerous to construct dams on geological fault lines.

Dam construction devastates lots of fertile land and causes the evacuation of rural populations. It is estimated that 50-80 million peoples have been displaced worldwide due to dam construction.

INDUS WATERS TREATY (INDIA-PAKISTAN)

The Indus Waters Treaty between India and Pakistan has been described as one of the most successful water sharing treaties ever accomplished. It is a unique treaty because it was able to get two countries with historically hostile relations to reach an agreement that has been in place since 1961. The treaty is also unique because of the role the World Bank played in brokering the agreement. It is therefore worth looking into for possible lessons for a future solution for the Central Asian countries.

The waters of the Indus basin begin in the Himalayan Mountains of Indian held Kashmir. The water flows from the hills through the arid states of Punjab and Sind, converging in

Pakistan and emptying into the Arabian Sea south of Karachi. Developments over the last century have created a large network of canals and storage facilities that provide water for more than 26 million acres - the largest irrigated area of any river system in the world.

The partitioning of the Indian subcontinent created a conflict over the entitlement of waters of the Indus basin. The newly formed states could not come to an agreement over how to share and manage what was essentially a unitary network of irrigation. Also, the geography of partition was such that the source rivers of the Indus basin were in India. Pakistan felt threatened by the prospect of Indian control over the tributaries that fed water into the Pakistani portion of the basin, as it threatened the country's main source of water to cultivate its land. This was a classic conflict situation between upstream and downstream riparian countries, and it was exacerbated by a lack of trust and intense territorial animosity between the two sides. Even though both countries tried to settle the matter bilaterally several times after partition, no lasting agreement was reached until the World Bank got involved as a mediating entity.

The World Bank volunteered to act as a benign go-between, but it did not intend, at least initially, to split the existing canal system and the basin unity. The World Bank's initial proposal was to have the Indus irrigation scheme administered as one unit by the two parties, irrespective of the new borders drawn as a result of the partitioning of the sub-continent. However, both parties turned down this proposal. After several years of negotiating, the two parties made progress towards an understanding that involved dividing the six rivers between the two parties. In addition, Pakistan was to receive financial assistance to construct storage reservoirs. This was to compensate for loss of water after rivers were divided.

The Indus Waters Treaty and the role of the World Bank

The Indus Waters Treaty was signed in 1960 and divided the six rivers comprising the Indus river system between the two countries. India was granted the three eastern tributaries (Ravi,

Beas, and Sutlej) and Pakistan assumed the flow of the three western rivers (Indus, Jhelum, and Chenab). A unique feature of the Indus Waters Treaty is that it is the only international waters-treaty co-signed by a third party, namely the World Bank. The World Bank signed the Treaty for certain specified purposes stated in the Treaty: Article V "Financial Provisions" deals with India's contribution to Pakistan for the replacement works to be constructed as a result of the termination of Pakistan's water rights to the Eastern rivers. India's contribution was made to the World Bank and credited to the Indus Basin Development Fund. Besides the contribution from India, the Fund consisted mostly of grant funding from a number of donors and World Bank loans. The Fund was used to finance the replacement works that Pakistan needed in order to end its reliance on the Eastern rivers and to augment the flow of the Western rivers. The funding for Development Fund is a very important aspect of the Treaty. The solution to get funding from the international community for replacement works, and not make India pay for it all, was the tipping point that made India accept the agreement,

RESOLVING THE BAGLIHAR DISPUTE THROUGH THE WORLD BANK

The procedural role of the World Bank was recently exercised when Pakistan approached the World Bank in 2005 stating that a dispute had arisen with regard to the Baglihar hydropower plant India was constructing on the Chenab River.

Although the Chenab River was allocated to Pakistan, India was allowed certain uses of the Western rivers, which include run-off-river hydropower plants.

It was the first time since the Treaty was signed that the Bank had been called upon by one of the parties to exercise its role and responsibilities under the Treaty with regard to a dispute settlement. In 2005 the World Bank informed the two parties that it had appointed Mr. Raymond Lafitte, a Swiss national, an engineer and professor, as the Neutral Expert to address the Baglihar difference. The Neutral Expert was able to deliver a decision that was accepted by the two parties and the Bank has been credited for its ability to play a fair, transparent and continued constructive role in its appointment of the Neutral Expert.

This case study can be related to the water dispute in Central Asia. It illustrates how shifting borders and the creation of independent states exacerbated what was initially an intra-national issue. It is also interesting to note that because hostility, mistrust and competing interests makes it hard to come to an agreement between the countries themselves, a possible solution could be the positive, active, and continuous involvement of a third party. The active participation of the World Bank was crucial to the success of the Indus Waters Treaty. The Bank offered a strong leadership role as well as providing support staff, funding, and, perhaps most important, its own proposals when negotiations reached a stalemate between India and Pakistan. It is therefore important to consider the Indus Waters Treaty as a potential model for environmental cooperation in Central Asia.

MEKONG RIVER BASIN (SOUTHEAST ASIA)

Foreign Policy Association, 2010

The Mekong is the longest river in Southeast Asia, the seventh longest in Asia, and the twelfth longest in the world. It originates in the Tanghla Shan Mountains on the Tibetan plateau, passes through southern China, Myanmar, Laos, Thailand, Cambodia, Viet Nam, and ends in the Indian Ocean. Roughly 70 million people of which some 62 million reside in the Lower Mekong Basin (almost all of Cambodia and Laos, one-third of Thailand, and one-fifth of Viet Nam) depend on the Mekong river system for their own subsistence. It is projected that in the following years, there will be an increase in the total number of people who depend on the Mekong River for food, water and transport.

Given the importance of the Mekong River Basin to all six riparian states, in 1957 the Mekong Committee was created. Whereas many inter-state water treaties have been designed in midst of potential open conflict, the Committee emerged during a time of relative peace in the region. Since its inception, the

Committee has operated in conjunction with many other international, regional and national organizations working in the Mekong River Basin. However, in 1995, Cambodia, Laos, Thailand and Vietnam signed the Agreement on the Co-operation for the Sustainable Development of the Mekong River Basin (MRC), making it the only legally constituted regional organization mandated from the highest political level to represent the interests of riparian states in Mekong River matters. In 1995 the MRC agreed to focus its efforts into three areas of priority. These are:

- Developing rules for the cooperative use of water through the Water Utilization Program.
- Basin Development Planning, facilitating cooperative sustainable development of water related resources.
- Environmental monitoring.

The MRC excels as a resilient paradigm that has withstood the test of time albeit with challenges: lack of accurate, timely data on Mekong River water quantity and quality: inadequate and incomplete policy and regulatory frameworks vis-à-vis the Basin's complex ecosystems and habitats, and weak enforcement capabilities. Another challenge that threatens the goals of the MRC is that the People's Republic of China and the Union of Myanmar are only dialogue partners to the MRC. Thus management of dams and downstream flows that severely affect the other Mekong countries are not given priority by the former two states. It is important to note that China has stressed that its eight dams would help, and not hinder, the MRC goals. Presently, China is reluctant to join the MRC, refuses to share more hydrological data related to the Mekong, and to be more transparent about its Mekong dams plans.

Interestingly, the Mekong water system, similarly to the Amu Darya River and Syr Darya River in Central Asia, has an ominous colonial legacy of large-scale exploitation by the French that supplied the large demand for Europe's industrialization process.

Notwithstanding the later, cooperation among the riparian Mekong countries has been a compelling force behind a common purpose: the promotion and coordination of integrated basin development through regional cooperation.

In spite of the fact that each of the riparian Mekong countries may have their own set of interests in the Mekong water and resources, they established a remarkable foundation to equitable sharing of common water resources by focusing on three elements. First, provide each country in the Mekong sub-region with equitable access to an important source of renewable energy-hydropower potential. Second, the MRC, fully aware of the importance of agriculture in the region, promotes a socio-economic agenda that focuses on greater efficacy of irrigated agriculture, diversification of the sector, and better quality of life for majority of rural population. The Mekong River is said to be the force behind the agricultural sector of Southeast Asia, and meets more than half of total water demand in the region. Third, given the Mekong River geographical dynamics, the MRC agenda focuses on developing transportation hubs among the riparian countries, which could facilitate regional and international trade, transparent borders, regional integration, and overall better regional relations between neighbors.

Relevant to the current water crisis in Central Asia is the way the water resources of the Mekong River Basin has been conducive to regional cooperation since 1957.

The MRC framework illustrates that joint water management agreements among riparian countries have an operational and effective role with regard to securing and promoting regional concord and development. The main lesson learned regarding the MRC is that an international water treaty among the Central Asia states is plausible, so long as the leadership at the highest political level put forward genuine resolve to settle any regional water-use disputes. The MRC framework should be an excellent example for the Central Asian countries should they decide to pursue a water cooperation agreement with special focus on equitable sharing of common water resources, so as to ensure the betterment of their own people. That is, with or without the involvement of an acceptable and neutral third-party mediator.

2

The Indus Water Treaty and River System

The 3rd World Water Forum held at Kyoto, Japan in March 2003 sent simultaneous messages of hope and distress regarding the availability of water to meet surging worldwide demand in the coming decades. Its significance is especially serious in the Indian subcontinent, a region that is home to one-fourth of humanity and to three of the mightiest rivers of the world: the Indus, Ganges and Brahmaputra. Although these rivers have been subject to significant water sharing treaties among the various riparian states in the past, currently four major treaties govern them. These include the Indus Water Treaty (1960) between India and Pakistan, Sankosh Multipurpose Project treaty (1993) between India and Bhutan, the Ganges Water Sharing Agreement (1996) between India and Bangladesh, and the Mahakali Treaty (1996) between India and Nepal.

Recent stresses and strains in the observance of the Indus Water Treaty (IWT) have had many analysts including this author believe that water sharing will take a politically charged dynamic and may even replace Kashmir as the primary source of conflict between India and Pakistan. Therefore it is important to have comprehensive understanding of the overall issues of the Indus system of rivers and the IWT as this article attempts to provide. It is formatted introduce the Indus river system, a brief overview of the principles of water sharing, the historical background leading up to the water crisis between India and Pakistan and the mediation by the World Bank, various provisions of the IWT, current disputes in water projects on the Indus River System bilaterally between India and Pakistan, and a look into the state of affairs of the Indus River System within Pakistan today.

THE INDUS RIVER SYSTEM

The northwestern part of the Indian subcontinent is dominated by the Indus River and its system of upper tributaries (collectively referred to as Indus River System in this article.) Originating 17,000 feet (518 m) above sea level in a spring near Lake Manasarovar at Mt. Kailash, the Indus river along with the Brahmaputra, Sutlej, and Karnali rivers are fed by massive Tibetan glacial waters to become a mighty river with further feeds from other glacial catchment areas in Karakoram and Zanskar ranges. The Indus then traverses a distance of 1800 miles (2900 km) through Tibet, India, Pakistan occupied Kashmir (PoK), and Pakistan before draining into the Arabian Sea south of Karachi. On its way, it is further enriched by the waters of several tributaries, the most important and discussed in this article are Beas, Sutlej, Ravi, Chenab and Jhelum rivers. The western tributaries of the Indus that include the Swat, Kurram, Gomal, Kohat, Zoab and Kabul are not discussed herein. The river has been variously known as the *Sengge* or Lion River by the Tibetans, *Abbasseen* or Father of Rivers by the Pathans of present NWFP Pakistan, and *Mitho Dariyo* or Sweet River by the denizens of the arid Sindh.

THE INDUS TRIBUTARIES

Sutlej : The longest of the five tributaries, the Sutlej originates near Mt. Kailash along with the Indus and runs a course of 964 miles (1550 km) through the Panjal and Siwalik mountain ranges and enters Pakistan through the plains of Indian Punjab. The Husseiniwala Headworks at Ferozepore is located downstream at the merger between of Beas and Sutlej, the closure of which on May 1, 1948 triggered the water crisis that prompted the IWT. These headworks supplied water to the then Princely State of Bikaner through a left-bank canal called Bikaner Canal and the state of Bahawalpur from the right-bank canal called Depalpur Canal. The huge 740 feet (225 m) high Bhakra Dam, which Nehru called "the new temple of resurgent India," is also situated on this river. In addition another important headwork located on this Sutlej is Harike that feeds the Sirhind and Rajasthan canals. Within Pakistan, these eastern tributaries of the Indus known as Panjand combine at Mithan Kot.

Chenab : This 675 mile (1086 km) long river originates in the Kulu and Kangra districts of Himachal Pradesh and is fed by the tributaries Chandra and Bagha as it enters J&K near Kishtwar. After cutting across the Pir Panjal range, it enters the Sialkot district in Pakistan that built the Marala barrage across the river in 1968 with a maximum discharge of 1.1 million cusecs.

Jhelum & Kishenganga (Neelum): The Kishenganga river rises in the mountain complex west of Dras and south of Deosai plateau and is fed by a number of tiny tributaries and merges with Jhelum near Muzaffarabad in PoK. The Jhelum itself originates in the foothills of Pir Panjal near Verinag and flows through the four major cities of Anantnag, Srinagar, Sopore and Baramulla. Some important tributaries of the Jhelum are Lidar, Sind and Vishav.

Ravi : This 475 mile (764 km) long river rises in Himachal Pradesh and runs a course of 102 miles (164 km) before joining Chenab in Pakistan after flowing past Lahore. The Thien Dam (Ranjit Sagar Dam) is located on this river at the tri-section of Punjab, Himachal Pradesh and J&K States and feeds the Upper Bari Doab Canal (UBDC) which irrigates Northwestern Punjab.

Beas : This 290 mile (467 km) long river originates near Rohtang Pass in Himachal Pradesh and flows through Kulu Valley and the Siwalik Range. The Pandoh Dam is situated on this and diverts water to Sutlej through the Beas-Sutlej link.

The original infrastructure built by the British to harness and efficiently distribute the waters of these tributaries with a series of canals, barrages, and headworks has been augmented with construction of dams since independence by both India and Pakistan.

THE INDUS WATER TREATY

The India Independence Act enacted in 1947 by British Parliament and the subsequent British withdrawal from India left the subcontinent partitioned between two independent states marred by demarcation problems along their international boundaries, the peculiar circumstances leading to the division, and the accession of a number of princely states especially that of Jammu & Kashmir straddling India and Pakistan as well as the complex riverine systems of Indus, Ganges, and Brahmaputra. Of these three rivers, the Indus presented a complicated set of issues stemming from thousands of kilometres of man-made irrigation canals and headworks that regulated the flow of its waters.

While all the rivers, except Indus and Sutlej, originated within Kashmir, the headworks located mostly in the Eastern Punjab were awarded to India. Aside from the Punjab Boundary Commission suggestion that the canal-headworks system be treated as a joint venture, a proposition rejected by both countries, it had not deliberated water sharing of Indus River Basin due to a hasty partition that was completed in a mere 73 days.

Water sharing issues of Indus River System would later take over a decade to resolve. Further complicating this issue, Pakistan covertly and later overtly sought to grab Jammu & Kashmir for various reasons including the desire to control the waters of these rivers that succeeded in instilling only distrust among Indian minds.

After the Partition, both the nations agreed to a "Standstill Agreement" on Dec. 30, 1947 freezing the existing water turn systems at the two headworks of Madhopur (on the Ravi) and Ferozepur (on the Sutlej) until March, 31, 1948. Any dispute that could not be resolved by the Punjab Partition Committee was to be decided by the Arbitral Tribunal (AT) which had been setup under Section Nine of the Indian Independence Act by the Governor General to sort out difficulties arising over the division of assets. However, on the expiry of the arrangement and after not receiving an encouraging response to a reminder for talks issued by the East Punjab Government on 29th March 1948, and in the absence of a new agreement, the then Indian Punjab Government promptly stopped the water supply through Madhopur on April, 1, 1948. By a coincidence, the Arbitral Tribunal's term also expired on the same day.

In the meanwhile, the AT had accepted India 's claims regarding seigniorage charges for the waters and ordered payment of the same by Pakistan. At the invitation of East Punjab, the Engineers of the two divided-Punjab States met in Simla on Apr. 15, 1948 and signed two Standstill Agreements regarding the Depalpur Canal and Central Bari Doab Canal to be in effect until Oct. 15, 1948. The West Punjab Government agreed to pay: (1) seigniorage charges, (2) proportionate maintenance costs, and (3) interest on a proportionate amount of capital. In its defence, the GoI cited such charges levied by the Punjab on the Bikaner state under the British.

However, the West Punjab Govt. refused to ratify the Agreement and the Prime Minister of Pakistan, then Liaqat Ali Khan, called for a meeting. The Finance Minister of Pakistan, Ghulam Mohammed, along with the Pakistani Punjab ministers, Shaukat Hayat Khan and Mumtaz Daulatana visited Delhi to work out an agreement in the Inter-Dominion Conference held on May, 3-4, 1948.

India agreed to resume release of water from the headworks, but made it clear that Pakistan could not lay claim to these waters as a matter of right and would levy seigniorage charges specified by the Prime Minister of India to be deposited in Reserve Bank of India, establishing Indian sovereignty over these rivers. The Indian side also made assurances that the waters would be diminished slowly giving enough time for West Punjab to develop alternate sources. The West Punjab Government, for its part, also recognized *"the natural anxiety of the East Punjab Government to discharge the obligations to develop areas where water is scarce and which were underdeveloped in relation to parts of West Punjab."* Soon the Pakistani Government falsely accused that they were coerced into signing this Agreement and made futile appeals to the Governor General Lord Mountbatten. However, due to the hostilities between India and Pakistan on account of Kashmir and in the general environment of distrust and animosity, no further talks took place. Pakistan 's suggestion in June 1949 to take the matter to the International Court of Justice at The Hague and widen the conflict across all rivers, was rejected by India. On November 1, 1949, Pakistan unilaterally invalidated the Delhi Agreement and by July, 1950 stopped seigniorage payments into RBI. However, India continued to abide by the Agreement and supplied waters.

In 1951, David Lilienthal, former chairman of the Tennessee Valley Authority and a former Chairman of Atomic Energy Commission, USA visited the two countries ostensibly to write a series of articles for the Colliers magazine *(since defunct)*. Having had access to both the Governments at the highest level, Lilientahl wrote in one of his articles, "*I proposed that India and Pakistan work out a program jointly to develop and jointly to operate the Indus Basin river system, upon which both nations were dependent for irrigation water. With new dams and irrigation canals, the Indus and its tributaries could be made to yield the additional water each country needed for increased food production. In the article I had suggested that the World Bank might use its good offices to bring the parties to agreement, and help in the financing of an Indus Development program.*" Inspired by this idea, Eugene R. Black, then President of the World Bank visited the two countries and proposed a Working Party of Indian, Pakistani and World Bank engineers to tackle the "functional", rather than the "political" aspects of water sharing. The two countries accepted this mediation (which also had the backing of President Truman who wanted to remove the "*kind of unfriendliness*" that existed then between the US and India) offer in March 1952 and sent their technical teams to Washington for further discussions. Subsequent meetings took place in Karachi in Nov., 1952 and New Delhi in Jan. 1953. The World Bank suggested that each side submit its own plans, which they did on Oct. 6, 1953. The two plans, while concurring on the available supply of water, differed widely on allocations. The table below, shows the initial, negotiated and final positions of both the countries.

Table : *Indus River System Estimates and Allocations*

Plan	India	Pakistan
Initial Estimate	119 MAF	118 MAF5
Initial Indian	29 MAF	90 MAF
Initial Pakistani	15.5 MAF	102.5 MAF
Revised Indian	All of the Eastern rivers + 7% of Western rivers	None of the Eastern rivers plus 93% of the Western rivers
Revised Pakistani	30% of Eastern rivers and none of the Western rivers	70% of the Eastern rivers + all of the Western rivers
World Bank	Entire flow of the Eastern Rivers	Entire flow of the Western Rivers

However, despite all efforts, the wide gaps in the stands of the two countries could not be bridged, mainly due to the intransigence of the Pakistani side as the revised and final allocations show clearly above. The World Bank felt that an ideal approach to joint development of an integrated plan for Indus Basin as proposed by David Lilienthal was now impossible. In order to resolve the dispute, it finally stepped in with its own "settlement" proposals on Feb. 5, 1954 offering the three Eastern rivers to India and the three Western rivers to Pakistan. India accepted the proposal *in toto* on Mar. 25, 1954 while Pakistan gave only a "qualified acceptance" on July 28, 1954. The settlement offered by the World Bank was closer to the Indian position as it repudiated the claims of Pakistan based on "historic usage". An angered Pakistan threatened to withdraw from further negotiations. The World Bank proposal was then transformed from a "settlement" to a "basis for further negotiations" and the talks eventually continued for the next six years. In the meanwhile, the two countries signed an Interim Agreement on June 21, 1955. As no conclusive agreement could be reached, the World Bank announced on Apr. 30, 1956 that the negotiation deadline has been indefinitely extended. As is its wont, Pakistan, through its then Prime Minister H.S.Suhrawardy, issued a direct threat of war with India over waters, escalating tensions.

Under the World Bank plan, Pakistan was asked to construct barrages and canals to divert the Western river waters to compensate the loss of Eastern rivers on the Pakistani side. During the period needed to do this, called the Transition Period, India was required to maintain the "historic withdrawals" to Pakistan The World Bank then suggested a "financial liability" for India as replacement costs by Pakistan for the loss of the three Eastern rivers.

In the 1958 meeting, the replacement works and the financial liability to India were considered. India rejected Pakistan 's proposal, known as the "London Plan", for two large dams on the Jhelum and the Indus and three smaller ones on Ravi and Sutlej and several canals, all in all totaling USD 1.2 Billion.

India 's alternate proposal, known as the "Marhu Tunnel Proposal", was unacceptable to Pakistan as leaving too much leverage on water flows in Indian hands. In May, 1959, the Bank's President visited both countries and suggested a way out which involved India paying a fixed amount of £ 62.060 Million to be paid in ten years in equal installments and the Bank assisting Pakistan with help from donor countries. The international consortium of donors pledged USD 900 Million for Pakistan and the drafting of the IWT began in Aug., 1959.

The treaty was signed in Karachi by Pandit Jawaharlal Nehru, Field Marshal Ayub Khan H.P., H.J. and Mr. W.A.B. Illif, President of the World Bank in a five-day summit meet starting Sep. 19, 1960. However, it was deemed effective from Apr. 1, 1960. The two governments ratified the same in January 1961 by exchanging documents in Delhi. Simultaneously an Indus Basin Development Fund was established with contributions from Australia, Canada, Germany, New Zealand, the UK and the US along with India 's share of the cost.

The Eisenhower Administration contributed roughly half the cost of the Fund, while the World Bank provided US$ 250 Million and the other donor countries together provided a similar amount. The Water and Power Development Authority (WAPDA) of Pakistan was entrusted with the task of completing these tasks. The fund was subsequently extinguished after the completion of the projects as per Article XI of the IWT. The May 4, 1948 accord stood annulled after the signing of IWT. The Indus Basin Project involved construction of two large dams, five barrages to transfer 14 MAF of water from the Western rivers. There are three systems of link canals. Two of the systems, the Rasul-Qadirabad-Balloki-Suleimanki System (R.Q.B.S.) and the Trimmu-Sidhnai-Mailsi-Bahawal System (T.S.M.B) connect the Jhelum River through to the Sutlej and the third system Chashma-Jhelum System (C.J) connects the Indus with the Jhelum.

The IWT also enunciated a mechanism to exchange regularly flow-data of rivers, canals and streams. A Permanent Indus Commission (PIC) was constituted, headed by two Commissioners, one from each country. The PIC is expected to meet at least once a year alternately in India and Pakistan and submit an annual report to their respective Governments before June, 30th every year. So far, the Commission has met 92 times. The IWT also sets out the procedures for settlement of differences and disputes both bilaterally and through International arbitration. Given below is an abridged version of the dispute settlement process that may be of interest in the present context:

A. Any question that might be a breach of IWT shall be first examined by the PIC.

B. A difference is deemed to have arisen if the PIC could not reach an agreement.

C. The difference shall be dealt with by a neutral expert who may opine if it is a dispute or not. If not, he shall resolve it. Such a neutral expert shall be a highly qualified engineer and appointed by the two Governments in consultation, or failing which, by the Bank. The expert's decision is final and binding.

D. In case of a dispute, the Commissioners report to their respective Governments which shall then strive to resolve the dispute.

E. A Court of Arbitration shall be setup to resolve the dispute, if no decision is reached by the above process.

F. Such a Court will consist of seven members, two from each party and three including a Chairman from a panel to be chosen by the two Governments. If no consensus on names can be arrived at, the IWT has given a list of persons from whom to choose such as the Secretary General of the U.N. or International Bank for Reconstruction and Development (IBRD) for the Chairmanship and the President of M.I.T., Cambridge, the Rector of Imperial College, London, the Chief Justice of the USA, or the Lord Chief Justice of England for panel membership.

Many Pakistanis feel that Pakistan surrendered to India the waters of the three Eastern rivers in 1960. Their argument is along the following lines.

On the basis of over fifty years' record the mean flow in Indus River System (IRS) totalled 175 MAF on the eve of Partition of Punjab in 1947. This comprised of 93 MAF including 27 of Kabul for Indus, 23 for Jhelum, 26 for Chenab, 6 for Ravi, 13 for Beas and 14 for Sutlej annually.

Out of this 175 MAF, 167 flowed into Pakistan at the time the boundaries of partitioned Punjab were fixed according to the Radcliffe Award. This means that the Indian East Punjab drew only 8 MAF of a total of 33 MAF of water that annually flowed in three eastern rivers Ravi, Beas and Sutlej. Under the Internationally agreed rights of lower riparian states and also Indian Independence Act 1947, the balance 25 MAF waters of three eastern rivers were to be shared between India and Pakistan. The Pakistanis feel that those who negotiated the IWT on their behalf did not sufficiently press for the sharing of this quantum of water.

However, there are several fallacies in these arguments. First, leaving the claim on the quantum of waters aside, the arrangement entered into at Partition time was interim in nature until a final agreement could be reached and the provisions of such an interim arrangement were in no way binding on the parties concerned. Secondly, the Indus Agreement was reached eventually in 1960 during that time the utilization of the waters of these rivers had grown enormously in the states of East Punjab, Rajasthan, and Jammu & Kashmir. To claim the waters on the basis of the flow thirteen years before, when agriculture and economy had been dictated by different circumstances of a united India is patently unfair. In fact, the IWT itself treats water flows and usage based on the situation existing as on Apr. 1, 1960, the effective date of the Treaty. Thirdly, as a lower riparian state, all the unused river waters would naturally flow to Pakistan. This, by itself, cannot bestow any rights on that country and again, a quantum of 80 MAF of water was reaching the Arabian Sea unutilized out of the total flow of the Indus River systems. All these are summarized by the following statement of N.D.Gulhati, the principal negotiator from the Indian side to the IWT, *"After ten years of hard and devoted work, we had secured almost a world-wide recognition of our claim to use in India all the waters of the Eastern Rivers, including the 12 MAF which was actually being let down for use in Pakistan as at the time of partition... In India, we had already allocated all these waters, including the 12 MAF referred to above, between Punjab (including the present Haryana), Rajasthan and Jammu and Kashmir. The scope of the Bhakra-Nangal project had been considerably increased, the Madhopur-Beas Link and the Sirhind Feeder had been completed and opened for operation, several new channels had been built on the Upper Bari Doab Canal and the Rajasthan Canal was under construction."*

CURRENT ISSUES ON INDUS WATER SHARING

Issues External to Pakistan

There are a host of factors external to Pakistan that could also affect the Indus River System. One is the climatic changes leading to reduced flows on the Indus *per se*. Another exogenous factor is the growing demand within India, especially the state of Jammu & Kashmir (J&K) where people feel that the IWT has wrongfully deprived them of water resulting retarding the growth of agriculture, power generation, and irrigation from rivers that originate and flow from their very state. There was also a widespread demand within India for abrogation of the IWT after the attack on the Indian Parliament on December 13, 2001 by terrorists supported directly by the Pakistani state apparatus.

The Tulbul Navigation Lock/Wullar Barrage Issue

The 74 Sq. Km. Wullar Lake (original size 202 Sq. Kms.) is the largest freshwater lake in India and is situated on the Jhelum and supplies 40% of J&K's fish catch. The stretch of 22 Km between Sopore and Baramulla becomes non-navigable during the lean winter season with a water depth of only 2.5 ft. It is only in spring that rainfall causes the snow to melt at higher elevations on the surrounding mountains and causes floods.

In order to improve navigation, India started constructing in 1985, a barrage 439 feet long and with a lock, at the mouth of the lake to raise the flow of water in winter to 4000 cusecs with a depth of 4 ft with an added storage of 0.3 MAF. Pakistan objected to this project and construction was halted in 1987. Pakistan's objection stems from two issues, one India needs to get concurrence of the design from Pakistan and two, it cannot store waters as per IWT on the Jhelum Main anything in excess of 0.01 MAF as "incidental storage work").

Pakistan 's real objections may be due to its fear that such a barrage may damage its own Triple-Canal project linking Jhelum and Chenab with the Upper Bari Doab Canal. Pakistan also says that such a barrage would be a security risk enabling the Indian Army to make the crossing of the river either easy or difficult through controlled release of water. India 's argument is that such a barrage would not reduce the quantum of water flow and it would also be beneficial to Pakistan by regulating water flow to Mangla Dam by controlling floods and also improve the Pakistani Triple-canal irrigation system.

The water flow would indeed double during the lean winter period from the current 2000 cusecs. Also, the project does not envisage building any new storage capacity as the Wullar lake already existed and the water is only for non-consumptive use (this term includes such usage as navigation, floating of timber, flood protection or control, and fishing with no diminution in volume of water returned to the river/tributaries after use) which is allowed by the IWT. The Wullar barrage is not a storage project but a control project permissible under the treaty. The two countries had indeed reached an agreement in October, 1991 but then Pakistan suddenly introduced an irrelevant element in February, 1992 by linking the termination of Kishenganga Hydroelectric project with further movements in the Tulbul Navigation Lock project and India 's refusal stalled further work.

The 1991 draft agreement stipulated that India would build a 40-feet wide lock but leave ungated 6.2 Metres of the lake at a crest level of 1574.9 Metres and would also forego 0.30MAF storage while Pakistan would allow the lake to fill to its full capacity at 1578 metres.

When the agreement was reached in 1991, the only contention that remained was the timing of the filling up of the lake. The crucial period was between June 21 and August 20 every year. Between October, 1987, and August, 1992, experts from the two countries met eight times to settle the issue. The matter was taken up during the Foreign Secretary-level talks between 1990 and 1994 also. The ninth round was held in July, 2004.

The Salal Hydroelectric Project

This was the first major dispute successfully resolved bilaterally under IWT. On April 14, 1978, the governments of India and Pakistan entered into a treaty on the Salal project. The Salal hydroelectric project on the Chenab in Jammu and Kashmir was negotiated by the Janata Party government in India and the Bhutto administration in Pakistan and has not been disputed by subsequent governments in Pakistan.

The negotiations and discussions took place for a period of four years between 1974 and 1978 between the Indus Commissioners and the foreign offices. The project provides waters to Pakistan in a regulated manner but involves no diversion by India.

However, Pakistan successfully objected to the building of the anti-siltation sluice gates, which were six low-level outlets normally used for controlling sedimentation, resulting in decreased power generation capacity of this project. India also agreed to reduce the heights of the spillway gates from 40 feet to 30 feet.

The Ranbir and Pratap Canals

The Ranbir Canal, built in 1870, was intended to feed the areas of Miran Sahib, Vijaypur and Madhopur. Poor maintenance has ensured that it can now carry just 300 cubic feet per second of water, rather than the 1,000 cusecs it was designed for when originally built. The Pratap Canal, meant to meet the needs of the Akhnoor-Sunderbani belt, has also silted up. These canals off take from Chenab between Salal and Marala headworks. These two canals need urgent repair work to restore their earlier capacities. Under the treaty, India is allowed to take out a fixed quantity of water for these channels. Many restrictions, such as quantum and dates of withdrawal have been imposed on India by the IWT.

The Kishenganga Project

India started the 330 MW Kishenganga hydroelectric projects across River Kishenganga after protracted negotiations between the Central Electricity Authority (CEA), the Defence Ministry, and the environmentalists who fear the loss of the serene Gurez valley. The project involves a 103 metre dam across the river before it crosses the Line of Control (LoC) and a channel and a 27 Km long tunnel through the North Kashmir ranges to bring the water to the Wullar lake where a hydroelectric power station will be built as part of an integrated project. The Kashmir Chief Minister Dr. Farooq Abdullah signed an MoU with the Union Power Minister in July, 2000 for the project. The National Hydroelectric Power Corp. (NHPC) was entrusted with this project on a Build-Own-Operate-Transfer (BOOT) basis. The CEA cleared the project only in June, 2004.

Pakistan objects to the Kishenganga project fearing an adverse impact on its envisaged 969-MW Neelum- Jhelum power plant to be constructed with Chinese assistance. This project was initially planned for 1994-1997 but lies dormant because of lack of funds. The Indian Kishenganga project is expected to lead to a shortfall of 21% loss of water flow in Neelum resulting in a 9% reduction in power for the Pakistani project. The IWT allows India to store waters on Neelum for power generation and so Pakistan wants to start its project first in order to deny waters to India claiming the principle of "prior appropriation", per Paragraph 15(iii), states *"where a Plant is located on a Tributary of The Jhelum on which Pakistan has any Agricultural use or hydroelectric use, the water released below the Plant may be delivered, if necessary, into another Tributary but only to the extent existing Agricultural Use or hydroelectric use by Pakistan on the former Tributary would not be adversely affected"*.

India also claims that the waters will ultimately reach Pakistan through Jhelum though not through Kishenganga (Neelum). In the meanwhile, Pakistan has felt the urgency to take up its USD 1.6 Billion Neelum –Jhelum Hydropower Project by appointing a private company, NESPAK, as consultants and complete the international bidding and evaluation by April 2005.

The Baglihar Project

This project, currently under construction by the Jammu & Kashmir Power Development Corp. on the Chenab in Doda Distt, will generate 450 MW of power when commissioned by end-December, 2005. The contract was extended in 2002 to raise the capacity to 900 MW by Dec., 2007.

Pakistan claims that this dam will result in a loss of 7000-8000 cusecs of water a day during the *rabi* season. India has assured Pakistan that the quantum of water will not be diminished in any way. Pakistan disputes India 's contention that this is a run-of-river project and the site is unsuitable for an ungated spillway.

The works involve the construction of a "Pondage" of 15 Million Cubic Metre (IWT allows for 'Pondage', a term meaning Live Storage, of only sufficient magnitude to meet fluctuations in the discharge of the turbines arising from variations in the daily and the weekly loads of the plant) capacity and an underground power station.

Pakistan claims that the submerged gate spillways of this 429-feet high 1046-feet long dam, allow India to increase the reservoir's storage capacity to 164,000 acre feet and the ability to stop water for about 26 days during December, January and February affecting canals taking off Marala headworks.

The IWT specifies the following with respect to gated spillways, *"If the conditions at the site of a plant make a gated spillway necessary, the bottom level of the gates in normal closed position shall be located at the highest level consistent with sound and economical design and satisfactory construction and operation of the works"*.

This project, Pakistan believes, could also lead to inundation of Bajwat Area above Marala headworks due to sudden synchronized releases from Dulhasti, Baglihar and Salal reservoirs on Chenab. Pakistan also claims that India adopted a stonewalling tactics by not allowing the Permanent Indus Commission members of Pakistan from visiting the dam site for four years after having been officially informed of the project in 1998, little recognizing that the 1999 Kargil conflict and the general mobilization of Indian troops as part of *Op.*

Parakram following the Dec. 13, 2001 Parliament attack, both events of Pakistan's own making, prevented such site visits. In fact, India suspended the site visit on Dec. 24, 2001 following the decision to mobilize troops. Pakistan also contests that it was informed only in 1998 about the Bagilhar project, though the GoI had informed Pakistan as early as 1992.

The Pakistani Commissioner of the Permanent Indus Commission had recommended to his government to appoint a neutral expert in Feb. 2003 and accordingly Pakistan claims to have served two notices to GoI in May and November of the same year. Following the February meeting, India allowed a visit by Pakistani experts to the Baglihar project site in October.

The Pakistani Commissioner is reported to have made the same recommendation to his Government in January 2004 after another round of PIC meeting. On December 15, 2004, India supplied Pakistan with more data on the project as a goodwill gesture and rejected Pakistan 's claims of violation of IWT. However, Pakistan rebuffed India 's explanations, refused India one week time to study and reply, and decided to discontinue the talks-illustrating Pakistani leadership uncompromising attitude and intransigence. By mid January 2005, Pakistan requested the World Bank to appoint a neutral expert under Article 9(2)(A) of the IWT, claiming one week later that the World Bank chief Mr.Wolfensohn, honored with Pakistan's highest award of Hilal-e-Pakistan during a visit to that country in early February 2005, had assured Gen. Musharraf that there would be no delay in appointing such an expert. While responding to enquiries from World Bank, India advised the Bank that rather it should allow the suspended bilateral course of action to resume rather than get involved at that stage especially as some convergence of views had appeared in the last round of talks in New Delhi. Meanwhile, Pakistan 's Minister for Education and former head of the ISI, Javed Ashraf Qazi, warned the Pakistani National Senate that the nation might go to war with India over Baglihar "controversy."

Embankment on Ravi

Pakistan claims that India has built a 15-Km long embankment (also known as River Training Works, RTWs) on river Ravi in the Narowal sector in 2002, in front of Kot Naina, a village in Shakargarh Distt. Pakistan claims that such a construction "so close to the international border" is violative of both the IWT and the Border Ground Rules, 1961 and has caused flooding on its side. By 2002, Pakistan had also decided to build a similar embankment on its side.

Issues Within Pakistan

The Indus River system, which accounts for 65% of water flow within an arid Pakistan, poses several major challenges to Pakistan today. Pakistan faces both political and non-political problems with respect to The Indus River System.

On the political front, there have been serious differences among the various provinces about sharing of the waters. In Sind, sea water has intruded as much as 54 miles into the estuary of the Indus river due to low or no flow. On the basis of a series of meetings among provinces in March 1991, an agreement, Water Agreement Accord (WAA), was reached on the sharing of the river waters. It stipulated the following allocations

Table : Water Allocation among Pakistani Provinces, 1991 (in MAF)

Province	Kharif	Rabi	Total
Punjab	37.07	18.87	55.94
Sindh *	33.94	14.82	48.76
NWFP **	3.48	2.30	5.78
Civil Canals	1.80	1.20	3.00
Balochistan	2.85	1.02	3.87

* - Including requirements of Karachi

** - Ungauged Civil Canals above the rim stations where measurements can be made

It was also decided to set up in 1992, an "Indus River System Authority" (IRSA), as per provisions of the 1991 Accord, with representation from all four provinces. However, actual water allocations have been made on the basis of "historic use" rather than on the 1991 settlement leading to more resentment in Sindh.

The climatic changes due to global warming have led to depleting flow in all Indus River system of rivers, especially the Indus, which depends on glacial runoffs for 90% of its waters. Generally, the Himalayan rivers also carry a very heavy sediment load especially during summer and rainy season, which in turn leads to river shifting and silting of dams and barrages.

The three largest dams in Pakistan, Tarbela, Mangla and Chashma have already lost ~ 25% of their capacity due to silting. This is a serious problem in a country which depends on river irrigation, rather than the monsoon rains, for 74% of its total cultivated land.

It is generally agreed that 40% of all the water drawn through the canals at barrage heads is lost because of seepage due to un-lined and porous beds and banks of the canals. Such problems exacerbate the already poor yield of the crops In addition, there is excessive system-loss of water due to improper and antiquated agricultural techniques and heavy cropping of water-intensive varieties like sugarcane and rice. While reeling under increasing drought for the last six years, it is also predicted that Pakistan will have a certain level of drought conditions for the next 15 years.. Since the dams mostly act as storage reservoirs during *Kharif* season and draw-down reservoirs during *Rabi*, there is an acute need within Pakistan for more storage.

There have been widespread protests against the proposed dams of Kalabagh at Mianwali, and Basha at Chilas, Gilgit area and the raising of the Mangla dam in Mirpur. Out of the four provinces of Pakistan, three viz. Sindh, Balochistan and NWFP are against these dams. Even the illegally occupied PoK and Balawaristan oppose the dam projects of Mangla and Basha. The proposed raising of the height of Mangla Dam in Mirpur, PoK, by another 40 feet, will further submerge that district. It is also possible that if India exercises its rights to store 1.5 MAF on Jhelum, the raised Mangla Dam will not fill up. The crux of the matter is the lack of agreement among provinces on the total water availability within the country.

Meanwhile, the dwindling flows of water and siltation have led to reduced power generation from the hydroelectric plants that are part of the Indus River System.. There is a real possibility of shutting down power generation permanently at Tarbela, leaving it for irrigation purposes only.

The dams, barrages and canals built to satisfy the increasing demands of water upstream have made water scarce in the Indus at the estuaries of the Arabian Sea causing the sea to push in and increase the salinity in 1.2 Million acres of farmlands. The discharge of freshwater from the Indus into the Arabian Sea has declined steadily from 85 MAF in the 1940s to about 10 MAF in the 90s and probably less today. Pakistan also uses the waters of the Indus rivers for another purpose, fortification of its defences along Indian borders. It has built a series of "defence canals" at strategic locations which are flooded at times of wars and tensions to prevent crossing by Indian armour and artillery. In 2002, after India mobilized its forces as part of Operation Parakram, Pakistan diverted waters to these "defence canals" accentuating the then already severe water shortage of 50% to over 70%.

The Indus remains important to both India and Pakistan in another less visible way. The extension of the exclusive economic zone (EEZ) beyond the 200 nautical mile (nm) limit from coastal baseline depends on the ability to prove the sedimentation of the Indus river into the sea and has to be claimed before May, 2009 The United Nations Convention on the Law of the Seas protocol allows the EEZ to be extended under several conditions. In places like the sedimentary basin of the Indus river, the sediment thickness of the rivers beyond the foot of the continental slope can be used to establish the outer limit of the continental shelf of a claimant. This requires baseline and bathymetry survey data. A crucial part of the claim is the delineation of the Territorial Sea Baseline (TSB) which is the set of coordinate points that define the line from which the seaward boundaries are to be measured. The continuing Pakistani wrangle with regards to Sir Creek has delayed the compilation and validation of the TSB thereby delaying the computation of the zone boundaries. This is important for India in view of the potential it has for national security, energy prospecting, mining, laying pipelines etc.

Conclusions

Pakistan faces one of the severest water shortages in the world as seen in its' per capita availability of water per annum fall from 5300 m^3 in 1951 to less than 1100 m^3 today. This figure is alarming given that it is below the internationally recommended level of 1500 m^3 and precariously close to the critical 1000 m^3 level. Compounded with the failure to fill the country's two largest reservoirs to capacity, declining flows in the Indus River System, elusive and contentious the inter-provincial water accord due to mutual suspicions among provinces, and an unsustainable population growth rate of 2% do not bode well for Pakistan's water situation. Disagreements on construction of new reservoirs, declining groundwater potential, and growing number of disputes with India after a relatively uneventful period of 44 years of water sharing will further complicate matters. In summation, the water situation in Pakistan (a country whose landscape is largely arid to semi-arid) is truly disastrous in spite of the Indus, its tributaries, and a treaty with generous concessions that has been implemented faithfully by upper riparian India to date in spite of grave provocations. Pakistani farmers may be forced to change to higher yielding earlier maturating crops, modify their sowing patterns, and employ micro irrigation in coming years to mitigate shortages-all of which will entail higher costs. Its frivolous objections to Indian projects and a general unwillingness to engage India constructively are partly to force India to amend the IWT to accommodate the emerging patterns of water use in Pakistan, such as water sharing during periods of shortage-a situation not envisaged in the treaty.

RIVERS WATER DISPUTE

The periodic scarcity of water in the Indus River System (IRS) gives rise to inter-provincial disputes especially between Punjab and Sindh which is the lower riparian of this system. Before proceeding further it is important to explain in common language certain technical terms used in case of flow, quantity and storage of water for irrigation and hydel power generation. The basic unit to measure the flow of water is 'cusec' which means a quantity of one cubic foot of water flowing in one second or commonly 6.24 gallons or 28 litres of clean water per second. The quantity of water is measured in terms of acre foot which equals the quantity of water needed to flood one acre of level ground to a depth of one Foot. This means 43560 cubic feet or 271,814 gallons or 1,223,165 litres of water. For very large quantities of water the term million acre feet (MAF) is used which equals a million or ten lakhs acre feet. In case of hydel-power, one cusec of water dropped from a height of 100 feet possesses gross potential energy to generate approximately 8.5 KW of electrical power and the amount of electricity produced is directly proportional to the height from which the same quantity of water is dropped. In the case of food production one acre foot of water applied to ordinarily levelled ground without any special inputs will produce 45 maunds of wheat. One cusec of water flowing continuously for 24 hours equals 1.98 acre foot of water.

These terms have been explained in order to enable ordinary readers to appreciate the potential that nature has hidden in the natural annual flow of water of a river both in terms of irrigation as well as hydel power. The flow of water in any river varies greatly from season to season and also from year to year. For this reason daily flows are recorded and tabled over a long period of time on weekly, monthly and annual basis. For the principle rivers of Indus River System, these records are available for seventy five years indicating maximum as well as minimum flows during different seasons. The rivers of this system are Indus itself and its tributaries Kabul, Jhelum, Chenab, Ravi, Bias and Sutlej. Since river Kabul merges with Indus at Attock ahead of classic Indus plains, therefore, the Indus River System is counted to comprise Indus below Attock and its tributaries the five rivers of Punjab.

There is one thing that must be very clearly understood. Allah Almighty holds into His exclusive discretion the quantity of water that flows into rivers at any time. Human ingenuity may make any device for storage and diversion of river flows but the sum total of the quantity shall always remain the same as Allah Almighty allows into the rivers. The construction of storage (dam) and diversion (barrage) schemes, therefore, solely depends on the total quantity of water that is available in a river during a year, particularly how these flows dovetail into the quantity of water needed during crop seasons.

This is the reason that has necessitated recording of river flows for long period of years. On the basis of over fifty years' record the mean flow in Indus River System (IRS) totalled 175 MAF on the eve of Partition of Punjab in 1947. This comprised 93 including 27 of Kabul for Indus, 23 for Jhelum, 26 for Chenab, 6 for Ravi, 13 for Bias and 14 for Sutlej in MAF annually. Out of this 175 MAF, 167 flowed into Pakistan at the time the boundaries of partitioned Punjab were fixed according to the Radcliffe Award. This means that the Indian East Punjab drew only 8 MAF of a total of 33 MAF of water that annually flowed in three eastern rivers Ravi, Bias and Sutlej before waters of these rivers entered West Punjab of Pakistan. Under the Internationally agreed rights of lower riparians and also Indian Independence Act 194, the balance 25 MAF waters of three eastern rivers were to be shared between India and Pakistan and India was also to guarantee non-interference in the existing supplies of canal waters flowing into Pakistan from Head Works (Madhopur and

Ferozpur) in India. The sordid tale must first be told as to how this life blood of Pakistan's agriculture was sold out to India first through the criminal conduct of Punjab Government in 1947 and later the infamous Indus Waters Treaty of 1960 which deprived Pakistan nearly one-sixth of its total surface water resources. This sell out is indeed a bigger act of treason against Pakistan than the separation of East Pakistan connived by 'patriots'.

Under Independence Act a Punjab Partition Council was set up comprising equal members from both East and West Punjab governments. An Arbitral Tribunal, with life up to March 31, 1948, was also set up to finally decide upon any contentious issues between the two governments. Committee B of the Partition Council was to decide upon the share of the three eastern rivers between the two governments and the canal waters. It was agreed between the representative of two governments that existing supplies of canal waters will not be disturbed and that the river waters shall be shared 'proportionally'. Under this formula the Rau Commission of 1941 had awarded East Punjab area of undivided Punjab construction of Bhakra Dam with a storage capacity of 4 MAF on river Sutlej. Both sides had, therefore, agreed to Pakistan's share of 21 MAF of three Eastern rivers and non-interference of supplies of waters of canals flowing into Pakistan from Madhopur and Ferozpur Head Works. The West Punjab government of Khan Mamdot with Daultana and Shaukat Hayat as key members, however, failed to draw out an agreement to this effect and register it with the Partition Council and relied only on the verbal assurances of their lingual brothers of East Punjab.

Consequently, as soon as the Arbitral Tribunal was abolished, India turned off the tap on canal waters on April 1, 1948 and on Pakistan's protest denied any agreement and claimed all waters of canals and eastern rivers to it. Chaudhri Muhammad Ali then Secretary General of Pakistan writes on the episode that on the part of East Punjab there was Machiavellian duplicity. On the part of West Punjab there was neglect of duty, complacency and lack of common prudence which had disastrous effects on Pakistan. In May 1948 a delegation led by Ghulam Muhammad with Daultana and Shaukat Hayat as members went to Delhi to sort out the issue. On May 4,1948 Ghulam Muhammad signed a statement which said that apart from the question of law involved, the governments were anxious to approach the problem in a practical spirit. The East Punjab government would progressively diminish its supplies to Central Bari Doab and Dipalpur canals in West Punjab to give it reasonable time to tap alternative sources. The legally agreed right of Pakistan to the waters of three Eastern rivers and the canals flowing into it from India, was thus abjectley surrendered by the delegation which went to discuss the problem with Indians.

When news of this reached Karachi, Liaquat Ali Khan in a telegram to Nehru immediately disowned the 'statement' as signed under duress and also informed UNO not to register it as an expression of government of Pakistan since the dying Jinnah was still alive. It should be remembered that the canal waters flowing into Pakistan from India irrigated less than ten percent of the total irrigated area in then West Punjab and contributed little to overall agricultural output. The Ghulam Muhammad Delegation, however, laid the basis for India to claim all the waters of Eastern rivers to which India stuck during all negotiations between the two countries. Pakistan persistently refused such claims until India finally assembled 90 percent of its army on West Punjab borders to brow beat Pakistan into submission. It was at this time that Liaquat challenged India for a fight to finish although the first Pakistani Commander-In-Chief of Army advised against war. Unable to confront a nation aroused to fight to finish, India withdrew its army and the canal supplies continued to flow.

It was at this juncture that Chairman of Tennessee Valley Authority in United States described the canal water dispute as 'Punjab powder keg' and went on to say that with such 'inflammables' around there is no chance of peace in the sub-continent. This made World Bank President, Eugene Black, contact the two governments in September 1951 and made India agree to Liaquat's demand that until a just solution is found the existing arrangement of water supplies to Pakistan shall not be disturbed.

However, no sooner the 'hurdle' of Liaquat was removed in October 1951, India started throttling the canal waters which the post Liaquat factional governments were not able to confront on 'principle', eventually ending in the anti-Pakistan Indus Waters Treaty of 1960. Indians, perhaps, waited for the assassination of Liaquat to squeeze Pakistan on canal waters much the same way as they waited till the death of Quaid-e-Azam to occupy Hyderabad in blatant disregard of its own Stand Still Agreement.

TRANSBOUNDARY WATER DISPUTES IN CENTRAL ASIA

Over the last decades, there has been a growing speculation about the likelihood of an acute conflict or even war over freshwater resources.

Scholars increasingly point out that the 21st century might see the battles fought due to water scarcity. Indeed, water is the only resource having no substitute, and the demand for it is constant and burning. All forms of the Earth's life, including humans, need water to survive. The fact that we inhabit the 'water planet' soothes little as only less than 3% of total water resources on the Earth are freshwater. Its distribution is obviously uneven, with some nations suffering severe droughts every year and the others blessed with water abundance.

It is no wonder then that through the whole history of human race, water allocation and quantity fuelled tensions between various states, with particular role played by transboundary river resources. And although history shows that full-scale wars over water, proving to be neither strategically rational nor hydrographically effective, have never been fought, water continues to be a source of intense disputes worldwide.

The problem grows harder when it comes to the relationships between two or more countries over river water as a result of the "internationalisation of a basin through political change. The number of international basins has grown from 214 in 1978 to 263 today. These international basins cover 45.3% of total land surface, affect about 40% of the world's population, and account for about 60% of global river flow.

Nineteen basins are shared by 5 or more riparian countries, with only the Danube being shared by 17 riparians, whereas five basins – the Congo, Niger, Nile, Rhine and Zambezi – are shared by between 9 and 11 countries.

In this situation, such long-negotiated instrument of international water law as the 1997 UN Convention on the Non-Navigational Uses of International Watercourses, is of little help as it provides for equally contradictory 'equitable use' and 'no significant harm' principles: while the former is favoured by upstream countries, downstream riparians insist on emphasising the latter because it protects their own rights.

It is also difficult to enforce the Convention in the absence of any international enforcing mechanisms. More importantly, the Convention hardly weighs out a variety of political, social, economic, demographic and environmental factors that encompass each shared river basin.

Negotiators whose task is to provide timely diplomatic intervention, or apply means of the so-called 'preventive diplomacy', in order to avoid the escalation of a dispute into open conflict need to be aware which basin is prone to water conflict well in advance. To do that, they need to identify potential indicators of conflict that incorporate a wide range of physical, social, economic and environmental variables, including those which can be analysed within a Geographic Information System (GIS), and to develop a comprehensive model to explore specific linkages between them. In particular, this method can be applicable in those cases of internationally shared rivers where progress towards successful resolution of a dispute was slow or unachievable.

Considering all factors having influence on the river basin regime is becoming crucial to elaborate meaningful and workable framework to provide resolution to the growing water conflict.

Since the collapse of the Soviet Union, Central Asia has become a tangle of unresolved transboundary water disputes. Water is the most critical resource in Central Asia and it "has more often been the source of competition rather than the focus of conservation.

The absence of mechanisms to handle the water problems has already resulted in various accusations of improper water use. Consequently, the whole region becomes the site of potential conflict that requires a framework which should incorporate a great many variables to identify the proneness to water conflict and to allow for the possibility of preventive diplomacy.

Such method which has never been used towards the specific problem of Central Asian water disputes can provide solutions based on a more holistic approach to natural resources, while recognising the historical, geopolitical and natural characteristics of the region.

This study seeks to identify potential indicators of water conflict and analyse some of them within the Geographical Information System (GIS).

Unlike other studies that involve global level analysis, the thesis will focus on Central Asia's regional and basin specific information. An attempt to answer a question of what indicators better point to water conflict will be taken.

Hypothesis

The study aims at testing the working hypothesis that proneness of a specific river basin to water conflict can be identified through a variety of indicators representing physical, political, environmental and socio-economic processes occurring in this specific region, thus providing better chance for using preventive diplomatic actions.

Methodology

The study's methodology is based on the concept of international river basins offered by the Transboundary Freshwater Dispute Database (TFDD), Oregon State University. The database contains a large collection of water treaties and agreements and is a sound foundation for transboundary water conflict research. For the purposes of this study, the Amu Darya Basin is examined. Taking the basin as a unit of research, the proposed study offers a model of relationship between water resources and social, political, economic and environmental patterns in Central Asia. There is also chance to explore the use of GIS such as ESRI Arc View for social research. A parallel analysis of water conflict related variables focuses on finding combinations of indicators that provide an indication of potential water conflict.

KASHMIR AND THE POLITICS OF WATER

The Indus River originates in the Tibetan plateau, making its 3,200km journey southwards along the entire length of Pakistan, before emptying into the Arabian Sea. The river basin is divided between Pakistan, which has about 60 per cent of the catchment area, India with about 20 per cent, Afghanistan with 5 per cent and around 15 per cent in Tibet. The two major riparians, Pakistan and India have extensively dammed the Indus River to provide for irrigation and hydro-electricity.

The Indus has five main tributaries. The Jhelum, the largest of these, originates in the Valley of Kashmir. The Chenab, a second tributary, flows through the Jammu region of the state of Jammu and Kashmir before entering the Indian state of Punjab. The remaining three tributaries (Ravi, Sutlej and Beas) either originate or flow through India's state of Himachal before entering Indian Punjab.

As a result, if the Line of Control (LoC) between India and Pakistan in Kashmir, were to move from being a defacto to a recognised international border, India would permanently become the upper riparian and Pakistan the lower riparian of the Indus River and all of its tributaries.

The Indus is a river system that sustains communities in both India and Pakistan. In Pakistan, it is the only river system supporting the country, where more than 92 per cent of the land is arid or semi-arid. In India, it is one of two main river systems supporting the country's northwest: Punjab, Haryana and Rajasthan (generally considered to be water deficient areas).

Given that over half of Pakistan's population is employed in the agricultural sector and that Punjab produces more than 20 per cent of India's wheat and is known as the "bread basket" of the Republic of India, the importance of the Indus River to the well-being and economy of both countries cannot be overemphasised.

In arbitrating the border between India and Pakistan in 1947, Sir Cyril Radcliffe, the chairman of the bodies set up to demarcate the borders, was unable to decide what to do with the Indus River system, given that it was likely to be vital to both states.

The biggest problem, of course, lay with the partitioning of the state of Punjab, as it contained a complex irrigation system built by the British to be run under a single administration. The task was eventually delegated to the Chief Engineers of East Punjab (India) and West Punjab (Pakistan) who agreed to allow the existing water sharing systems to continue until the following year. This Standstill Agreement between India and Pakistan expired on March 31, 1948. On the following day Indian Punjab cut off water flow to Pakistan.

The conflict in Kashmir overlapped with the water disputes, and by January 1948 India had taken the Kashmir issue to the United Nations Security Council (UNSC). On April 21, 1948, a resolution calling for a ceasefire and withdrawal of all troops was passed.

The Kashmir dispute and disputes over the sharing of water resources are intertwined. From independence to the present day, they remain the two biggest challenges when it comes to normalising relations between the states of India and Pakistan.

Later in 1948, Eugene Black, then president of the World Bank, offered the services of his organisation to help negotiate a solution to the water-sharing dispute between the two countries. Although India was not eager to allow third-party involvement, both countries eventually agreed to this proposal.

Evidence and records from the time suggest that in 1948, when the Kashmir issue was taken to the UNSC and the canal dispute between East and West Punjab first arose (in April of that year), they were treated as distinctly separate political and economic issues.

In the early days of independence, the fact that India was able to shut off the Central Bari Doab Canals at the time of the sowing season, causing significant damage to Pakistan's crops, exposed a central weakness and vulnerability in the newly created state that was desperately trying to establish its independence.

As noted by one British general on a visit to the area in 1948, the dispute centres around the "water insecur[ity]" of Pakistan, as all of its rivers either originate in or pass through India.

Experts agreed, saying that resolving water disputes under the auspices of the World Bank was "one way to reduce hostility" over Kashmir.

Nevertheless, military and political clashes over Kashmir in the early years of independence appear to be more about ideology and sovereignity, rather than sharing water resources. A communique from the British High Commissioner's office in Karachi, then capital of Pakistan, from November 1951 seems to suggest otherwise, however:

"But one assumption they have refused to entertain: that India should have control over Kashmir. By having such control India could ruin Pakistan, simply by refusing to operate Mangla at the headworks. It is almost certain therefore that Pakistan would reject any solution of the Kashmir problem which would give these powers; she would rather embark on a war which she fully understood to be suicidal."

Indian ministers at the time were also issuing statements, saying that controlling the entire flow of the Indus river would be impossible, "even if India controlled Kashmir".

It would appear that somewhere along the ideological path, as negotiations on water were being held, politicians worked out that a resolution to the water dispute may well directly influence the Kashmir problem.

Indeed some experts have suggested that Pakistan thought that it could solve the Kashmir dispute through solving canal-related issues, but India completely denied this route of resolution.

Consequently, the Indus Water Treaty was signed by both countries in September 1960, giving exclusive rights over the three western rivers of the Indus river system (Jhelum, Chenab and Indus) to Pakistan, and over the three eastern rivers (Sutlej, Ravi and Beas) to India.

The signing of the treaty and the FINANCING of various water storage projects to benefit Pakistan and India meant that tensions were minimal and to a great degree much of Kashmir's water importance was forgotten for the next couple of decades.

As the populations of both countries increased exponentially, however, water resources came under increasing stress. With India preparing ambitious irrigation project plans, it was possible to see how, by the 1990s, Kashmir's hydrological importance had once again become a serious issue.

The fact that, unlike India, all of Pakistan is wholly dependent upon the Indus River system is a geographical reality. Another reality that compounds this one is the fact that, as the upstream riparian on all five of the main Indus tributaries that flow into Pakistan, India has the strategically advantageous position with regards to control and flow of water.

John Briscoe, a subcontinental water expert, former World Bank senior water expert and currently a professor at Harvard University, recognised Pakistan's unhappy position in the following words: "This is a very uneven playing field. The regional hegemon is the upper riparian and has all the cards in its hands." Pakistan is all too aware of its vulnerable position vis-a-vis water and the fact that more than half of independent Pakistan's time has been spent under military rule has not helped to de-escalate or 'de-securitise' the water discourse in the country.

Over the years, water has been raised as an issue directly linked to Kashmir. Pakistan's political leaders and military elites have emphasised that if they are forced to let go of their claim to Kashmir, that will mean letting go of the source of Jhelum and Chenab as well and being at the mercy of India for water. Though it is unrealistic to assume that India could readily and easily violate the terms of the Indus Water Treaty, Briscoe emphasises that Pakistan and India do not have "normal, trustful relations". The trust deficit along with the fact that India once blocked water flows to Pakistan has the military establishment convinced that they must hold on to their claim to Kashmir in an effort to maintain the country's water security.

Interestingly enough, another Pakistani organisation that has been vociferous in defending Pakistan's rights over Kashmir and criticising India's "aggression" against Pakistan through reduced water flows is the 'charity' Jammat-ud-Dawa (JuD). The JuD is widely believed to be a front group of the militant outfit Lashkar-e-Taiba (LeT) that has been linked to the Mumbai attacks of 2008.

Though there is widespread conjecture on the organisation's close association with Pakistan's intelligence agencies, officially, such a relationship has always been denied. It is worth noting that the JuD has publicly declared India's "occupation" of Kashmir unacceptable and has also termed its policy of blocking water to Pakistan a justification to wage jihad. In most public statements, however, the JuD tends not to link water and Kashmir, in contrast to the Pakistani military's position on the argument.

India has consistently and emphatically maintained that it has never meddled with Pakistan's share of the Indus waters. Even as the Indus Water Treaty was being negotiated, with the Indian government assuring Pakistan and the World Bank that water was not being blocked, Chintamanrao Deshmukh, the then IndianFINANCE minister, stated in a 1953 parliamentary address that the serious food shortage in Pakistan was not a result of India blocking river flows.

"Even if it were assumed that some mistakes were made at some short period, which in any case did not exceed one or two weeks," he said.

Throughout the history of the dispute, India has rarely, if ever, acknowledged that it has tampered with the supply of water flowing into Pakistan. Since there is also a large amount of secrecy that surrounds the governance of the Indus waters and data is not readily shared, there is no definitive way to prove whether India has just got caught up in Pakistani sensationalism or whether the seeds of resentment and securitisation of water were sowed and are being maintained by the Indian side.

In negotiations and meetings with Pakistani counterparts on the wider Indo-Pak relationship, India does not deal with water and Kashmir as the same issue. In fact, it has often been suggested by analysts that a more consolidated agreement on water might perhaps be a more readily achievable goal in India-Pakistan composite dialogue as COMPARED to Kashmir.

Briscoe finds that the Indian press seems to have a uniform view on water issues, in relation to Pakistan. He says that it was explained to him as follows: "When it comes to Kashmir - and the Indus Treaty is considered an integral part of Kashmir" - the ministry of external affairs (India's foreign ministry) instructs the media about what they are allowed to say. In certain cases, India is happy to conflate the Kashmir and water issues, whereas in negotiations with Pakistan it would like to deal with them as distinct and separate.

Currently, India is in the process of building a number of dams on the Jhelum and Chenab Rivers (both of which originate in Kashmir), such as the Kishenganga, Dal Huste, Sawalkot etc. The Indus Water Treaty allows India to harness the hydropower potential of the Jhelum and Chenab Rivers, as long as it does not reduce or delay the supply to Pakistan. India therefore maintains that its projects are in compliance with the treaty and sees no conflict with Pakistan on these issues.

The region of Kashmir sees itself losing considerably from the Indus Water Treaty because it is not allowed to fully exploit the hydropower potential of its own rivers.

In June 2011, a Chinese news agency reported that the state government of Kashmir was looking for reputed multi-national consultancies to calculate the exact loss to Kashmir from the Indus Water Treaty so that the government will have a number it can take to the Indian federal government. Given that both Pakistan and India are dangerously energy and water starved and nowhere close to an agreement on Kashmir, teamed with the impact of climate change and population pressures, the prognosis on the Indo-Pak water problem involving Kashmir is anything but positive.

INDUS RIVER SYSTEM AND ITS IMPORTANCE FOR INDIA AND PAKISTAN

Indus river basin drains the highland of four riparian countries, Pakistan, India, Afghanistan and China. The rough terrains surrounding the river in China and Afghanistan has so far minimized these states ability to develop the river within their border but China and Afghanistan are asserting their rights to a reasonable and equitable share of the Indus tributaries flowing through their territory. Afghanistan has started to build a dam on Kabul River for hydropower generation but mainly India and Pakistan are dependent on the Indus river system. Out of about 193 million total populations, 72% of Pakistan and 23% of Indian live in Indus basin system.

For Pakistan, Indus River is the main source for domestic, industrial and agricultural water. Agriculture is vital for Pakistan's welfare and its role is like a backbone in national economy. This sector employed 43% of Pakistan's labour force and contributed about 25% of Pakistan GDP. In spite of the fact, Pakistan agriculture is mostly dependent on irrigation network because of little rainfall, low quality ground water etc. Of the total irrigated area of Indus River, 74 % is located in Pakistan that provides over 60% of the water utilized for irrigation purposes through the world best and largest irrigational network. The irrigational network comprises of 3 reservoirs (Tarbela, Chashma on Indus River and Mangla on Jhelum River), 19 large river barrage and 45 independent irrigational canal commands, some 1.6 million km water courses and 144 large dams. The irrigational network almost spread out more than one third part of country. About 78% of Pakistan's cultivated area is under irrigation and it ranks second in the world after Egypt.

Background

The canals and barrages built under the British rule to serve Indo-Pak continent were under partition in 1947. As a result of partition, these canals network is divided into East Punjab that is in India and West Punjab in Pakistan. For India, the real problem arose when out of 26 million acres of land annually irrigated by Indus and its tributaries, 21 million acres became part of Pakistan. But, the headworks of the entire network remained in India. During the division of Punjab into East and West regions, Punjab partition committee was established to settle down the dispute related to division of assets between East and West Punjab provinces. In 1947 both east and west Punjab were agree that water shall be divided equally.

Pakistan and India disputes over Indus water erupted soon after eight months of independence, when India cut off the water coming across the border into Pakistan in 1948. East Punjab cut off the supplies of every single canal that crossed the border and declared its decision not to restore the flow of these canals, unless west Punjab recognized that it had no rights to the water and resumed the flows only after Pakistan made a payment to India. This situation was extremely stressful for west Punjab farmers dependent upon them.

In May1948, Simla agreement was signed but, Pakistan rejected it in early 1950s arguing that it has been forced upon them. From the early 1950s the situation had reached to a deadlock and there was no communication over water between both countries for a long period of time.

INDUS RIVER BASIN

The Indus river basin is one of the largest basins in Asia covering an area of 1,165,000 km2. The river flows through four countries in south Asia including, China in north- east, India in east, Afghanistan in north-west and Khyber Pakhtunkhwa and majority of plains of the Punjab and Sindh in Pakistan. The Indus river basin comprise of Indus river, its two western tributaries the Kabul and Kurram rivers and five eastern tributaries the Jhelum, Ravi, Beas, Sutlej and Chenab rivers. Indus and Sutlej originate from Lake Manasarovarin in Tibet. Chenab River originates from Himachal Pradesh in India and flows through Kashmir valley and into Pakistan. Ravi also originates from Himachal Pradesh but directly flows into Punjab and then Pakistan. Beas originates and flows entirely in India. Jhelum originates in the Kashmir valley of India and flows to Pakistan.

Kabul River rises in Afghanistan and flows through the Peshawar valley to join the Indus at Attock. These five main left bank tributaries have an aggregate length of more than 2,800 miles and Kabul River and Kurram River together cover more than 700 miles.

The basin is the home to three world's mightiest mountain ranges (Karakoram, Himalayan and Hindukush). The basin originates at 17,000 feet above sea level in Tibetan plateau. The river pass through Indian occupied Jammu and Kashmir, enters into north area of Pakistan and finally merge into an Arabian sea. Most of its flows around 69% originate from India, compared to 12% for Tibet and Afghanistan and 19% for Pakistan.. The drainage area which extends into india is 45,000 square miles and contribute to an average annual inflow (including all rivers) of 175 million acre feet.. The snow melting in the Himalayan- Hindukush regions and precipitations in mountains are the major components of the annual flow of these rivers. Climate is not uniform over Indus basin region. It varies from arid to semi arid to temperate sub-humid in the plains of Sindh and Punjab provinces. Annual precipitations ranges maximum 2000 mm on mountain slopes and between 100 to 500 mm in the lowlands. Abundant flow is during the monsoon season (July- September), which contributes 51% of annual flow.

INDUS WATER TREATY (IWT)

The president of International Bank of Reconstruction and Development, Mr. Eugene Black offered his good office to settle the water dispute. After close to eight years of negotiation the IWT came into existence. The IWT was concluded by India and Pakistan with the World Bank's mediation on 19th of September 1960. IWT based on the allocation of Indus and its tributaries. According to IWT the three Eastern Rivers (Ravi, Beas and Sutlej) allocated to India and three Western Rivers (Indus, Jhelum and Chenab) allocated to Pakistan. India has unrestricted use of the Eastern Rivers and Pakistan has a right for the exclusive use of Western Rivers. India can use the water of Western Rivers for hydropower generations, to meet the domestic, Industrial and irrigation requirements of Jammu-Kashmir and also develop these tributaries for flood protection, floating of timbers and fishing. It clearly mentioned in IWT that, Pakistan has to construct infrastructure to meet the Eastern Rivers needs from the Western Rivers and India has to pay fixed amount of money to Pakistan to build infrastructures. Both parties have to regularly exchange flow data.

A permanent Indus commission (PIC) established to supervise implementation of the IWT. Implementation of IWT with the involvement of PIC is one of the successful agreements for resolving trans-boundary water issues. PIC worked very well for maintaining the soul of treaty. The commissioners are obliged to meet once a year, altering their meetings places between the two countries. During their meetings, they plan and organize their tours, exchange data and information regarding the current and future developments. If either of the countries have questions, regarding the projects and maintenance work, the problems can be referred to PIC. If PIC is unable to resolve the issues, then the question becomes a difference and could be referred to a Neutral expert, either appointed by two members of commission or by a third party. If the neutral expert failed to solve the difference then it should be treated as disputes and then International Court of Arbitration (ICA) could be establish to resolve the disputes..

WATER CRISIS IN THE INDUS BASIN

Pakistan is one of the world's most arid countries with an average rainfall of less than 240 mm. Indus water is the only source of water for domestic agriculture and industrial needs. Agriculture importance is like the backbone in Pakistan's economy. Indus flow plays a major contribution in maintaining and developing Pakistan's economy as it provides over 60% of the water utilized for irrigation purposes. Continuation in population growth with high demand of food, water and energy increasing strains on limited water resources. Now a day Pakistan faces a very severe water crisis. One third of the country population is living under water stress condition. An estimated report of November 2008 shows that out of 165 million population of Pakistan, 25% are below poverty level, 98 million rely on agriculture, 50 million do not have access to safe drinking water and 74 million have no sanitation. The gap between demand and supply is widening. In 2004, water shortfall was 11 MAF which is expected to ascend to 31 MAF in 2013. Water availability has been declining at an alarming rate from 5000 cubic meter per capita in 1951 to about 1100 cubic meter currently and it has been projected to less than 700 cubic meter by 2025. Pakistan's total water demand in 2025 is projected to 338 bcm suggesting a gap of 100 bcm.

Compared to Pakistan, India is a semi arid country. Over 70% of Indian's live in rural areas and agriculture is the primary source of their livelihood. About 200 million people are directly employed by agriculture (Government of India Ministry of Agriculture 2005). Population is growing rapidly after China, India is the second largest country having population of 1,241 million (2011 world population datasheet).

Rising population with high demand of water put more pressure on limited resources. India's per capita water availability has declined from 5000 cubic meters in 1950 to 1800 cubic meters in 2005 and it has been assumed that per capita water availability will fall below 1000 cubic meters by 2050. Growing demand of food and energy pushed India to concentrate for water conservation and power generation projects.

Many analysts argue that GDP growth of 7% per year requires a 10 % increase in annual supply. India booming economy needs energy to grow particularly in Jammu and Kashmir that has many potential hydroelectric sites despite the fact that, Jammu and Kashmir faces energy crisis. Despite the potential of 30,000MW of power, 25% of our population has no access to electricity and 75% is getting episodic electricity.

High demands of water to meet the challenges of rapid increase in population, increased urbanization and industrialization creating a competing environment for a limiting water resource. Limited water availability with high demand also creates some sort of intrastate tensions in Pakistan and India. Both countries desperately need water for booming their economy and trying hard to get access as much as they can. Although, the Indus water treaty has been successful in managing the war between Pakistan and India two and half times and worked very well for more than 50 years. But, there are series of disagreement going on between both these riparian countries.

Baglihar Hydroelectric Dam

Baglihar Dam was one of the most controversial issues. India planned to build Baglihar dam on the Chenab River 60 miles up streams from the Pakistani border. Under the IWT India has a right to build upstream non storage facilities but it must not alter or influence the flow of the river. Pakistan had a number of objections over the construction of this dam. Pakistan claimed that dam design did not following the criteria (a), (c), (e) and (f) of paragraph 8 to the treaty.

- Criteria (a) states that the work shall not be capable of raising the water level artificially above the full pondage level specified in design. Pakistan claimed that dam design is excessive and provided ability to India for raising artificial water level above the full pondage level.
- Criteria (c) requires that the maximum pondage in the operating pool not to exceed twice the pondage required for firm power and Pakistan claimed that the pondage in operating tool mentioned by India is excessive. So it should be reduced.
- Criteria (e) state that if the conditions for gated spillway is necessary, the bottom level of gates in normal closed position shall be located at the highest level consistent with sound and economical design. Bone of contention on this point, Pakistan claimed that design was not based on reality and correct estimates of flood discharge. Pakistan claimed that spillway was not necessary. Either un-gated or surface gated spillway could be provided with the bottom of the gates with the highest level.
- Criteria (f) require that intake for the turbine shall be located at the highest level coherent with sufficient and economical construction and operation of the plant as

run off river plant. Pakistan had an objection that the location of intake power is not at the highest level as mandated in IWT.

Although, both countries tried hard to settle the issue by themselves but bilateral negotiation did not bear any productive result. So, first time in the history of IWT, on January 15, 2005, Pakistan asked for World Bank to appoint a neutral expert to resolve the differences over Baghliar dam. After five months of the original request, Raymond Lafitte, professor of Swiss Institute of Technology in Lausanne was appointed as a neutral expert to address the differences regarding Baglihar project.

In February, 2007, Lafitte delivered his final decision to both parties and also one copy of decision to World Bank. In his report he partly addressed some objections of Pakistan like, reduced the pondage capacity, increased 3m height of power intake and acknowledged India's right to construct gated spillway. Both countries agreed to follow the final descision of the neutral expert.

But, the dispute again activated when, India filled the dam during the dry season in 2008, that seriously disturbed the livelihood and agriculture production of Pakistan. Pakistani media and local people blamed that India stole water having rights of Pakistan. The filing of Baglihar dam above Marala reduced the flow as low as 20000 cusec, whereas India obliged to maintain the minimum inflow at the level of 55,000 cusec.

Pakistan lost about 2 MAF of water from August, 25, 2008 to September, 4, 2008 and it adversely affected Pakistan's wheat crop. President of Pakistan even raised the issue in his speech to the UN General Assembly.

Pakistan strongly protested and claimed that India is violating the IWT. But this time, Pakistan decided to solve the issue by negotiation. Indian commission admitted that reduction was because of unavailability of any mechanism to pass the flow at the low level. He explained that this happened because we were expecting heavy rainfall during these days. Pakistan's Indus commissioner in an interview told that although "Pakistan felt that parameter and procedure mentioned in IWT were not followed during the initial filling of the dam. We have resolved the differences on the initial filling of the dam in a spirit of cooperation and good will and India gave us the insurance that it will be careful in future".

Wullar Barrage/ Tulbul Navigation Project

Wullar barrage or tulbul navigation project being constructed by India on Jhelum River just below Wullar lake located 25 kilometers north of Srinagar at 5180 feet above sea level. The project has been started by government of Indian state of Jammu and Kashmir. The dispute emerged in 1985 when Pakistan learnt through the notification of tender notice in newspaper. Pakistan calls it a Wullar barrage constructed by India for storage purposes and India refer it as a Tulbul Navigation project for transportation of fruits and timbers.

Pakistan strongly opposed the construction of this project. Pakistan claimed that construction of such a project on that site had a potential to unfavorably affect the triple canal project in Pakistan namely, Upper Chenab Canal, Upper Jhelum Canal and lower Bari Doab Canal. Pakistan believed that construction of this barrage would provide India with the means to control over River Jhelum that could facilitate India to stop water flow during winter. The Mangla Dam on Jhelum River, which is a main source of irrigation and electricity for Punjab, would be adversely affected. Moreover, Pakistan has an apprehension that India could close the gate of barrage during war so, enhancing the ability of Indian troops to come in Pakistan. Pakistan remembered in the connection of 1965 war, when Indian army had failed to cross the Bambanwali Ravi Bedian Link Canal because of its full flow.

Indian government argues that, the purpose of Tulbul project is only to improve the navigations in Jhelum River during lean month in order to connect Srinagar with Baramula. Indian claimed that 90 percent of this project would be beneficial to Pakistan, as it would increase the power generation capacity of Mangla. The project would regulate the supply of Mangla dam as well as increase the efficiency of irrigation network in Pakistan Punjab. India argues that the Tulbul Project would be effective in reducing the flow of water during the flood seasons and suggest that Pakistan should bear the share of construction. Pakistan assert that the Wullar barrage capacity is more than 300,000 acre feet and according to IWT, the India is only allowed to construct storage work on western tributaries, if it does not exceed 100000 acre feet and the design has been approved by Pakistan. Pakistan referred this issue to the Indus commission in 1986, but commission failed to resolve it. Pakistan then decided to take the case to a International court of arbitration (ICA), but India postponed the construction. About ten rounds of talk have already been done but only with little progress. Pakistan gave an option to stop the construction of Kishanganga project on Neelum River, which would affect the Neelum-Jhelum Project constructed by Pakistan.

Kishanganga Hydroelectric Project (KHEP)

Now the current controversy is related to Kishanganga hydroelectric project (KHEP) that entangled two countries in conflict. This is the 330 MW Hydropower project in India about 160 km upstreasm of Muzaffarabad. The KHEP involves the 100 km diversion of Kishanganga River (called the Neelum Riverin Pakistan) to a tributary named Bunar Madumati Nullah of Jhelum near Bunkot, through a 22 km tunnel. The water will rejoin the Jhelum through Wullar Lake near the town of Bandipur in Baramula district. Neelum is the greatest tributary of Jhelum River and runs about 150 km in Pakistan controlled Kashmir before it joins the Jhelum River near Muzafarabad. Because of this diversion, instead of Muzafarabad it will rejoin Jhelum in Indian controlled Kashmir. This diversion will change the direction of river about 204 km before it joins the Jhelum River near Muzafarabad, the site where Pakistan Neelum-Jhelum hydel Project is situated.

PAKISTAN'S APPREHENSIONS

Pakistan first received a report about the Indian's plan of this project in 1988, while India officially confirmed it in 1994. Pakistan claims that India is violating the IWT by diverting the water and water drawn from a given tributary must be return to the same river. According to IWT, upstream must release as much water as downstream have the capacity to store it and the diversion will also affect the ecosystems, it submerged the Pakistan controlled Kashmir and entire Neelum valley. It will affect 133, 000 hectors of irrigation in the Neelum valley. Pakistan also claims that 11 percent of water flow in summer and 27 percent flow in winter would reduce due to Kishanganga project. The Hydropower generation capacity of 969 MW Neelum-Jhelum Project which Pakistan is constructing on Jhelum River would reduce by 11 percent. The Kishanganga dam could reduce Pakistan's total water availability from an estimated 154 MAF per year and may affect a significant portion of the Mangla dam storage capacity besides declining the pressure required to generate electricity in Neelum-Jhelum Power Project. Pakistan also claims that the feasibility study of Neelum-Jhelum project has acquired right in favor of Pakistan..

INDIA'S APPREHENSIONS

India argues that the diversion will not affect the flow of water because the quantum of water will be the same as it before. The diversion of river is not matter instead of meeting in Pakistan controlled Kashmir it would meet in Indian controlled Kashmir. India also rejected Pakistan's objection of favoring feasibility study by quoted the Indus water treaty according to that the project authorized first would give top priority.

In May 2004, India promised to freeze all its work on the site and hold a meeting with Pakistan to remove its objections. Pakistan raised six objections of which one related to the power generation scheme, two to the diversion of water and three related to the design of dam. The issue was discussed in five meetings from November 2004 to November 2005 but it did not bear any prolific results. In 2006, India submitted the revised plan of the project, brought down the storage capacity by reducing the height of dam from 75.48m to 35.48 m. Pakistan rejected the revised plan having objection over the diversion of the water. Because, it will adversely affect the Neelum-Jhelum Project capacity, that Pakistan has a plan to complete in 2015 one year before the completion of KHEP.

According to the press report Pakistan Indus water commission Sayed Jamat Ali Shah said that New Dahli is not cooperating with us. Indian Government is not providing any project information before according to Indus water treaty the states have to share information on any new project before six month of starting.

"India never stole or blocked Pakistan's share of waters and has assured Pakistan that New Delhi would implement Indus Water Treaty in letter and spirit". Indus Water Commissioner of India G. Auranganathan.

Chairman Indus Water Treaty Council Hafiz Zahoor-ul-Hassan Dahr has stated that like the 131 round talk between Pakistan and India under Indus water treaty not bore any fruit and the latest series of dialogue would meet the same result. India is still willing and in favor of bilateral talk but Pakistan decided to take this issue to World Bank. So, Pakistan sent a legal notice to India on 20 May 2010 on Kishanganag hydropower project.

Because of the technical and legal objections, first time in the history of IWT, Pakistan took this issue to ICA. Pakistan nominated Jan Paulsson, head of Norwegian international law firm, and Bruno Simma, of the International Court of Justice, as its arbitrators in the Court of Arbitration. India nominated Peter Tomka, Vice-President of the International Court of Justice at Geneva and Lucius Caflisch, a Swiss international law expert who is a professor at the Graduate Institute of International Studies to represent it in the dispute. Although the two countries have rejected each other's nominees for the Court of Arbitration, they decided to set up a panel comprising a chairman, a legal member and an engineer to select the umpires, by drawing lots. In response to the Pakistan appeal, ICA on 25th September, 2011 has barred India from going ahead to work on controversial KHEP on Neelum River.

Limitations in IWT

Agreements on water have the prime importance in water allocation. It brings the national and international community to the same table for the joint management of their common resource. Signing agreements over water sharing might be easy but the real problem is to keep alive the agreements in letter and spirit. Agreements over share water resource not only motivate the riparian states to work together but also can be a source to promote peace and cooperation among states on other mutual issues. But the validity of agreements depends on the mutual interest of all the stakeholders, strength of their relationship, level of interdependency and cooperation. States with a good political relationship and mutual interest tend to co-operate more affectively then adversarial states. Agreements with good characteristics need to be workable for a long period of time. Only then they can positively contribute in peace and cooperation within a basin by addressing the future water needs of the riparian countries.

The 1960, Indus water agreement (IWT) signed for water allocation of Indus River between Pakistan and India. IWT worked very well for more than forty five years. During this time period both states have a difference on many issues but they settle the dispute by themselves. PIC tried hard to work in letter and spirit for the implementation of IWT. But one of the main drawbacks is the amputation surgery of the Indus basin into two. According to IWRM the whole basin should be treated as a single unit so that states can cooperate in more effective way for the sustainable management of river and land resources. But, this division reduced the level of cooperation among states. Although both state are highly interdependent on each other for the construction of infrastructure and pollution control etc. But in this agreement the level of joint basin management seems to be missing.

Another drawback is missing the perception of all stakeholders, their needs and future demands. Jammu and Kashmir is a disputed territory of which major part is under the control of India. At the time of treaty the population of Jammu and Kashmir was 3.5 million which now has increase three times. Increase population demanding more water and energy for boosting their economy. While, according to IWT Jammu and Kashmir can use only 10% of hydroelectric potential and 40% of cultivable land. Due to this restrictive use, people in Jammu and Kashmir facing high energy crisis.IWT signed in 1960, with the simple division of Indus basin without considering the future need. According to IWT, annually 135 MAF water were allocated to Pakistan. Compare to that time Pakistan population now has grown three times. Population growth result in declining per capita water availability. Now, Pakistan is under water scarce situation and the situation become worst in future if the current circumstances go as such.

Lack of Trust and Cooperation

Effective transboundary cooperation over shared water resources is closely related to the establishment of institutional organizations. Sufficient institutional capacities within an enabling environment are necessary for promoting good cooperation in order to manage the international river basins. Cooperation over shared water resource maintains regional stability by promoting peace and improving economic efficiency. Cooperation will enable better management of ecosystem, providing benefits to the river and underpinning all other benefits that can be derived. Cooperation over shared water resource can ease tension and provide gains in the form of savings that can be achieved.

Sustainable international rivers development depends on the cooperative management strategies. The IWRM concept of building cooperation at political, institutional and technical level within an enabling environment is the complimentary element for sustainable river basin management. Transboundary cooperation depends on the political, geographic and cultural circumstances. The countries having a bad history of political relations are less cooperative than others. Even in the presence of bilateral agreements, such countries are more reserve to cooperate unconditionally because of trust deficits. The establishment of an internationally acceptable legal principle to share the common rivers may itself not bring a solution. Complex water disputes can only be solved by co-operations and compromises.

IWT 1960 agreement is a successful bilateral agreement that obliged both states to cooperate on water management issues under the supervision of PIC. The commission is trying hard to monitor and implement of the IWT. As both states are striving to utilize limited resources with full potential by constructing hydropower projects and storage reservoirs. Pakistan claimed that India is not providing fair information on time as obliged in IWT to share information on any project before six month to start. Pakistan as a lower riparian has a fear of flood and drought by the construction of Indian's projects on western rivers and have a perception that India would be able to harm Pakistan during war time. These unilateral actions performed by upstream bear a fear of water scarcity to lower riparian.

Although, India is denying Pakistan's objections but this distrust environment is a result of lack of joint river basin management institutions, poor political relations and lack of cooperation. Due to poor historical political relations and lack of information exchange, a trust deficit environment has been developed between both states, that's became a major obstacle to achieve potential cooperation. This lack of trust and cooperation has led to several negative social, environmental and economic impacts, creating regional instabilities by affecting the livelihood of local people in Pakistan.

High politics

International rivers are more prone to conflict because of the involvement of more than one state interest. Poor state relations and lack of trust makes the water issue more politicize. States focused on other issues like nation security instead of considering the overall cooperative management of shared water resources. The involvement of political bodies in policy making and implementation put the water in less priority.

Indus river system also has the same effect. Because of the hostile relationship between Pakistan and India the element of effective joint cooperation seems to be missing. Kashmir issue and Pressure of fundamentalist group of people from both sides is the major obstacles in resolving water related issues jointly.

Moreover, as Indus seems to be a more political case; lack of accountability and transparency is highly observable in Indus water issue. Water governing authorities from India fear to give relevant information before time. All these Situations are the hindrance in joint management of Indus River Basin.

Revision of treaty

Many analysts from Pakistan claim that IWT is not in favor of Pakistan and experts from Kashmir have opinion that IWT is limiting their right to use water. The 1960 agreement of IWT does not fulfill the requirement of IWRM. IWRM is holistic and participatory approach; focus on the integration of all the sectors in decision making and implementation by considering the perspective of all stakeholders for sustainable management. This element of all stakeholder participation seems to be missing in 1960 agreement. The other major limitation of IWT is missing the considerations of future water demands. Treaty was signed when water was abundance and now due to high population growth and climate change both countries are facing water scarcity. Some experts also argue that IWT is not supporting the concept of IWRM because of the partition of Indus into two parts. According to IWRM, the whole basin should be taken as a single unit and it is essential to consider its social, economic and environmental interest for sustainable management. The partition of Indus basin into two has divided the interest of the users and also affected the environment and ecosystem of Indus basin.

IWT worked very well for more than forty five years, till now both countries are striving to implement the treaty with soul and spirit. The current circumstances reveal that IWT does not seem to work efficiently in future. Both countries have high water need for boosting their economy and to meet the future demands. To prevent the future disasters of acute water shortage, there is a dire need to revise the treaty according to the present and future demand of all the states while keeping in mind the environmental sustainability and equity.

Although, IWT obliged both countries to be interdependent before taking any action on Indus river but the level of cooperation is very low. The unilateral actions of India like construction of dams for hydropower generation and navigation projects extremely affecting the livelihood of Pakistan. As Indus is the life blood for Pakistan, is facing a high water scarcity situation and the conditions will become worst in near future. Now, there is a need for both countries to come forward and reconsider the IWT in a comprehensive way by involving the participation of all major stakeholders and considering their interests, needs and future demands.

Sustainable river basin management needs an effective role of river basin organizations. Organizations for managing share water resources could work efficiently, if they are independent to make decisions and willing to cooperate fairly. Under the revised treaty, a joint river basin organization should be established for sustainable and efficient utilization of Indus water resource. The organization should be independent and free to make decisions without any political pressure. There should not be any political interference in decision making and management of river resources. Working efficiency of joint river basin organization become strong by the participation and joint work of technical staff from riparian countries in analyzing the situation and decision making process.

As, in case of Columbia River, the 1964, Colombia river treaty between USA and Canada has provided significant benefits through the coordinated river basin management to both countries. To analyze the future flood and power situation both countries are cooperating on joint river basin management. There is no interference from political sides, only technical staffs are responsible to analyze the future needs and management requirements. After analyzing the whole situation the member of technical staff is free to take decision that is beneficial for both countries (U.S Army Corps of Engineers, 2009). There is a need to organize such type of joint Indus river basin organization for the sustainable management of limited Indus water resource. Establishment of joint river basin organization could be a catalyst to build trust among these two hostile riparian and will also enhance the benefit sharing. Sharing the benefits of cooperative water management is an integral part of the successful treaty design and implementation. In revised treaty, whole basin should be considered as a single unit and all states should oblige to cooperate fairly.

Cooperation at political, institutional and technical level is vital to manage share water resources effectively. Effective cooperation between states on shared resource not only improves the better management, it also enhances the regional stability by reducing the tensions at international levels. Establishment of joint river basin organization will be helpful in promoting cooperation by improving the level of transparency and accountability.

3

Indus Waters Treaty : An Indian Perspective

The Indus Waters Treaty is regarded internationally to be a successful instance of conflict-resolution between two countries that have otherwise been locked in mutual antagonism. That favorable view of the Treaty is by and large shared in India as well as in Pakistan, but there is a measure of dissatisfaction in both countries regarding matters of water-allocation in the Treaty. Furthermore, the operation of the Treaty has been characterized by a series of differences. Should we regard it as a success or a failure?

The Treaty has settled the water-sharing dispute, and it has managed to survive four wars. In that sense it must be regarded as a success. Dividing the river system into two segments was perhaps not the best thing to do; the better course might have been for the two countries jointly to manage the entire system in an integrated and holistic manner.

However, given the circumstances of Partition and the difficult relationship between the two newly formed countries, it would have been naïve to expect that such a joint, integrated, cooperative approach would work. If the best course is unavailable, then we have to settle for the second best – that is what the Treaty represents. The Treaty is essentially a partitioning agreement, not a grand instrument of inter-country cooperation. The land was partitioned in 1947, and the waters were partitioned in 1960.

TECHNICAL DIFFERENCES OVER PROJECTS

The water-sharing has been settled, but differences have continued to arise about certain design and engineering features of Indian projects on the western rivers. The Treaty allows India limited use of the waters of those rivers, but the use is subject to fairly stringent technical conditions and stipulations to safeguard Pakistan's interests.

Thus, the Treaty is both permissive and restrictive toward Indian projects – particularly big projects – on the western rivers. India tries to use the permissive provisions to the fullest, whereas Pakistan tries to apply the restrictive provisions stringently. The two countries are thus pulling in two opposite directions. This leads to a permanent tug of war in the Indus Commission. As the lower riparian on the Indus system, Pakistan tends to look with anxious eyes at any attempts by India to build structures on the western rivers that may enable India either to reduce water flows or to release stored waters and cause floods. Pakistan's objections are thus partly water-related and partly security-related. The Indian position is that the security fears are misconceived because India cannot flood Pakistan without flooding itself first; that its capacity to reduce flows to Pakistan is very limited; and that the record of the last half-century gives no basis for any such apprehensions.

An important political dimension to these differences is that the projects are – or will be – located in Jammu and Kashmir. Pakistan can hardly be enthusiastic about facilitating Indian projects in what it regards as disputed territory.

Where do we go from here?

Abrogation of the Treaty, occasionally advocated by some, does not merit serious discussion. Should there be a renegotiation of the Treaty, as is often urged in both countries? It is difficult to envisage an outcome that would be better than before, from the points of view of both countries. Unfortunately, water-sharing is a zero-sum game: One side cannot increase its share without diminishing that of the other. The best course would perhaps be to leave things as they are and hope that, with improving political relations, a more reasonable and constructive spirit on both sides toward the operation of the Treaty will prevail in the future.

Until a few years ago, while there were arguments about certain Indian projects on the western rivers and their conformity to the provisions of the Indus Treaty, no one in Pakistan talked about water as being a major issue between their country and India. From early 2010 onwards, Pakistan has been projecting water as being a major issue between the two countries, indeed as a new "core issue" that is as important as Kashmir, if not more so.

Why has it decided to do so? We can only guess. Focusing public attention on the water issue may act as a powerful mobilizing factor and rally the people as a whole behind the government and/or the army. The government of Pakistan perhaps hopes to distract attention from bitter inter-provincial water-sharing disputes within its own country. Raising water as a new core issue may also be a counter move in response to the focus that India has been maintaining on terrorism.

The view seems to be widely held that if Pakistan faces a present or imminent water crisis, India is an important factor in that development. This could have a serious impact on India-Pakistan relations, even at the people-to-people level.

SOME PAKISTANI CONCERNS

Leaving aside popular misconceptions in Pakistan, let us take note of some of the concerns expressed in Track II meetings by thoughtful, well-informed members of Pakistani civil society and academia, including those who want good relations with India.

- Popular perceptions or misperceptions about the diversion of water by India seem to receive unwitting corroboration in reported findings by Pakistani scholars of a trend of reduction in the flows in the western rivers. The tendency is to assume that the upper riparian must be responsible for that reduction. The only answer to this is to institute a joint study by experts from both countries to determine whether in fact flows in the western rivers have diminished, and if so, to identify the factors responsible.

- Other popular beliefs in Pakistan are: that the Indus Waters Treaty never envisaged the construction of a large number of major projects by India on the western rivers; that what was intended to be a minor concession has been stretched by India unduly; and that because of this stretching, every Indian project on the western rivers is in violation of the Treaty. These accusations arise from a misreading of the Treaty, which clearly envisages major Indian projects on the western rivers, as documented by the massive annexes to the Treaty. So long as India conforms to the stringent restrictive provisions of the Treaty, it cannot be charged with stretching or violating the Treaty.
- A third point on which much anxiety is expressed is the cumulative impact of a large number of projects on the western rivers. India might argue that if each project conforms to the Treaty, there can be no such thing as the "cumulative impact" of a large number of projects. However, Pakistani apprehensions on this score cannot be lightly dismissed. Many in India have been worried about the cumulative impact of a large number of hydroelectric projects on the Ganges River, and studies have been commissioned to address the issue. What applies to the Ganges applies equally to the Indus system. The issue needs to be carefully considered. Here again, a joint study by experts from both countries seems desirable.
- In recent years, pleas have been made for a holistic, integrated management of the entire system, joint watershed management, etc. These are unexceptionable ideas, but a completely different "holistic" Treaty will have to wait for better times. Current concerns such as environmental impacts, minimum or ecological flows, etc., are as applicable to the Indus system as to other systems, and demands for them should not be brushed aside merely because the Indus Treaty did not foresee

them. Presumably, environmental impact assessments are being made for each of the hydroelectric projects that are being planned on the western rivers. Environmental impacts do not stop at the border; a project on the Indian side can have impacts across the border, and a project on the Pakistani side – for instance the Neelum Jhelum hydroelectric project that Pakistan is planning – may have impacts on the Indian side of the border.

Conclusion: The Indus Waters Treaty in an age of climate change

Global climate change and its possible impact on water availability in the Indus river system are matters of vital concern, and the two countries must begin immediately to work together on these. There has already been a measure of cooperation between them during international negotiations on climate change, but this must go beyond the limited issue of emission reductions. This cannot be brought within the ambit of the Indus Waters Treaty but must be a separate exercise.

Summing up, agreed solutions can be found for the differences that have arisen during the course of operation of the Treaty, but they become difficult because of fluctuating political relations between the two countries. An improvement in those relations and the harmonious operation of the Treaty are interrelated, and each will facilitate the other. The newer emerging concerns that were not foreseen in 1960 – and in particular climate change and its impact on water resources – call for inter-country cooperation beyond the Treaty.

THE INDUS WATERS KISHENGANGA ARBITRATION (PAKISTAN V. INDIA)

A Partial Award was rendered in the *Indus Waters Kishenganga Arbitration* between Pakistan and India on February 18, 2013. The inter-State dispute under the 1960 Indus Waters Treaty (IWT) arises from India's proposal to build a 330 megawatt hydroelectric project on the Kishenganga River" a tributary of the Jhelum River in the India-administered part of Jammu and Kashmir.

Upon crossing the Line of Control between India and Pakistan, the Kishenganga is rechristened the Neelum River in Pakistan-administered Kashmir, before finally joining the Jhelum. India's Kishenganga Hydro-Electric Project (KHEP) involves the diversion of water from the Kishenganga/Neelum River (the River), at a point in the Gurez Valley, through a network of tunnels to the powerhouse at a distance of 23 kilometers from the River, before emptying the water into another tributary of the Jhelum at a lower elevation.

Downstream, Pakistan has also sought to harvest the hydroelectric potential of the River by constructing the 969 megawatt Neelum-Jhelum hydroelectric project (NJHEP). The Jhelum is an important river within the over-burdened Indus river system, which irrigates large areas of India and Pakistan. Concerned by the impact of the KHEP on its water supply, Pakistan filed a Request for Arbitration under the IWT in May 2010.

THE INDUS WATERS TREATY

The 1960 IWT an outcome of decade-long negotiations between India and Pakistan facilitated by the World Bank sets out the rights and obligations of the Parties for the utilization of the Indus river system's water resources. In a rather unusual approach, the Treaty allocates entire streams, instead of water volumes. India is permitted unrestricted use of the Eastern Rivers (the Sutlej, the Beas and the Ravi), while the Western rivers are allocated to Pakistan (the Indus, the Jhelum and the Chenab), subject to certain exceptions contained in the Treaty. By focusing on the Parties' rights to use the streams, the Treaty avoids addressing the controversial question of sovereignty over the disputed parts of Jammu and Kashmir through which the rivers flow.

The Treaty also establishes the Permanent Indus Commission, comprising a commissioner from each State, for its implementation. Article IX provides for a multi-tiered dispute resolution process based upon a hierarchy of disputes. A "question" between the Parties relating to the interpretation or application of the IWT or the existence of certain facts, if unresolved by the Commission, gives rise to a "difference." If, however, a difference does not relate to the listed technical matters, or if the Neutral Expert considers appropriate, then a "dispute" arises. Such a dispute may be settled by formal negotiations, failing which, or if the Parties agree, it is to be resolved by a seven-member arbitral tribunal called the "Court of Arbitration."

THE DISPUTE AND PROCEEDINGS

This is the first time a dispute under the IWT has been referred to a Court of Arbitration. In its Request for Arbitration, Pakistan identified two questions: first, whether India's proposed inter-tributary transfer as part of the KHEP breached its obligations under the IWT, as interpreted and applied under international law (First Dispute); and, second, whether the IWT allowed India to deplete the reservoir level of a run-of-river plant below the "Dead Storage Level" in circumstances other than unforeseen emergencies.

To answer these, a Court of Arbitration was constituted on December 17, 2010. In June 2011, Pakistan submitted an application for provisional measures, leading to an Order on Interim Measures by the Court on September 23, 2011. Subsequently, the Court undertook two site visits and oral hearings on the merits were held at the Permanent Court of Arbitration in.

The Hague from August 20-31, 2012. The Partial Award of February 18, 2013 allowed India to proceed with the construction and operation of the KHEP, subject to certain operational constraints to be determined in the Final Award. While both Parties agreed that the awards should be published, Pakistan opposed the publication of the pleadings.

The Award

The First Dispute concerned the permissibility of India's KHEP and the inter-tributary transfer under the IWT. The IWT obliges India to "let flow" the waters of the Western Rivers, except for limited, enumerated uses. In the Court's view, these exceptions give India the right to utilize the Western Rivers in some ways, subject to its obligations under the IWT.

The Court began by considering India's general obligations under Articles III and IV(6) of the IWT. Pakistan argued that, since the power generated by the KHEP would be supplied to the whole of India's northern electricity grid, the Project did not conform with Article III(2), restricting India's use of the Western Rivers to "the drainage basin thereof." The Court disagreed: though Article III(2) imposed a geographical restriction on India's use of the Western River waters, such a restriction did not extend to the products (such as electricity) generated from the use of these waters. Pakistan also argued that, by failing to adequately assess the environmental impact of the inter-tributary transfer, India breached its general obligation to "use its best endeavours to maintain the natural channels of the Rivers" under Article IV(6). Although noting that Article IV(6) was obligatory, the Court considered it of no direct relevance as it only required the preservation of the natural, unobstructed paths of the rivers, and not the volume or timing of the flow.

Next, the Court turned to Pakistan's arguments of the IWT prescribing requirements for the design and operation of run-of-river plants. Pakistan contended that, first, permit the permanent diversion of a tributary; second, even if such diversion was permitted, the KHEP did not qualify as a "Plant" under Paragraph 15(iii); and, finally, even if the KHEP was a "Plant," it failed the test of necessity contained in Paragraph 15(iii).

The Court rejected all three arguments. It found that the plain text of Paragraph 15(iii) allowed inter-tributary transfers, provided that the diverting works complied with three conditions. First, the work must be a run-of-river plant. The Court noted that the KHEP was designed and notified to Pakistan as a run-of-river plant. Second, the plant must be "located on" a tributary of the Jhelum. Pakistan pointed out that the actual electricity generation was to take place at a distance of 23 kilometers from the Kishenganga. The Court however saw no reason for "disaggregating the elements" comprising the KHEP, designed to operate as an "integrated whole," and concluded that the condition was satisfied since the works that trapped the water were "located on" the Kishenganga" a tributary of the Jhelum.

Finally, the Court noted that Paragraph 15(iii) required the diversion of water into another tributary to be "necessary" for generating hydroelectricity. On the threshold for necessity, the Court considered "inapposite" the concepts of necessity developed in other branches of international law, such as international trade law, investment law and the law of State responsibility, adopting instead the plain meaning of "necessary" to describe action that was "required, needed or essential." Against this threshold, it found that the diversion was necessary for India to utilize the difference in elevation between the two tributaries in order to generate significant power.

The Court next turned to the "essence" of the First Dispute: the requirement under Paragraph 15(iii) that any Indian inter-tributary run-of-river plant operate "only to the extent that the *then existing* Agricultural Use or hydro-electric use by Pakistan on the former Tributary would not be adversely affected." Pakistan argued for an "ambulatory" interpretation of "then existing use" in Paragraph 15(iii), calling for a "dynamic assessment by India of the agricultural and hydro-electric uses of Pakistan whenever water is released by the KHEP." By contrast, India argued for a "static" approach, focusing on a "critical date," when India communicated to Pakistan its "firm intention" to proceed with a project, such that Pakistan's agricultural and hydroelectric uses must be "frozen" at the stage when design was finalized.

In answering whether the NJHEP constituted "then existing use" by Pakistan, which restricted India's right under Paragraph 15(iii), the Court did not accept either interpretation in entirety. With respect to Pakistan's approach, it noted that the "overall structure" of that "the general permissibility of any new Plant's design is determined prior to the commencements of its construction." It ultimately rejected Pakistan's interpretation because it would subject the viability of India's works to the "unilateral will and action of another party."

With respect to India's approach, the Court considered that, in practice, it could be "very difficult to pinpoint" the exact moment at which a firm intention to proceed with a project crystallizes, keeping in mind the "continuum of design, financing, government approval, construction, completion and operation" associated with large infrastructure projects such as the KHEP. Instead, the Court proposed a "'critical period,' wherein a cumulation of facts â•" tender, financing secured, government approvals in place and construction underway â•" has achieved a level of certitude indicating that a project will proceed 'firmly' as proposed." Applying this "critical period" approach to India's KHEP and Pakistan's NJHEP, it found that the KHEP preceded the NJHEP such that the NJHEP did not constitute a "then existing use" by Pakistan. India was therefore permitted to effectuate an inter-tributary transfer under Paragraph 15(iii).

However, the Court accommodated elements of the dynamic approach by subjecting India's right to operate the KHEP to certain operational constraints. In doing so, it recognized that India's rights to divert water for the operation of the KHEP are "tempered" by Pakistan's right to a minimum flow of water for hydroelectric and agricultural uses. The Court observed that Paragraph 15 "delineates a number of operational constraints" for new works and seems to be "operational in character," such that the Treaty imposed a duty on India to ensure that a minimum flow of water reaches Pakistan at all times.

The Court also found support for such a duty in "contemporary customary international law," which requires States to take "environmental protection into consideration when planning and developing Projects that may cause injury to a bordering State." Acknowledging that the IWT must be interpreted and applied in light of the "customary international principles for the protection of the environment in force today," the Court noted that general international law imposes a duty on States "to prevent, or at least mitigate" significant harm to the environment when pursuing large-scale construction activities. Crucially, it recalled the International Court of Justice's observations that the "duties of due diligence, vigilance and prevention" imposed by the principle of sustainable development continue "once operations have started and ¦ throughout the life of the project." It acknowledged that India recognized this continuous duty by committing to ensure a minimum downstream flow of water. However, the information presently at its disposal did not allow the Court to objectively fix the exact rate of the minimum downstream flow, and it requested the Parties to provide the relevant information to fix this rate in its Final Award.

Second Dispute

Although Pakistan framed the Second Dispute as relating to the permissibility of reservoir depletion in the abstract, the Court noted that Pakistan in essence took issue with the use of a sediment management technique called "drawdown flushing" by India at the KHEP and other future projects. It clarified that while its findings could not reverse the Neutral Expert's 2007 Determination (permitting this technique for India's *Baglihar* project), or retrospectively affect any plant already in operation or under construction, they would apply to the KHEP and any future Indian run-of-river plants on the Western Rivers.

India put forth two objections to the admissibility of the Second Dispute. First, it argued that except when the two Permanent Indus Commissioners were in agreement to pursue an alternative, the IWT required a Neutral Expert to initially determine whether a matter was a technical "difference" or a "dispute" to be referred to arbitration. With respect to Pakistan's claim, no such initial determination was made. Second, in India's view, the subject matter of the Second Dispute was objectively among the questions consigned to a Neutral Expert. The Court dismissed both objections. In its view, the text of Article IX(2)(a), as confirmed by its object and purpose, did not impose "an additional procedural hurdle" to access the arbitral process, and it was not open to India to assert at this late stage that the Second Dispute was a "difference" and not a "dispute."

Looking at the treaty context, the Court noted that several provisions strongly suggested that some limitation on India's use and depletion of dead storage" a consequence of drawdown flushing technique" was intended. Specifically, it identified a "decisive prohibition" in the Treaty against the depletion of dead storage, except in unforeseen emergencies. Noting that both Parties agreed that sediment accumulation did not constitute an unforeseen emergency, the Court concluded that the text of the Treaty prohibited the depletion of dead storage for drawdown flushing. Next, the Court juxtaposed its understanding of the limitations on the use of dead storage with another object of the Treaty: to allow India to harness the hydroelectric potential of the Western Rivers. Agreeing that "anything you build needs to work," it considered whether drawdown flushing was indispensable to the sustainable generation of hydroelectricity on the Western Rivers. Based on the evidence, it concluded that India's right to utilize the Western Rivers could be "meaningfully exercised without drawdown flushing." In particular, the Court suggested the use of another technique called "sluicing" for sediment management.

WATER SUPPLY AND SANITATION IN INDIA

Water supply and sanitation in India continue to be inadequate, despite longstanding efforts by the various levels of government and communities at improving coverage. The level of investment in water and sanitation, albeit low by international standards, has increased during the 2000s. Access has also increased significantly. For example, in 1980 rural sanitation coverage was estimated at 1% and reached 21% in 2008. Also, the share of Indians with access to improved sources of water has increased significantly from 72% in 1990 to 88% in 2008. At the same time, local government institutions in charge of operating and maintaining the infrastructure are seen as weak and lack the financial resources to carry out their functions. In addition, no major city in India is known to have a continuous water supply and an estimated 72% of Indians still lack access to improved sanitation facilities.

A number of innovative approaches to improve water supply and sanitation have been tested in India, in particular in the early 2000s. These include demand-driven approaches in rural water supply since 1999, community-led total sanitation, a public-private partnerships to improve the continuity of urban water supply in Karnataka, and the use of micro-credit to women in order to improve access to water.

Access

In 2008, 88% of the population in India had access to an improved water source, but only 31% had access to improved sanitation. In rural areas, where 72% of India's population lives, the respective shares are 84% for water and only 21% for sanitation. In urban areas, 96% had access to an improved water source and 54% to improved sanitation. Access has improved substantially since 1990 when it was estimated to stand at 72% for water and 18% for sanitation.

As of 2010, the UN estimated based on Indian statistics that 626 people practice open defecation. In June 2012 Minister of Rural Development Jairam Ramesh stated India is the worlds largest "open air toilet". He also remarked that Pakistan, Bangladesh and Afghanistan have better sanitation records.

According to Indian norms, access to improved water supply exists if at least 40 litres/capita/day of safe drinking water are provided within a distance of 1.6 km or 100 meter of elevation difference, to be relaxed as per field conditions. There should be at least one pump per 250 persons.

Service Quality

Water and sanitation service quality in India is generally poor, although there has been some limited progress concerning continuity of supply in urban areas and access to sanitation in rural areas.

Water Supply

Challenges. None of the 35 Indian cities with a population of more than one million distribute water for more than a few hours per day, despite generally sufficient infrastructure. Owing to inadequate pressure people struggle to collect water even when it is available. According to the World Bank, none have performance indicators that compare with average international standards. A 2007 study by the Asian Development Bank showed that in 20 cities the average duration of supply was only 4.3 hours per day. No city had continuous supply. The longest duration of supply was 12 hours per day in Chandigarh, and the lowest was 0.3 hours per day in Rajkot. In Delhi residents receive water only a few hours per day because of inadequate management of the distribution system. This results in contaminated water and forces households to complement a deficient public water service at prohibitive 'coping' costs; the poor suffer most from this situation. For example, according to a 1996 survey households in Delhi spent an average of 2,182 (US$39.5) per year in time and money to cope with poor service levels. This is more than three times as much as the 2001 water bill of about US$18 per year of a Delhi household that uses 20 cubic meters per month.

Achievements. Jamshedpur, a city in Jharkhand with 573,000 inhabitants, provided 25% of its residents with continuous water supply in 2009. Navi Mumbai, a planned city with more than 1m inhabitants, has achieved continuous supply for about half its population as of January 2009. Badlapur, another city in the Mumbai Conurbation with a population of 140,000, has achieved continuous supply in 3 out of 10 operating zones, covering 30% of its population. Thiruvananthapuram, the capital of Kerala state with a population of 745,000 in 2001, is probably the largest Indian city that enjoys continuous water supply.

Sanitation

Most Indians depend on on-site sanitation facilities. Recently, access to on-site sanitation have increased in both rural and urban areas. In rural areas, total sanitation has been successful. In urban areas, a good practice is the Slum Sanitation Program in Mumbai that has provided access to sanitation for a quarter million slum dwellers. Sewerage, where available, is often in a bad state. In Delhi the sewerage network has lacked maintenance over the years and overflow of raw sewage in open drains is common, due to blockage, settlements and inadequate pumping capacities. The capacity of the 17 existing wastewater treatment plants in Delhi is adequate to cater a daily production of waste water of less than 50% of the drinking water produced. Of the 2.5 Billion people in the world that defecate openly, some 665 million live in India. This is of greater concern as 88% of deaths from diarrhoea occur because of unsafe water, inadequate sanitation and poor hygiene.

Environment

As of 2003, it was estimated that only 27% of India's wastewater was being treated, with the remainder flowing into rivers, canals, groundwater or the sea., For example, the sacred Ganges river is infested with diseases and in some places "the Ganges becomes black and septic. Corpses, of semi-cremated adults or enshrouded babies, drift slowly by.". News Week describes Delhi's sacred Yamuna River as "a putrid ribbon of black sludge" where fecal bacteria is 10,000 over safety limits despite a 15-year program to address the problem. Cholera epidemics are not unknown.

Health Impact

The lack of adequate sanitation and safe water has significant negative health impacts including diarrhoea, referred to by travellers as the "Delhi Belly", and experienced by about 10 million visitors annually. While most visitors to India recover quickly and otherwise receive proper care, the World Health Organisation estimated that around 700,000 Indians die each year from diarrhoea. The dismal working conditions of sewer workers are another concern. A survey of the working conditions of sewage workers in Delhi showed that most of them suffer from chronic diseases, respiratory problems, skin disorders, allergies, headaches and eye infections.

Water Supply and Water Resources

Depleting ground water table and deteriorating ground water quality are threatening the sustainability of both urban and rural water supply in many parts of India. The supply of cities that depend on surface water is threatened by pollution, increasing water scarcity and conflicts among users. For example, Bangalore depends to a large extent on water pumped since 1974 from the

Kaveri river, whose waters are disputed between the states of Karnataka and Tamil Nadu. As in other Indian cities, the response to water scarcity is to transfer more water over large distances at high costs. In the case of Bangalore, the 3,384 crore (US$612.5 million) Kaveri Stage IV project, Phase II, includes the supply of 500,000 cubic meter of water per day over a distance of 100 km, thus increasing the city's supply by two thirds.

Responsibility for Water Supply and Sanitation

Water supply and sanitation is a State responsibility under the Indian Constitution. States may give the responsibility to the Panchayati Raj Institutions (PRI) in rural areas or municipalities in urban areas, called Urban Local Bodies (ULB). At present, states generally plan, design and execute water supply schemes (and often operate them) through their State Departments (of Public Health Engineering or Rural Development Engineering) or State Water Boards.

Highly centralised decision-making and approvals at the state level, which are characteristic of the Indian civil service, affect the management of water supply and sanitation services. For example, according to the World Bank in the state of Punjab the process of approving designs is centralised with even minor technical approvals reaching the office of chief engineers. A majority of decisions are made in a very centralised manner at the headquarters. In 1993 the Indian constitution and relevant state legislations were amended in order to decentralise certain responsibilities, including water supply and sanitation, to municipalities. Since the assignment of responsibilities to municipalities is a state responsibility, different states have followed different approaches. According to a Planning Commission report of 2003 there is a trend to decentralise capital investment to engineering departments at the district level and operation and maintenance to district and gram panchayat levels.

Policy and Regulation

The responsibility for water supply and sanitation at the central and state level is shared by various Ministries. At the central level, The Ministry of Rural Development is responsible for rural water supply through its Department of Drinking Water Supply (DDWS) and theMinistry of Housing and Urban Poverty Alleviation is responsible for urban water supply. However, except for the National Capital Territory of Delhi and other Union Territories, the central Ministries only have an advisory capacity and a very limited role in funding. Sector policy thus is a prerogative of state governments.

Service Provision

Urban areas. Institutional arrangements for water supply and sanitation in Indian cities vary greatly. Typically, a state-level agency is in charge of planning and investment, while the local government (Urban Local Bodies) is in charge of operation and maintenance. Some of the largest cities have created municipal water and sanitation utilities that are legally and financially separated from the local government.

However, these utilities remain weak in terms of financial capacity. In spite of decentralisation, ULBs remain dependent on capital subsidies from state governments.

Tariffs are also set by state governments, which often even subsidise operating costs. Furthermore, when no separate utility exists there is no separation of accounts for different activities within a municipality. Some states and cities have non-typical institutional arrangements. For example, in Rajasthan the sector is more centralised and the state government is also in charge of operation and maintenance, while in Mumbai the sector is more decentralised and local government is also in charge of planning and investment.

Private sector participation. The private sector plays a limited, albeit recently increasing role in operating and maintaining urban water systems on behalf of ULBs. For example, the Jamshedpur Utilities & Services Company (Jusco), a subsidiary of Tata Steel, has a lease contract for Jamshedpur (Jharkhand), a management contract in Haldia, another contract in Mysore (Karnataka) and since 2007 a contract for the reduction of non-revenue water in parts of Bhopal (Madhya Pradesh). The French water company

Veolia won a management contract in three cities in Karnataka in 2005.

In 2002 a consortium including Thames Water won a pilot contract covering 40,000 households to reduce non-revenue water in parts of Bangalore, funded by the Japan Bank for International Cooperation.

The contract was scaled up in 2004. The Cypriot company Hydro-Comp, together with two Indian companies, won a 10-year concession contract for the city of Latur City (Maharashtra) in 2007 and an operator-consultant contract in Madurai (Tamil Nadu). Furthermore, the private Indian infrastructure development company SPML is engaged in Build-Operate-Transfer (BOT) projects, such as a bulk water supply project for Bhiwandi (Maharashtra).

Rural areas. There are about a 100,000 rural water supply systems in India. At least in some states responsibility for service provision is in the process of being partially transferred from State Water Boards and district governments to Panchayati Raj Institutions (PRI) at the block or village level (there were about 604 districts and 256,000 villages in India in 2002, according to Subdivisions of India. Blocks are an intermediate level between districts and villages). Where this transfer has been initiated, it seems to be more advanced for single-village water schemes than for more complex multi-village water schemes. Despite their professed role Panchayati Raj Institutions, play only a limited role in provision of rural water supply and sanitation as of 2006. There has been limited success in implementing decentralisation, partly due to low priority by some state governments. Rural sanitation is typically provided by households themselves in the form of latrines.

Innovative Approaches

A number of innovative approaches to improve water supply and sanitation have been tested in India, in particular in the early 2000s. These include community-led total sanitation, demand-driven approaches in rural water supply, a public-private partnerships to improve the continuity of urban water supply in

Karnataka, and the use of micro-credit to women in order to improve access to water.

Community-led Total Sanitation

In 1999 a demand-driven and people-centered sanitation program was initiated under the name Total Sanitation Campaign (TSC) or Community-led total sanitation. It evolved from the limited achievements of the first structured programme for rural sanitation in India, the Central Rural Sanitation Programme, which had minimal community participation. The main goal of Total Sanitation Campaign is to eradicate the practice of open defecation by 2017. Community-led total sanitation is not focused on building infrastructure, but on preventing open defecation through peer pressure and shame. In Maharashtra where the program started more than 2000 Gram Panchayats have achieved "open defecation free" status. Villages that achieve this status receive monetary rewards and high publicity under a program called Nirmal Gram Puraskar.

Demand-driven Approaches in Rural Water Supply

Most rural water supply schemes in India use a centralised, supply-driven approach, i.e. a government institution designs a project and has it built with little community consultation and no capacity building for the community, often requiring no water fees to be paid for its subsequent operation. Since 2002 the Government of India has rolled out at the national level a program to change the way in which water and sanitation services are supported in rural areas. The program, called *Swajaldhara,* decentralises service delivery responsibility to rural local governments and user groups. Under the new approach communities are being consulted and trained, and users agree up-front to pay a tariff that is set at a level sufficiently high to cover operation and maintenance costs. It also includes measures to promote sanitation and to improve hygiene behaviour. The national program follows a pilot program launched in 1999.

According to a 2008 World Bank study in 10 Indian states, *Swajaldhara* results in lower capital costs, lower administrative costs and better service quality compared to the supply-driven approach. In particular, the study found that the average full cost of supply-driven schemes is Rs 38 (US$0.7) per cubic meter, while it is only Rs 26 (US$0.5) per cubic meter for demand-driven schemes. These costs include capital, operation and maintenance costs, administrative costs and coping costs incurred by users of malfunctioning systems.

Coping costs include travelling long distances to obtain water, standing in long queues, storing water and repairing failed systems. Among the surveyed systems that were built using supply-driven approach system breakdowns were common, the quantity and quality of water supply were less than foreseen in designs, and 30% of households did not get daily supply in summer. The poor functioning of one system sometimes leads to the construction of another system, so that about 30% of households surveyed were served by several systems. As of 2008 only about 10% of rural water schemes built in India used a demand-driven approach. Since water users have to pay lower or no tariffs under the supply-driven approach, this discourages them to opt for a demand-driven approach, even if the likelihood of the systems operating on a sustainable basis is higher under a demand-driven approach.

Achieving Continuous Water Supply with the Help of a Private Operator in Karnataka

In the cities of Hubli, Belgaum and Gulbarga in the state of Karnataka, the private operator Veolia increased water supply from once every 2–15 days for 1–2 hours, to 24 hours per day for 180,000 people (12% of the population of the 3 cities) within 2 years (2006–2008). This was achieved by carefully selecting and ring-fencing demonstration zones (one in each city), renovating the distribution network, installing meters, introducing a well-functioning commercial system, and effective grass-roots social intermediation by an NGO, all without increasing the amount of bulk water supplied. The project, known by its acronym as KUWASIP (Karnataka Urban Water Sector Improvement Project), was supported by a US$39.5 million loan from the World Bank.

It constitutes a milestone for India, where no large city so far has achieved continuous water supply. The project is expected to be scaled-up to cover the entire area of the three cities.

Micro-credit for Water connections in Tamil Nadu

In Tiruchirapalli in Tamil Nadu, the NGO Gramalaya, established in 1987, and women self-help groups promote access to water supply and sanitation by the poor through micro-credit. Among the benefits are that women can spend more time with their children, earn additional income, and sell surplus water to neighbours. This money contributes to her repayment of the WaterCredit loan. The initiative is supported by the US-based non-profit Water Partners International.

The Jamshedpur Utilities and Services Company

The Jamshedpur Utilities and Services Company (JUSCO) provides water and sanitation services in Jamshedpur, a major industrial centre in East India that is home to Tata Steel. Until 2004 a division of Tata Steel provided water to the city's residents. However, service quality was poor with intermittent supply, high water losses and no metering. To improve this situation and to establish good practices that could be replicated in other Indian cities, JUSCO was set up as a wholly owned subsidiary of Tata Steel in 2004.

Efficiency and service quality improved substantially over the following years. The level on non-revenue water decreased from an estimated 36% in 2005 to 10% in 2009; one quarter of residents received continuous water supply (although the average supply remained at only 7 hours per day) in 2009; the share of metered connections increased from 2% in 2007 to 26% in 2009; the number of customers increased; and the company recovered its operating costs plus a portion of capital costs. Identifying and legalising illegal connections was an important element in the reduction of non-revenue water. The utility prides itself today of the good drinking water quality provided and encourages its customers to drink from the tap. The utility also operates a wastewater treatment plant that meets discharge standards. The private utility pays salaries that are higher than civil service salaries and conducts extensive training programs for its staff. It has also installed a modern system to track and resolve customer complaints. Furthermore, it conducts independent annual customer satisfaction surveys. JUSCO's vision is to be the preferred provider of water supply and other urban services throughout India. Together with Ranhill Malaysia it won a 25-year concession contract for providing the water supply in Haldia City, West Bengal.

Efficiency

There are only limited data on the operating efficiency of utilities in India, and even fewer data on the efficiency of investments.

Concerning operating efficiency, a study of 20 cities by the Jawaharlal Nehru National Urban Renewal Mission with the support of the Asian Development Bank showed an average level of non-revenue water (NRW) of 32%. However, 5 out of the 20 cities did not provide any data. For those that provided data there probably is a large margin of error, since only 25% of connections are metered, which makes it very difficult to estimate non-revenue water. Also, three utilities show NRW levels of less than 20%, two of which have practically no metering, which indicates that the numbers are not reliable and actual values are likely to be higher. In Delhi, which was not included in the ADB study, non-revenue water stood at 53% and there were about 20 employees per 1000 connections. Furthermore, only 70% of revenue billed was actually collected.

Concerning labour productivity, the 20 utilities in the sample had on average 7.4 employees per 1,000 connections, which is much higher than the estimated level for an efficient utility. A survey of a larger sample of Indian utilities showed an average ratio of 10.9 employees per 1,000 connections.

Tariffs, Cost Recovery and Subsidies

Water and sewer tariffs in India are low in both urban and rural areas. In urban areas they were set at the equivalent of about US$0.10 per cubic meter in 2007 and recovered about 60% of operating and maintenance costs, with large differences between cities. Some cities such as Kolkata do not bill residential users at all. In rural areas the level of cost recovery often is even lower than in urban areas and was estimated at only 20% in rural Punjab. Subsidies were estimated at US$1.1 billion per year in the mid-1990s, accounting to 4% of all government subsidies in India. 70% of those benefiting from the subsidies are not poor.

Urban Areas

Metering. Water metering is the precondition for billing water users on the basis of volume consumed. According to a 1999 survey of 300 cities about 62% of urban water customers in metropolitan areas and 50% in smaller cities are metered (average 55%). However, meters often do not work so that many "metered" customers are charged flat rates. Bangalore and Pune are among the few Indian cities that meter all their customers. Many other cities have no metering at all or meter only commercial customers. Users of standposts receive water free of charge. A 2007 study of 20 cities by the Jawaharlal Nehru National Urban Renewal Mission with the support of the Asian Development Bank (ADB) showed that only 25% of customers of these utilities were metered. Most other customers paid a flat tariff independent of consumption. Some utilities, such as the one serving Kolkata, actually do not bill residential users at all.

Tariff levels. According to the same ADB study the average tariff for all customers – including industrial, commercial and public customers – is Rs. 4.9 (US$0.1) per cubic meter. According to a 2007 global water tariff survey by the OECD the residential water tariff for a consumption of 15 m^3 was equivalent to US$0.15 per m^3 in Bangalore, US$0.12 per m^3 in Calcutta, US$0.11 per m3 in New Delhi and US$0.09 per m^3 in Mumbai. Only Bangalore had a sewer tariff of US$0.02 per m^3. The other three cities did not charge for sewerage, although the better-off tend to be the ones with access to sewers.

Tariff structure. The tariff for customers that are effectively metered is typically a uniform linear tariff, although some cities apply increasing-block tariffs. Affordability. Urban water tariffs were highly affordable according to data from the year 2000.

A family of five living on the poverty line which uses 20 cubic meter of water per month would spend less than 1.2% of its budget on its water bill if it had a water meter. If it did not have a water meter and was charged a flat rate, it would pay 2.0% of its budget. This percentage lies below the often used affordability threshold of 5%. However, at that time the average metered tariff was estimated at only US$0.03 per m^3, or less than three times what it was estimated to be in 2007. Apparently no more up-to-date estimates on the share of the average water bill in the budget of the poor are available.

Cost recovery. According to a 2007 study of 20 cities the average rate of cost recovery for operating and maintenance costs of utilities in these cities was 60%. Seven of the 20 utilities generated a cash surplus to partially finance investments. Chennai generated the highest relative surplus. The lowest cost recovery ratio was found in Indore in Madhya Pradesh, which recovered less than 20% of its operating and maintenance costs.

Delhi example. In Delhi revenues were just sufficient to cover about 60% of operating costs of the city's utility in 2004; maintenance has, as a result, been minimal. In the past, the Delhi utility has relied heavily on government financial support for recurrent and capital expenditures in the magnitude of Rs. 3 billion (US$54.3 million) per year and Rs. 7 billion (US$126.7 million) respectively.

As financial support for both capital and recurrent expenditures has been passed on as loans by the Government of the National Capital Territory of Delhi, the utility's balance sheet is loaded with a huge debt totalling about Rs. 50 billion (US$905 million) that it is unlikely to be able to service. Accounts receivable represent more than 12 months of billing, part of it being non recoverable. The average tariff was estimated atUS$0.074/$m^3$ in 2001, compared to production costs of US$0.085/$m^3$, the latter probably being a very conservative estimate that does not take into account capital costs. Challenges faced in attempting to increase tariffs. Even if users are willing to pay more for better services, political interests often prevent tariffs from being increased even to a small extent. An example is the city of Jabalpur where the central government and the state government financed a Rs. 130 million (US$2.4 million) water supply project from 2000–2004 to be operated by the Jabalpur Municipal Corporation, an entity that collected only less than half of its operational costs in revenues even before this major investment.

Even so the municipal corporation initially refused to increase tariffs. Only following pressure from the state government it reluctantly agreed to increase commercial tariffs, but not residential tariffs.

Rural Areas

Cost recovery in rural areas is low and a majority of the rural water systems are defunct for lack of maintenance. Some state governments subsidise rural water systems, but funds are scarce and insufficient. In rural areas in Punjab, operation and maintenance cost recovery is only about 20%. On one hand, expenditures are high due to high salary levels, high power tariff and a high number of operating staff. On the other hand, revenue is paid only by the 10% of the households who have private connections. Those drawing water from public stand posts do not pay any water charges at all, although the official tariff for public stand post users is Rs. 15 (US$0.3) per month per household.

Subsidies and Targeting of Subsidies

There are no accurate recent estimates of the level of subsidies for water and sanitation in India. It has been estimated that transfers to the water sector in India amounted to Rs. 5,470.8 crore (US$990.2 million) per year in the mid-1990s, accounting for 4% of all government subsidies in India. About 98% of this subsidy is said to come from State rather than Central budgets. This figure may only cover recurrent cost subsidies and not investment subsidies, which are even higher. There is little targeting of subsidies. According to the World Bank, 70% of those benefiting from subsidies for public water supply are not poor, while 40% of the poor are excluded because they do not have access to public water services.

Investment and Financing

Investment in urban water supply and sanitation has increased during the first decade of the 21st century, not least thanks to increased central government grants made available under Jawaharlal Nehru National Urban Renewal Mission alongside with loans from the Housing and Urban Development Corporation.

Investment

The Eleventh Five-Year Plan (2007–2012) foresees investments of Rs. 127,025 crore (US$23 billion) for urban water supply and sanitation, including urban (stormwater) drainage and solid waste management.

Financing

55% of the investments foreseen under the 11th Plan are to be financed by the central government, 28% by state governments, 8% by "institutional financing" such as HUDCO, 8% by external agencies and 1.5% by the private sector. Local governments are not expected to contribute to the investments. The volume of investments is expected to double to reach 0.7% of GDP. Also, it implies a shift in financing from state governments to the central government. During the 9th Plan only 24% of investments were financed by the central government and 76% by state governments. Central government financing was heavily focused on water supply in rural areas.

Institutions

State Financing Corporations (SFC) play an important role in making recommendations regarding the allocation of state tax revenues between states and municipalities, criteria for grants, and measures to improve the financial position of municipalities. According to the Planning Commission, SFCs are in some cases not sufficiently transparent and/or competent, have high transactions costs, and their recommendations are sometimes not being implemented. An important source of financing are loans from Housing and Urban Development Corporation Ltd

(HUDCO), a Central government financial undertaking. HUDCO loans to municipal corporations need to be guaranteed by state governments. HUDCO also on-lends loans from foreign aid, including Japanese aid, to states. The Jawaharlal Nehru National Urban Renewal Mission initiated in 2005 also plays an increasingly important role in financing urban water supply and sanitation through central government grants.

The current system of financing water supply and sanitation is fragmented through a number of different national and state programs. This results in simultaneous implementation with different and conflicting rules in neighbouring areas. In rural areas different programs undermine each other, adversely affecting demand driven approaches requiring cost sharing by users.

External Cooperation

In absolute terms India receives almost twice as much development assistance for water, sanitation and water resources management as any other country, according to data from the Organisation for Economic Co-operation and Development. India accounts for 13 per cent of commitments in global water aid for 2006–07, receiving an annual average of about US$830 million (•620 million), more than double the amount provided to China. India's biggest water and sanitation donor is Japan, which provided US$635 million, followed by the World Bank with US$130 million. The annual average for 2004–06, however, was about half as much at US$448 million, of which Japan provided US$293 million and the World Bank US$87 million. The Asian Development Bank and Germany are other important external partners in water supply and sanitation.

In 2003 the Indian government decided it would only accept bilateral aid from five countries (the United Kingdom, the United States, Russia, Germany and Japan). A further 22 bilateral donors were asked to channel aid through nongovernmental organisations, United Nations agencies or multilateral institutions such as the European Union, the Asian Development Bank or the World Bank.

Asian Development Bank

India has increased its loans from the Asian Development Bank (ADB) since 2005 after the introduction of new financing modalities, such as the multitranche financing facility (MFF) which features a framework agreement with the national government under which financing is provided in flexible tranches for subprojects that meet established selection criteria.

In 2008 four MFFs for urban development investment programs were under way in North Karnataka (US$862 million), Jammu and Kashmir (US$1,260 million),Rajasthan (US$450 million), and Uttarakhand (US$1,589 million). Included in these MFFs are major investments for the development of urban water supply and sanitation services.

Germany

Germany supports access to water and sanitation in India through financial cooperation by KfW development bank and technical cooperation by GTZ.

Since the early 1990s both institutions have supported watershed management in rural Maharashtra, using a participatory approach first piloted by the Social Centre in Ahmednagar and that constituted a fundamental break with the previous top-down, technical approach to watershed management that had yielded little results. The involvement of women in decision-making is an essential part of the project. While the benefits are mostly in terms of increased agricultural production, the project also increases availability of water resources for rural water supply. In addition, GTZ actively supports the introduction of ecological sanitationconcepts in India, including community toilets and decentralised wastewater systems for schools as well as small and medium enterprises. Many of these systems produce biogas from wastewater, provide fertiliser and irrigation water.

Japan

As India's largest donor in the sector the Japan International Cooperation Agency (JICA) finances a multitude of projects with a focus on capital-intensive urban water supply and sanitation projects, often involving follow-up projects in the same locations.

Current projects. Projects approved between 2006 and 2009 include the Guwahati Water Supply Project in Assam, the Kerala Water Supply Project (Phased II and III), the Hogenakkal Water Supply and Fluorosis Mitigation Project (Phases I and II) in Tamil Nadu, the Goa Water Supply and Sewerage Project, the Agra Water Supply Project, the Amritsar Sewerage Project in Punjab, the Orissa Integrated Sanitation Improvement Project, and the Bangalore Water Supply and Sewerage Project.

Evaluation of past projects. An ex-post evaluation of one large program, the Urban Water Supply and Sanitation Improvement Program, showed that "some 60%–70% of the goals were achieved" and that "results were moderate". The program was implemented by the Housing and Urban Development Corporation, Ltd. (HUDCO) from 1996 to 2003 in 26 cities. The evaluation says that "state government plans were not based on sufficient demand research, including the research for residents' willingness to pay for services", so that demand for connections was overestimated. Also fees (water tariffs) were rarely increased despite recommendations to increase them. The evaluation concludes that "HUDCO was not able to make significant contributions to the effectiveness, sustainability, or overall quality of individual projects. One of the reasons that not much attention was given to this problem is probably that there was little risk of default on the loans thanks to state government guarantees."

World Bank

Current projects. The World Bank finances a number of projects in urban and rural areas that are fully or partly dedicated to water supply and sanitation. In urban areas the World Bank supports the Andhra Pradesh Municipal Development Project (approved in 2009, US$300 million loan), the Karnataka Municipal Reform Project (approved in 2006, US$216 million loan), the Third Tamil Nadu Urban Development Project (approved in 2005, US$300 million loan) and the Karnataka Urban Water Sector Improvement Project (approved in 2004, US$39.5 million loan).

In rural areas it supports the Andhra Pradesh Rural Water Supply and Sanitation (US$150 million loan, approved in 2009), the Second Karnataka Rural Water Supply and Sanitation Project (approved in 2001,US$151.6 million loan), the Uttaranchal Rural Water Supply and Sanitation Project (approved in 2006, US$120 million loan) and the Punjab Rural Water Supply and Sanitation Project (approved in 2006, US$154 million loan).

Evaluation of past projects. A study by the World Bank's independent evaluation department evaluated the impact of the World Bank-supported interventions in the provision of urban water supply and wastewater services in Mumbai between 1973 and 1990. It concluded that water supply and sewerage planning, construction and operations in Bombay posed daunting challenges to those who planned and implemented the investment program. At the outset, there was a huge backlog of unmet demand because of under investment. Population and economic growth accelerated in the following decades and the proportion of the poor increased as did the slums which they occupied. The intended impacts of the program have not been realised. Shortcomings include that "water is not safe to drink; water service, especially to the poor, is difficult to access and is provided at inconvenient hours of the day; industrial water needs are not fully met; sanitary facilities are too few in number and often unusable; and urban drains, creeks and coastal waters are polluted with sanitary and industrial wastes."

4

Water Wars

INDIA AND PAKISTAN SQUARING OFF OVER THEIR RIVERS

India's Wular Lake, a popular picnic and tourist spot nestled in the Kashmir Valley, is an unlikely site for conflict. But India's plan to build a structure on the Jhelum River at the mouth of the lake that will allow it to release water during the river's lean winter months has outraged neighboring Pakistan, which believes the project will give India the power to control how much water flows downstream to its farmers. After two and a half decades of deadlock and 15 marathon rounds of bilateral talks — the most recent occurring in late March — the countries appear a long way from finding common ground.

The dispute isn't the first of its kind, nor will it be the last. The waters of the Indus River and tributaries like the Jhelum — and the dams built on them by India — have long been one of the main points of contention between the rival neighbors, along with the disputed region of Kashmir itself and cross-border terrorism. Pakistan, whose agriculture-dominated economy is heavily reliant on the Indus and its tributaries, fears upstream dams allow India to manipulate the flows of water as it sees fit. Many in Pakistan accuse New Delhi of wantonly exacerbating the country's dire water shortages, choking its agricultural production and ruining livelihoods.

India dismisses these accusations as paranoid and without scientific backing. Its dams are run-of-the-river, it says, aimed at generating hydroelectricity, or in the case of the Tulbul navigation project on the Jhelum, meeting other development needs like facilitating year-round trade. India's Indus Water Commissioner G. Aranganathan says that after India fills its reservoirs in the initial stages of each project, it only uses the water it needs to run its turbines and doesn't prevent any from flowing into Pakistan. "There is absolutely no question of interrupting or reducing Pakistan's water supply," he tells TIME.

The countries' early leaders anticipated this fierce rivalry over the waters that straddle their volatile border. Following protracted and painstaking negotiations, they signed an accord in 1960 called the Indus Waters Treaty that determined exactly how the region's rivers are to be divided. In the treaty, control over the three "eastern" rivers — the Beas, Ravi and Sutlej — was given to India and the three "western" rivers — the Indus, Chenab and Jhelum — to Pakistan. More controversial, however, were the provisions on how the waters were to be shared. Since Pakistan's rivers flow through India first, the treaty allowed India to use them for irrigation, transport and power generation, while laying down precise do's and don'ts for Indian building projects along the way.

The treaty has been widely hailed as a success, having survived three post-independence wars between the hostile nuclear neighbors. But its resilience is increasingly being tested by challenges thrown up by the 21st century. For one, Pakistan is on the brink of water scarcity. Its once-lush agricultural fields, which employ half of all Pakistanis and account for a quarter of its GDP, are now frequently parched. This predicament, experts say, is attributable in large part to the country's haphazard water management policies, unproductive agricultural practices, dilapidated infrastructure and grossly inadequate water storage facilities. Climate change, too, has begun to have an impact. A recent Dutch study found that by 2050, shrinking glaciers are predicted to reduce the flows of the Indus by 8%. But in Pakistan, which is deeply distrustful of its larger and more powerful neighbor, the country's crippling water shortage is seen as a direct result of India's upstream dams and water projects.

Indeed, India has ramped up its hydroelectricity projects in recent years to try to boost its woefully inadequate power supplies. The government has a total of 45 projects either already completed or in the proposal stage on the western rivers, some as large as 1000 megawatt and many as small as 2 and 3 megawatt. This expansion has irked Islamabad. "India is putting more and more restrictions and constrictions on Pakistan's waters," Kamal Majidulla, Pakistani Prime Minister Yousuf Raza Gillani's special assistant on water resources and agriculture, tells TIME.

A 2011 U.S. Senate Foreign Relations Committee report said that studies show no single dam will affect Pakistan's access to water, but the cumulative effect of multiple hydroelectric projects could give India the ability to store enough water to limit Pakistan's supply at crucial moments in the growing season. India has never abused its water supplies in this way, the report adds, and New Delhi rejects the theory as an unsubstantiated hypothesis. But the report's observations serve as a suitable analogy for India and Pakistan's water conflicts overall. While no single legal or diplomatic tussle will rupture the fragile relations between the countries, the cumulative effect of a series of standoffs could cause tensions to boil over.

The countries have already been embroiled in two high-profile legal fights over water. In 2005, Pakistan challenged India's 450-megawatt Baglihar dam before a World Bank-appointed neutral expert and lost. And last year, the countries went head to head at the International Court of Arbitration over India's 330-megawatt Kishanganga project in Jammu and Kashmir. The court has ordered India to temporarily stop some constructions on the dam while assessments are being made. Pakistan is also considering arbitration to iron out differences over another dam — the Nimoo Bazgo — on the Indus.

"Unfortunately, we are going towards conflict and not conflict resolution," says Majidulla, who heads a body called the Pakistan Trans-border Water Organization, formed in September to monitor what he calls "increased activity" on the Indian side of the border. The countries' antagonistic political relationship has certainly not helped to ease their differences over water. "Given the mutual hostility between the two countries, it is not surprising that there is a tendency in Pakistan to believe that the scarcity it is experiencing or fearing is partly attributable to upper riparian actions," Ramaswamy Iyer, India's former secretary for water resources, wrote in an op-ed in the *Hindu* newspaper. At times, the rhetoric has even reached a fevered pitch, such as when Hafiz Saeed, head of the Pakistani militant group Jamaat-u-Dawa and alleged mastermind of the 2008 Mumbai attacks, whipped up public sentiment against India's so-called "water terrorism" in 2010 by using slogans like "water flows or blood." Few believe India and Pakistan will actually go to war over the disputes, but one thing is for certain: water is making it harder for the long-time rivals to put their enmity behind them.

INDIA AND PAKISTAN FEUD OVER INDUS WATERS

The countries have harmoniously shared the waters of the Indus River for decades. A 50-year-old treaty regulating access to water from the river and its tributaries has been viewed as a bright spot for India and Pakistan, which have gone to war three times since 1947.

Now, the Pakistanis complain that India is hogging water upstream, which is hurting Pakistani farmers downstream. Pakistani officials say they will soon begin formal arbitration over a proposed Indian dam. At a meeting that started Sunday, Pakistan raised objections to new Indian dam projects on the Indus River and asked for satellite monitoring of river flows.

"Water I see emerging as a very serious source of tension between Pakistan and India," said Shah Mehmood Qureshi, Pakistan's foreign minister, in an interview Friday. He said he has raised the issue with Indian Prime Minister Manmohan Singh.

A senior Indian government official denied India is violating the treaty. He blamed Pakistan's water shortage on changing weather patterns and the country's poor water management. He called the strident rhetoric from Pakistani officials a "political gimmick...designed to place yet one more agenda item in our already complex relationship." Indian officials declined comment on the record.

The latest dispute revolves around India's plans to build a 330-megawatt hydroelectric power project on the Kishenganga River, a tributary of the Indus. India says it is well within its rights to build the dam. The project has been on the drawing board since the late 1980s and is expected to cost about $800 million.

Water Woes

Pakistan says New Delhi's plans to divert the course of the river will reduce its flow by a third in the winter. That would make it unfeasible for Pakistan to move ahead with its own plans for a hydroelectric dam downstream.

Pakistan wants to put the Kishenganga project before an arbitration panel—the first time that mechanism of the treaty will have been used. If India agrees, a seven-person court of arbitration would include two members appointed by each country, and three outsiders. India hasn't yet responded formally to the proposal, according to the Pakistan delegation to the meeting.

"We're already a water-stressed country," Jamaat Ali Shah, Pakistan's Indus waters commissioner, said ahead of this week's meeting. India's construction of new dams is "aggravating the stresses."

The water dispute comes as the relationship between the nuclear-armed neighbors is at an inflection point. India last month invited Pakistan to discuss the resumption of regular peace talks, and the two countries' foreign secretaries met in Delhi Feb. 25. A water squabble could upset those peace efforts.

That would deal a major blow to Indian Prime Minister Singh, who views engagement with Pakistan as the best way to contain terrorism. Mr. Singh wants Pakistan's aid in bringing to justice Pakistan-based militants that New Delhi believes carried out the November 2008 attacks in Mumbai, a bloody siege that killed 166 people.

Further deterioration of relations between New Delhi and Islamabad would also be a setback for Washington's efforts to stabilize the region. Pakistan has told the U.S. that tensions with India on its eastern border over the disputed territory of Kashmir have prevented it from cracking down more aggressively on Taliban and al Qaeda leaders directing the insurgency in Afghanistan.

Islamist groups in Pakistan have taken up the water issue as a new focus. "If our government doesn't act to resolve this issue then the people will take it in to their own hands. If water doesn't flow in to these rivers, then blood will," said Hafiz Khalid Waleed, the political affairs chief of Jamaat-ud-Dawah, an Islamic charity. India and others call the charity a front for Lashkar-e-Taiba, the militant group it says orchestrated the Mumbai terrorist attacks in Nov. 2008. Mr. Waleed denies any link to terrorism, calling it "American propaganda."

Water scarcity is a growing political issue across the globe, from the Middle East to the U.S. West. South Asia's water politics date back to Britain's partition of the Indian subcontinent in 1947, when newly created nations India and Pakistan wrangled over how to divide resources.

The Indus River, whose waters Britain had harnessed through a vast system of irrigation canals, was a crucial lifeline to farmers in the Punjab region stretching across both countries. But India and Pakistan were fighting over control of Kashmir, where several Indus tributaries begin.

After years of tense negotiations, India and Pakistan signed the Indus Waters Treaty in 1960 with the help of the World Bank. As part of the treaty—which is widely viewed by water experts as a model of how water conflicts can be managed—each side got unrestricted use of three rivers and rights to use the others for nonconsumptive purposes such as flood control, navigation and bathing. India was granted limited agricultural usage of Pakistan's rivers, plus the right to build hydroelectric projects, as long as they don't store or divert large amounts of water.

The treaty provides for bureaucrats appointed by both governments to meet regularly, exchange data, and resolve disputes. Commissioners have held more than 200 site inspections and meetings since 1960, even during times of war.

Yet Pakistan's rows with India have intensified as its water situation has worsened over the years. Water availability in Pakistan has fallen 70% since the early 1950s to 1,500 cubic meters per capita. It is expected to reach the 1,000-cubic-meter level considered officially "scarce" by international standards in 25 years, according to a report last year by the Woodrow Wilson International Center for Scholars.

Pakistani officials acknowledge their water woes aren't caused by India's damming of rivers alone. Major reservoirs are filling with sediment picked up by the rivers on their routes to the sea. Canals are aging and breaking down. The World Bank says soil erosion and poor irrigation are sapping roughly 1% from Pakistan's Gross Domestic Product growth.

Skeptics in India say Pakistan is simply looking for a scapegoat as it struggles to manage its internal water politics.

The especially arid province of Sindh, for example, blames the powerful upstream province of Punjab for consuming too much.

"Their water management is in terrible shape, and it's convenient to put the onus on India," said G. Parthasarathy, a former Indian envoy to Pakistan.

But Pakistani officials say New Delhi's actions are exacerbating a precarious situation.

This year the Pakistan province of Punjab—the political heartland of the nation and a major producer of wheat, rice, maize and sugar cane—is facing unprecedented water shortages. At harvest time in Mandi Bahauddin, an area in the north of Punjab province of relatively prosperous farmland, the wheat still grows waist-high.

But farmers here complain that yields and incomes have dropped by a third in the past five years because of water shortages. In the past, canals used to supply water for irrigation year-round. They are now empty for about four months each year. That forces villagers to pump groundwater, which is fast turning brackish and causing diseases like hepatitis, said Tariq Mehmood Allowana, a local farmer and member of the provincial assembly. In the past, the area's only problem was regular flooding. India's dams stopped this, causing a dearth of water instead, says Mr. Allowana, who owns 25 acres of wheat fields. The farmer represents the Pakistan Peoples Party of the late former Prime Minister Benazir Bhutto. Farmers say they have stopped cultivating rice—a water-intensive crop—except for personal use. Nearby, more than half of the Chenab river bed has become a dusty plain where children play with the flow reduced to a trickle.

"India is engaged in an economic warfare against Pakistan. If the problem persists for another five years the whole area will become barren," said Mr. Allowana, as a group of farmers nearby filled irrigation channels from groundwater supplies using a diesel-fueled pump.

Over the years, tensions have built as Pakistan has objected to the size and technical design of various Indian projects. India says it has 33 Indus-related hydrological projects at various stages of implementation, and all have been contested in one way or another by Pakistan. India also says it has yet to make use of its limited rights to store water on Pakistan's rivers or use it for limited irrigation.

"We've found there's a pattern in Pakistan of raising technical issues ad nauseam to stall a project or delay a project indefinitely," the senior Indian official said Friday.

In 2005 Pakistan raised issues with the Baglihar dam, an Indian power project on the Chenab river—one of those allotted to Pakistan—saying it would store too much water upstream and reduce downstream flow to Pakistan. The countries agreed in 2007 to let the World Bank appoint an independent expert, who ruled that India had to make minor modifications to the dam, such as lowering its height. Pakistan now contends the dam, which began operations in 2008, is reducing the flow of the Chenab below levels stipulated in the treaty. India denies this.

Pakistan wants Washington to play a mediating role with India—in the water dispute and wider issues like the Kashmir conflict. The U.S. is pushing for tighter relations with Pakistan as it steps up pressure on the Taliban in Afghanistan but has to balance this with its close ties to India. For now, the U.S. is treading carefully, offering Pakistan stepped-up economic aid and military hardware supplies.

Pakistan raised the water issue in Washington during an official visit last week. Secretary of State Hillary Clinton has signaled that Washington isn't interested in mediating on water issues.

A State Department spokesperson pointed to an interview Mrs. Clinton recently did with a Pakistani news channel in which she said it would be "sensible" to stick to the Indus Waters Treaty for resolving disputes.

The Indian projects that Pakistan says are draining its water resources are primarily on Indus tributaries in Kashmir. Some experts say the water issue is a back door way for Islamic militants to push their political agenda regarding Kashmir.

"They're saying, 'We must liberate Kashmir to save our water,'" said B.G. Verghese, a veteran journalist who has studied water issues closely and is a visiting professor at the Center for Policy Research, a New Delhi think tank.

THE INDUS WATER TREATY IS A SUCCESSFUL INSTANCE OF CONFLICT-RESOLUTION

After the Partition of India and Pakistan in 1947, an understanding on the sharing of water of Indus River between the two countries became necessary to facilitate the development of water resources of this basin. After prolonged talks between the two Governments, the Indus Water Treaty was signed in September According to this Treaty, waters of the three western rivers (the Jhelum, the Chenab, and the Indus itself) were allocated to Pakistan, and those of the three eastern rivers (the Ravi, the Beas and the Sutlej) were allocated to India. Certain restrictions about water utilization were placed on India which is the upper riparian country. The highlights of the Treaty are:

- India has not been allowed to build storages on the rivers where water has been allocated to Pakistan.

- Restrictions have also been imposed on the extension of irrigation development in India. Less significant restrictions have been placed on Pakistan, being the lower riparian.
- The Treaty contains provisions regarding the exchange of data on project operation, extent of irrigated agriculture, etc.
- The Treaty provides for certain institutional arrangements. A permanent Indus Commission consisting of a Commissioner each for India and for Pakistan has been set up and there are periodical meetings and exchanges of visits between the two sides.
- Detailed guidelines were included in the Treaty for conflict-resolution. The Indus Commission is the first step for conflict resolution. If an agreement cannot be reached at the Commission level, the dispute is to be referred to the two governments. If the governments too fail to reach an agreement, the Treaty provides an arbitration mechanism.

The Indus Water Treaty is a successful instance of conflict-resolution. It has been working reasonably well despite the strained political relationship between India and Pakistan. Importantly, it continued to be honoured even during wars between the two countries. Undoubtedly differences do arise from time to time, but these usually get resolved within the framework of the Treaty. Minor differences are settled within the Commission, and major disputes go to the two Governments.

KASHMIR'S RAGING RIVERS

A resolution of the Kashmir conflict seems as elusive today as it did in 1951. Since 1989, armed Kashmiri separatists, some with Pakistani support, have waged a low-grade, off-and-on insurgency against Indian security forces. (Protests last summer against India's heavy-handed rule in the Kashmir Valley roiled the region for several weeks, leading to the deaths of at least 110 Kashmiris, many of them teenage boys.) * Still, without the IWT, Kashmir might have been the source of even wider conflict.

Lilienthal recognized a truth that remains little discussed but as relevant as ever: The struggle for Kashmir was motivated in large part by Pakistan's desperation to control the rivers that flowed through the region. "The starting point should be ... to set to rest Pakistan's fears of deprivation and a return to desert," he wrote. The treaty would defuse these tensions at a critical point in the young nations' relations, by clearly spelling out how much water each was entitled to use from the rivers that crossed the western border.

India and Pakistan signed the IWT in 1960, after protracted negotiations facilitated by the World Bank. Before the partition of British India in 1947, each province had jurisdiction to build dams and other infrastructure for electricity and irrigation on the portions of the rivers that flowed through their land; after partition, a series of patchwork agreements left several key issues, such as whether and how much Pakistan should pay India for water and canal maintenance costs, unresolved. The IWT gave "unrestricted use" of the basin's three western rivers (the Indus, the Jhelum, and the Chenab) to Pakistan and the three eastern rivers (the Ravi, the Beas, and the Sutlej) to India. Today, the treaty governs the use of roughly 55 trillion gallons of water per year, which sustains more than 210 million people in the basin.

The IWT has since solidly weathered three Indo-Pakistani wars (including two over Kashmir) and countless flare-ups between the now nuclear-armed neighbors. The Indian and Pakistani members of the treaty-stipulated Indus Waters Commission have met at least once every year, conducting amicable discussions and sharing important hydrological data even when their nations' diplomatic relations have been severed.

Yet the treaty shows signs of strain. In 2005, Pakistan invoked the arbitration provisions of the treaty—for the first time in its history—in response to India's construction of a large hydropower project on the Chenab River. Pakistan has since raised objections to several other power projects on IWT-governed rivers, spurred by its ancient fears that India's storage of water in those dams could threaten its agricultural production. While the treaty's existing provisions have largely been able to contain these disputes, two emerging trends—climate change and Kashmiris' desire for greater control over their water resources—threaten to undermine the very foundations of the treaty as a tool for averting conflict.

The Indus receives at least 30 percent of its flow from the region's shrinking glaciers—more than any other Asian river. As global warming plods on, experts expect increased flows and possibly flooding in the near term as the glacial "water towers" melt. But this spike will be followed by a long, painful tail of perennial scarcity as the glaciers' role in providing water during the dry season becomes greatly diminished.

The Indus basin's overwhelming dependence on snow and ice melt has led Shakil Romshoo, a professor of geophysics and geology at the University of Kashmir in Srinagar, to conclude that global warming will destabilize the IWT within the next few decades. In Kashmir, "the surface runoff ... is decreasing," he says. "And on this surface water depends the entire economy of Pakistan."

About 80 percent of Pakistan's cultivated lands are irrigated by water from the Indus system, the lion's share being governed by the IWT. Of the IWT water, more than 70 percent of flows from the Indian state of Jammu and Kashmir. The math gets worse for Pakistan: The country's population is projected to increase by 82 percent, from 184 million in 2010 to 335 million in 2050; per capita water availability was nearly 80 percent lower in 2005 than 1947, plunging from 5,600 cubic meters to 1,200 cubic meters, dangerously close to the 1,000-cubic-meter-per-person-per-year "water scarcity" threshold defined by the widely used Falkenmark index. A growing alarm in Pakistan over this hydrological straitjacket has in recent years spurred jihadi leaders based there to frame their attacks against India as a struggle to secure the rivers that form Pakistan's "lifeline."

The stakes are high for Kashmiris as well. A recent study in the journal *Science* concluded that the eventual reduced flow of meltwater from glaciers and snowfields threatens the food security of close to 30 million people living in the Indus basin. Many Kashmiri farmers have switched from grain production to less-thirsty horticulture in recent years due to the increasingly uncertain availability of water at critical times in the growing season.

Rising local resentment is the second factor jeopardizing the IWT. Kashmiri perspectives have never had a prominent voice in IWT-related discussions. Their frustration stems in part from the way the treaty limits the construction of new irrigation works and storage facilities for hydropower on the Indian side of the three western rivers (the ones granted to Pakistan for unrestricted use). But Kashmiris are also unhappy with the Indian government's decision to retain control over most of the existing hydro plants in their state, thus depriving the local government and economy of a critical source of revenue.

Any wider effort to industrialize Jammu and Kashmir's economy will depend on greater exploitation of the state's hydropower potential. The state potentially has up to 15,000 megawatts of exploitable hydropower, less than 10 percent of which has been tapped. But India hasn't allowed the state to access international financing to develop and operate more power plants on its rivers. It "is non-negotiable for us that ... Kashmir will have to have control of its power resources," says Arjimand Hussain Talib, a Kashmiri newspaper columnist working on a book about Kashmir's water politics.

The state government recently hired an international consultant to do a thorough study of the economic losses incurred by Jammu and Kashmir due to restrictions on hydropower and agricultural development imposed by the treaty. Past speculative estimates have put the number around $1.5 billion per year. More detailed and credible numbers could give Kashmiris more leverage to wrest financial compensation from New Delhi.

Talib predicts that ongoing talks between India and Pakistan will ultimately result in "a kind of joint collaborative approach to the basin's management." This might take the form of a new successor agreement to the IWT, as some analysts call for. A more likely scenario than total renegotiation, according to Talib, would be India and Pakistan signing an "extension agreement." In this event, the countries would extend the IWT in a separate, complementary treaty to include joint planning and oversight in the early stages of infrastructure projects on the six rivers—even across Kashmir's militarized Line of Control.

This vision echoes a proposal Lilienthal floated sixty years ago. "The whole Indus system must be ... designed, built and operated as a unit," Lilienthal argued, to benefit both India and Pakistan optimally. This objective, he insisted, "cannot be achieved by the countries working separately; the river pays no attention to partition."

INDIA AND PAKISTAN AT ODDS OVER SHRINKING INDUS RIVER

"Pakistan's entire economy is driven by the textile industry," said Michael Kugelman, a South Asia expert at the Woodrow Wilson International Center for Scholars. "The problem with Pakistan's economy is that most of the major industries use a ton of water—textiles, sugar, wheat—and there's a tremendous amount of water that's not only used, but wasted," he added.

The same is true for India

That impact is an important part of a complex water equation in countries already under strain from booming populations. More people means more demand for water to irrigate crops, cool machinery, and power cities. The Indus River, which begins in Indian-controlled Kashmir and flows through Pakistan on its way to the sea, is Pakistan's primary freshwater source—on which 90 percent of its agriculture depends—and a critical outlet of hydropower generation for both countries.

Downstream provinces are already feeling the strain, with some dried-out areas being abandoned by fishermen and farmers forced to move to cities. That increases competition between urban and rural communities for water. "In areas where you used to have raging rivers, you have, essentially, streams or even puddles and not much else," said Kugelman.

In years past, the coastal districts that lost their shares of the Indus' flows have become "economically orphaned," the poorest districts in the country, according to Pakistani water activist

Mustafa Talpur. Because Pakistani civil society is weak, he says, corruption and deteriorating water distribution tend to go hand in hand.

In the port city of Karachi, which depends for its water on the Indus, water theft—in which public water is stolen from the pipes and sold from tankers in slums and around the city—may be a $500-million annual industry.

In the balance is the fate not only of people, but important aquatic species like the Indus River dolphin, which is now threatened to extinction by agricultural pollution and dams, among other pressures. Scientists estimate that fewer than 100 individuals remain.

Threat to Peace?

One of the potentially catastrophic consequences of the region's fragile water balance is the effect on political tensions.

In India, competition for water has a history of provoking conflict between communities. In Pakistan, water shortages have triggered food and energy crises that ignited riots and protests in some cities. Most troubling, Islamabad's diversions of water to upstream communities with ties to the government are inflaming sectarian loyalties and stoking unrest in the lower downstream region of Sindh.

But the issue also threatens the fragile peace that holds between the nations of India and Pakistan, two nuclear-armed rivals. Water has long been seen as a core strategic interest in the dispute over the Kashmir region, home to the Indus' headwaters. Since 1960, a delicate political accord called the Indus Waters Treaty has governed the sharing of the river's resources. But dwindling river flows will be harder to share as the populations in both countries grow and the per-capita water supply plummets.

Some growth models predict that by 2025, India's population will grow to triple what it was—and Pakistan's population to six times what it was—when the Indus treaty was signed. Lurking in the background are fears that climate change is speeding up the melting of the glaciers that feed the river.

Mountain glaciers in Kashmir play a central role in regulating the river's flows, acting as a natural water storage tank that freezes precipitation in winter and releases it as meltwater in the summer. The Indus is dependent on glacial melting for as much as half of its flow. So its fate is uniquely tied to the health of the Himalayas. In the short term, higher glacial melt is expected to bring more intense flooding, like last year's devastating deluge.

Both countries are also racing to complete large hydroelectric dams along their respective stretches of the Kashmir river system, elevating tensions. India's projects are of a size and scope that many Pakistanis fear could be used to disrupt their hydropower efforts, as well as the timing of the flows on which Pakistani crops rely.

"Many in Pakistan are worried that, being in control of upstream waters, India can easily run Pakistan dry either by diverting the flow of water by building storage dams or using up all the water through hydroelectric power schemes," said Pakistani security analyst Rifaat Hussain.

For years, Pakistani politicians have claimed India is responsible for Pakistan's water troubles. More recently, militant groups have picked up their rhetoric. Hafiz Saeed, the founder of the Pakistani militant group allegedly responsible for the 2008 terror attack in Mumbai, even accused India of "water terrorism."

Hope for the Future

In the past few months, however, the situation has improved, according to Kugelman. "We've been hearing nearly unprecedented statements from very high-level Pakistani officials who have essentially acknowledged that India is not stealing Pakistan's water, and that Pakistan's water problems are essentially a function of internal mismanagement issues," he said. Militants are still griping, he said, "but not as shrilly."

This may be because the two countries are cooperating on water and other issues better than before, and because militants are now focusing less on their archenemy in India and more on coalition forces in Afghanistan.

"But I imagine this is momentary," said Kugelman. "The facts on the ground—the water constraints in both India and Pakistan—have not abated. They're both still very serious and getting worse."

What's needed, he says, is more conservation and adaptation—a smarter way of doing business.

WATER WARRIORS OF INDIA - INITIATIVE TOWARDS PURE AND AMPLE WATER

No water or contaminated water is commonplace news in the national or regional dailies of India. Such incidents are termed by newspapers as mismanagement of the government, bureaucrats calls it unfortunate incidents and the governing authorities term it as accident. Whatever the term used its the shame to the whole mankind that even being in 21st century, with such high development of technology some of our fellow beings living in certain sections of the society has a threat to ill health and in some cases succumb their lives to shackles of death because of water which itself is the originator of life.

Rainwater harvesting is what India can choose, and the youth consortium which will bring paradigm shift in this process will be Water Warriors of India Its an irony that India being surrounded by water bodies on three sides, house of 13 major rivers, largest river island (Majuli), highest rainfall (Mausingram) and many other facts which reflects Indias dominance in water resources, yet we face shortages every year.

Consider this the per capita water availability in India was 3450 cu m in 1952. It stands at 1800 cu m now and by estimates by 2025 it will fall to 1200 1500 cu m per person. Even though the rate of urbanization in India is among the lowest in the world, the nation has more than 250 million city-dwellers. Experts predict that this number will rise even further, and by 2020, about 50 per cent of India's population will be living in cities. This is going to put further pressure on the already strained centralized water supply systems of urban areas.

The urban water supply and sanitation sector in the country is suffering from inadequate levels of service, an increasing demand-supply gap, poor sanitary conditions and deteriorating financial and technical performance. Supply of water is highly erratic and unreliable.

Transmission and distribution networks are old and poorly maintained, and generally of a poor quality. Consequently physical losses are typically high, ranging from 25 to over 50 per cent. Low pressures and intermittent supplies allow back siphoning, which results in contamination of water in the distribution network. Water is typically available for only 2-8 hours a day in most Indian cities. The situation is even worse in summer when water is available only for a few minutes, sometimes not at all.

Looking at the condition at metro cities of India: Mumbais demand for water is expected to rise to 7,970 MLD (million litres daily) by 2011, current supply is 3100 MLD which already constitutes a substantial shortfall as the city receives only 2,500 MLD, the balance lost on account of leakages and pilferage. In the capital itself Delhi the supply of water is around 650 million gallons of water per day against the demand of 750 million. According to a World Bank study, of the 27 Asian cities with populations of over 1,000,000, Chennai and Delhi are ranked as the worst performing metropolitan cities in terms of hours of water availability per day, while Mumbai is ranked as second worst performer and Calcutta fourth worst

All these was regarding the shortage of water but the analysis remains incomplete if we dont emphasize on the quality of water available for drinking. Whether the water is potable? The fact is that it is deteriorating fast. As early as in 1982 it was reported that 70 per cent of all available water in India was polluted. The situation is much worse today. There are daily news reports on prime dailies showing the pictures of the contaminated water available in various localities of the city for drinking. The colour of the contaminated water supplied to these areas is worse to urine. Over extraction of ground water has led to salt water intrusion into coastal aquifers. It has also resulted in problems of excessive fluoride, iron, arsenic and salinity in water affecting about 44 million people in India. Ground water is facing an equally serious threat from contamination by industrial effluent as well as pesticides and fertilizer from farm run-offs.

Sanitation and water management should be looked at simultaneously. Too often attention is focused on drinking water supply, leaving sanitation and wastewater treatment for later. However, for every 100 litres of water going into a house about 90 litres will have to leave the plot again. Unless priority is given quickly to creating an infrastructure to assure availability of water, there may be no water to meet the agricultural, domestic and industrial needs of a population that has tripled in 50 years to more than a billion.

Water management in terms of availability and most importantly quality is therefore major challenge not only for town planners, state and central governments but being citizen of the worlds largest democracy its our supreme duty to overcome the hurdles regarding the water management and water warriors will take initiative in gratifying this duty. Water supply is an institutional process and an institutional framework for effective water supply and sanitation has to comply with the functions of policy, regulation and sector organization, management of quality, infrastructure and on-site sanitation.

So we discuss about the major issues and their solution concerning institutional options in water problem and sanitation in Indian community, analysis can be further extended to other developing countries: First issue: Water supply should treat to all sections of society, but poor people are neglected

Institutions in developing countries dealing with water and sanitation issues have rarely been designed to cater for large numbers of poor people. At the level of operations, public utilities are often constrained by bureaucratic requirements. For instance there is often considerable inflexibility in the management of human resources within public utilities. Given the complexity of the problem in many countries there are a number of separate agencies responsible for wastewater and sanitation, particular in the case of public sector provision. For this, the role of Non-governmental organizations (NGOs) such as ours, particularly in low cost sanitation, community participation and creating public awareness has to be very positive. In cities, community toilets has to be constructed and managed mainly by NGOs or private firms, based on the user pays principle or as a charity. We will be active in raising awareness concerning health, hygiene, slum development, solid waste collection and disposal issue and equitable distribution of facilities. The challenge remains to increase the impact of these initiatives by multiplying them on a larger scale or mainstreaming the approach in the leading institutions for water and sanitation in India.

Second issue: Should privatization of water be done and confusion regarding the delegation of roles between public and private sector? An important issue according to this is the division of responsibilities between the government and the private sector. Ideally the government would set the framework, but there is often market failure. Then governments get involved and find it difficult to pull out. Also the type and scale of technology is important and has consequences for the management and financing. The larger the scale, the bigger the financial implications. In that case governments will also be more inclined to involve the private sector.

But majority of the public opinion favors water as a common resource while showing reservation about policy that seeks to make water a commodity of the state. Water policies adopted by states like Maharashtra and Rajasthan are being opposed by several groups including the environmentalists. A largely felt perception held by the people is that governments in India are buckling under pressure from the World Bank. These policies, it is felt, help declare water as a state property, which later facilitates its conversion into private property. But is the privatization of water the only viably efficient solution to our shoddy management of water resources?

The division between the public and private sector requires answering the question which tasks each one is fulfilling? To ensure effective provision of sanitation services it is imperative to have a good understanding of the roles and responsibilities of every entity (be it public or private) and the technologies used to perform its task. The emergence of the private sector and the users themselves as alternative providers leads to a formulation of a large number of institutional modes for the provision of services with private sector involvement. These modes vary from simple service contract to complete divestiture to the private sector, and a large variety of models for user involvement as owners or in the management.

On the other hand we as participants of the youth movement in water through our ways of harvesting water along with water activists, environmentalist and policy makers will work to provide alternatives to water policies so that the government and people are made aware that there are ways other than privatization to manage the countrys water resources.

Third issue: Willingness to pay or to contribute for water supply and sanitation is minimal. Effective demand for water and sanitation is often weak if measured by the willingness to pay or contribute to for example the installation of sanitary services. Public demand in context of making payments for water supply and sanitation services systems is low in spite of the high social cost assigned to the polluted sites. The public sector has also become increasingly aware of the high political risk of a significant raise in basic rates for providing these services. Key constituting elements of such systems are appropriate policies, laws and regulations, institutions, technologies and cost recovery systems. There is a need to look for appropriate technological solutions and to involve the people at the preparation and implementation stage.

In general the public is interested in getting sanitation facilities, but not very much concerned about the treatment of wastewater or the necessary off plot sanitation facilities. This usually means a limited willingness to pay and a negative attitude towards involving private parties. Water warriors in its programme will organize campaign stressing on bringing water democracy by ensuring that every drop is conserved, harvested and shared by the people.

Fourth issue: water supply and waste water management should be looked in an integrated way It is desirable to think of water supply, sanitation and wastewater in an integrated way.

This implies that the cost of an integrated solution will be much lower than a solution at a later stage by a separate institution based on different cost recovery system. In big cities dealing with wastewater and offsite sanitation is often integrated. However, in the Indian case we also learn that this tends to be limited to the area of the Municipal Commission, leaving the rest of the city to the development authorities or even district authorities, who tend to have less money and no money raising responsibilities.

As a result we at our movement will make government and people aware to manage useable water and waste water with same assiduousness.

Fifth issue: there is a need for regulation in the system. The need for well-defined roles and responsibilities is clear. It is also necessary to make the institutional arrangements between the municipality and the private sector explicit. There needs to be a regulatory framework and the authorities need to take their responsibility. As public utilities are not usually subject to the disciplines of the market, they have fewer incentives to minimize costs (and maximize tariff collection rates). Regulatory arrangements can stimulate them to look at their cost, for example through a system of benchmarking.

The design of an effective institutional framework is a challenge in large metropolitan areas. If not done well, the existence of multiple institutions with primary or secondary responsibilities in sanitation can become a hindrance to effective development and management of sanitation services. A case in point is Bangalore where mandates not only overlap, but have also been defined at different levels, and for different technologies. Here, effective co-ordination is absent, as a result of which the services cannot be run effectively. So, if each section of the society is made aware of its role, such commotion wont arise at all, this is also an area where water warriors will emphasize.

Sixth issue: Finances cannot be ignored. Financing is crucial. What is the financial basis for supplying water and sanitation services? Some of the cost recovery mechanisms currently used includes infrastructure charges, connection fees, environmental user fees and local taxes. Raising sufficient revenue to cover for the cost is difficult. As already emphasized, the costs of these services are high and at the same time, the demand is usually little developed and the willingness to pay is low, and lower than that for other services.

In addition, enforcement of payment for sanitation and waste water services is difficult, as one cannot simply disconnect as is done with other utilities such power and telecoms. Yet, any sustainable water management initiative must address the key issues of financing and cost recovery.

In this context, raising the awareness of the need to have adequate wastewater and sanitation services, of the range of technologies, and of the cost of such services and of the inevitability of cost recovery in return for good service quality is a precondition for effectiveness. User participation is yet another key to success in wastewater services: several urban case studies have shown that willingness to pay is above expected levels in cases where the users have been given a chance to consciously participate in the selection and establishment of the sanitation system.

Various cost recovery mechanisms or economic instruments can be applied to recover (at least) the operational cost of urban sanitation and the treatment of wastewater. These include user charges, effluent charges and taxation. There should be provision of 'polluter pays' in which the costs of wastewater management charged to a customer are calculated in function of wastewater quantity and pollution load.

Household charges may be uniform and based on an assumed pollution equivalent, or a volumetric rate based on recorded water consumption.

High charges may encourage pre-treatment and even process-redesign by industries in an effort to optimize water and wastewater costs. (Too) high charges may also have undesired effects such as illegal discharges inside or outside the wastewater system. So water warriors through advocating such policies will ensure maximizing of utility under the constraints of minimizing cost.

The youth consortium of water warriors will cater specifically to all the above concerned issues. Having discussed the current scenario, reasons and the issues and their specific solution regarding the water management in India, now we shift our emphasis on the ways in which an individual or a locality can take measures to solve its own major water problem

Urban centres in India are facing an ironical situation today. On one hand there is the acute water scarcity and on the other, the streets are often flooded during the monsoons. This has led to serious problems with quality and quantity of groundwater.

This is despite the fact that all these cities receive good rainfall. However, this rainfall occurs during short spells of high intensity. (Most of the rain falls in just 100 hours out of 8,760 hours in a year). Because of such short duration of heavy rain, most of the rain falling on the surface tends to flow away rapidly leaving very little for recharge of groundwater. As water shortage increases, alternative sources of water supply are gaining importance. These include sewage recycle, rainwater harvesting, generating water form humidity in the atmosphere etc.

Water recycle through rain water harvesting is a simple, effective and economical solution to conserve water so that more fresh water is available for essential uses drinking, bathing, cooking and laundry. Population, industrialization and pollution are putting pressure on our limited fresh water resource. There is limit to increasing water supply because we are running out of sources and cost of additional facilities is prohibitive. The best way to solve water problem therefore is by conserving water and recycling it wherever possible. Recycling must be made mandatory far all new projects- industrial or domestic and even should be promoted to existing buildings also.

One of the solutions to the urban water crisis and the best way to recycle water is *Rainwater Harvesting - capturing the runoff.* Rain harvesting will be really efficient in areas where there is inadequate groundwater supply or surface resources are either lacking or insufficient, it drastically reduces urban flooding from which our two major cities Mumbai and Chennai suffered drastically last year

Rain water harvesting is an ancient concept, the implementation of it does not requires any major technology and the cost is even low, as compared to the benefits cost should not even be considered. At this juncture its worth mentioning the ways in which an individual of the society can take part in such a process.

Rainwater harvesting can be harvested from the following surfaces:

Rooftops: If buildings with impervious roofs are already in place, the catchment area is effectively available free of charge and they provide a supply at the point of consumption.

Paved and unpaved areas i.e., landscapes, open fields, parks, storm water drains, roads and pavements and other open areas can be effectively used to harvest the runoff. The main advantage in using ground as collecting surface is that water can be collected from a larger area. This is part of the community project to be undertaken

Water bodies: The potential of lakes, tanks and ponds to store rainwater is immense. The harvested rainwater can not only be used to meet water requirements of the city, it also recharges groundwater aquifers.

Storm water drains: Most of the residential colonies have proper network of storm water drains. If maintained neatly, these offer a simple and cost effective means for harvesting rainwater.

Rain water though stored will only serve the purpose if properly filtered to meet the major drinking water needs. For this effect major invention in the field has been made which provides proper rain water purification mechanisms. These purification system works on the normal treatment method involving screening, flocculation sedimentation and filtration.

These purification systems are also available for micro scale projects to serve the need of a household. Such purification systems are simple in installing and easy to operate. The most important feature is that they dont require electricity.

Many entrepreneurs of industries tend to forget the fact that they are part of the living society and in turn they tend to foster the production of negative externality. It should be made mandatory for each industry to install water management solutions to recycle its waste water for reuse. Major step in this front is through the development of Industrial effluent recycle solution which integrates physiochemical, biological and membrane separation processes for optimum water recovery. They achieve water management through water recycle and source reduction, and waste management through product recovery and waste minimization. They are cost effective as they recover valuable products for reuse while recycling which gives industries a good return on their investment while protecting the environment and even the common people as it reduces the water usage of industries and transmittance of waste to water bodies.

After emphasizing the ways of tackling the problem through rain water harvesting and other recycling options, the following paragraphs paves the way to the essence of the whole discussion; it illuminates the role of the youth in curbing the problem of such a magnitude which can pose a threat to the very existence of the mankind in this world.

Any amount of government expenditure cannot solve this problem unless and until the community as a whole in its full might rise to the occasion and work for it.

In India the role of youth cannot be under estimated as India in its demography cycle has a position of Young India with more than half of Indias population below the age of 35 years. The youth of the nation has to take part in mass movement of awareness; they have to be the Water warriors of India

In this approach the youth will be enlightened to serve their locality and curb the water problem. Each locality in city will have its own group of members named as the water warriors whose primary work will be to impart awareness among the residents regarding rain water harvesting. Charity begins at home, so in the first step the members have to set up rain water harvesting system in their respective houses, so that they can put forward examples and other people can replicate these. Water warriors of respective localities will provide assistance in setting up of the system of rain water harvesting. In certain cases possible community projects can be taken as a whole where large tanks are to be constructed to store rain water. Major foray of water warriors will be in water harvesting but it will also simultaneously ensure that water is being properly utilized.

The promotion techniques will include the most believable of all- word-of-mouth, apart from other conventional means of imparting awareness such as newspapers, hoarding etc., as water warriors will be a youth forum, the awareness and membership will be imparted through the largest network of World Wide Web.

The major question which remained unanswered is that why will any youth join this consortium of water warrior? The answer to this question can be traced from last year experience of major cities of west and south India, which were struck by floods, the irony was that there was water everywhere but there was no water to drink, no water to cook food, no water to survive life. This incident in major way has brought into notice the major problem of water management in our country, and its the younger generations who have to foray into the scene, join the consortium and solve the problem simply because of the reason that we are the people who have to destine the future of ours as well as coming generation. It was first time that major important cities of India had confronted such a problem which made youth aware of the reality, and steps has to be taken to overcome the harsh realities of water mismanagement.

Among the factors that constrain performance of water management in India are: poor levels of service particularly for sanitation, inadequate pricing policies (poor cost recovery), undue political interference with service provision, highly centralized character of the sector, lack of accountability, lack of continuation in policies and programmes, low levels of productivity and efficiency and inadequate training or management and sector staff. These factors are exacerbated by external factors such as of population growth, urbanization, and economic development that jointly drive a growth in demand that providers fail to cope with. Successful approaches that has to be considered at macro level for policies should be effective decentralization, integration of hygiene and sanitation activities, demand-driven approaches, cost recovery and good governance, and focus on poverty alleviation, equitable distribution of health services, and gender-sensitive approaches.

It is heartening to note that in India, the water supply sector is at last moving away from an infrastructure- creation approach to a consolidation approach. But India still needs to make substantial infrastructure is that its growth has not been accompanied by an improvement in the quality of governance of water services in the country and that the water sector suffered from a policy of build- neglect and rebuild. Therefore, government and its agencies should not merely concern them with fixing pipes but also fixing institutions that fix pipes

These were the approaches at macro level but for effective utilization of these policies the work has to start from micro level, from each and every household itself. We as youth through our voice need to create awareness about the importance of water in the community so that mindset, attitudes, and habits change proactively rather than wait for legislation and regulation. Together we must work to see that waste of this precious resource is minimizes and we are able to conserve fresh water for future generations.

There is need to grab the water problem by the scruff of its neck. Enough has been written, discussed about the problem, hardly anybody takes a look at the solution. Residents of the locality blame it on the government; government on the other hand overlooks it as a seasonal or short term problem. Therefore, there is a need of a paradigm shift from problems to the solution, from despair to problem solving, form now to future. This is what the youth movement of water warriors will be about.

The water warrior campaigns, ultimate goal will be to see a world as an agglomeration of ecological - water harvesting - democracies.

WATER CRISIS LOOMS COUNTRYWIDE

Water has become the most commercial products of the century. This may sound bizarre, but true. In fact, what water is to the 21st century, oil was to the 20th century. The stress on the multiple water resources is a result of a multitude of factors. On the one hand, the rapidly rising population and changing lifestyles have increased the need for fresh water. On the other hand, intense competitions among users in agriculture, industry and domestic sector is pushing the ground water table deeper.

To get bucket of drinking water is a struggle for most women in the country. The virtually dry and dead water resources have lead to acute water scarcity, affecting the socio-economic condition of the society. The drought conditions have pushed villagers to move to cities in search of jobs, whereas women and girls have to trudge further. This time lost in fetching water can very well translate into financial gains, leading to a better life for the family. If opportunity costs were taken into account, it would be clear that in most rural areas, households are paying far more for water supply than the often-normal rates charged in urban areas. Also, if this cost of fetching water which is almost equivalent. to 150 million women days each year, is covered into a loss for the national exchequer, it translates into a whopping 10 billion rupees per year.

The government has accorded the highest priority to rural drinking water for ensuring universal access as a part of policy framework to achieve the goal of reaching the unreached. Despite the installation of more than 3.5 million hand pumps and over 116 thousand piped water supply schemes, in many parts of the country, the people face water scarcity almost every year, there by meaning that our water supply systems are failing to sustain despite huge investments.

In India, there are many villages either with scarce water supply or without any source of water. If there is no source of potable water in 2.5 kilometres, then the village becomes no source water village or problem village. In many rural areas, women still have to walk a distance of about 2.5 kms to reach the source of water. She reaches home carrying heavy pots, not to rest but to do other household chores of cooking, washing-cleaning, caring of children and looking after livestock. Again in the evening she has to fetch water. Thus a rural woman's life is sheer drudgery.

Water is the biggest crisis facing India in terms of spread and severity, affecting one in every three persons. Even in Chennai, Bangalore, Shimla and Delhi, water is being rationed and India's food security is under threat. With the lives and livelihood of millions at risk, urban India is screaming for water. For instance, water is rationed twice a week in Bangalore, and for 30 minutes a day in Bhopal; 250 tankers make 2,250 trips to quench Chennai's thirst. Mumbai routinely lives through water cuts from January to June, when some areas get water once in three days in Hyderabad.

Harrowing midnight for a precious bucket of drinking water is a regular feature for many families of Vypuri, an Island off the mainland of Kochi. Women have to queue up in front of the public water taps, being at the lag end of the pipeline system, they get water only after the users ahead in the pipeline finish collecting water. There are nights when water pressure dips so low that some women get it after midnight. They split their day between household chores and collecting water.

Apart from the water scarcity caused by Coca-cola in Plachimada, the other districts in the state are facing a water crisis. For instance, in Kottayam district at some places, the water scarcity is so acute that people hesist to offer a glass of water to the visitor, which hitherto was a common custom. In the upper Kuttanadu area of the district during summer people collect water from a distance of 3-4 kms. Water supply from public taps is erratic and very often even after standing for an hour in the queue; people are not able to get a bucket of water. Most women and girls in Rajasthan find themselves searching water for much of the year. They trudge bare foot in the hot sun for hours over wastelands, across thorny fields, or rough terrain in search of water, often life the colour of mud and brackish, but still welcome for the parched throats back home. On an average, a rural woman walks more than 14000 km a year just to fetch water. Their urban sisters are only slightly better off- they do not walk such distances, but stand in the long winding queues for hours on end to collect water from the roadside taps on the water lorries.

In every household, in the rural areas in Rajasthan, women and girl children bear the responsibilit of collecting, transporting, storing, and managing water. In places, where there is no water for farming, men migrate to urban areas in search of work leaving women behind to fond for the old and the children. Women spend most of their time, collecting water with little time for other productive work. This impacts on the education of the girl child, if the girl is herself not collecting water, she is looking after the home and her siblings when her mother is away.

In brief:

- Water source being open dug well, the quality of water is poor; dirty, saline and has turbidity
- Women have to make at least three trips at 5 am, 11 am and 5 pm
- Sometimes, the number of trips is more
- Total distance traveled is 9-10 km, even higher
- Total Time spent is 6-9 hours
- Total number of pots/buckets is about 3 pots, 30-45 litres (one pot of 10-15 litres per trip)
- Due to long distance, they have to take rest in the middle of the way. Dust storms aggravate their problem
- At some villages water from tubewells is too saline to drink. Even animals particularly cow gets indigestion after drinking this water, so the villagers add water from the dug well. The entire life of women in rural areas like Jaisalmer is spent on water collection and cooking. Even the girls of 8-10 years cannot be spared. They cannot afford the luxury of school. For instance for Pappu a girl of hardly 10 years, water collection has become her main job. In the words of her grandmother "Water fetching is the schooling for Pappu." There are so many Pappus in the villages and dhaanis of Jaisalmer.

In Sriganganagar, the Indira Gandhi canal is the main source for drinking water. However, during the crisis period (either because of no water in the main canal/sub canal or due to the erratic power supply), the rich remain unaffected. In such crisis women from poorhouse hold draw water from the village diggis, which is totally unfit for any kind of human activity. They use this water not only for washing cloth and bathing but also for drinking. Due to the formation of algae, water becomes greenish and filthy. Women add alum to purify it.

In Orissa drinking water is being privatized. The government first insists on the formation of water associations and conveniently pass the responsibilities on to these association. When this proves inefficient, water distribution rights are given away to private contractors. For example, the Orissa government initially stressed on the formation of Paani Panchayats (water associations).

Later using police the government suppressed these panchayats justifying this by claiming that the villages were not being responsible enough. Titlagarh is the hottest town of India, but it has no water, causing great misery to the women. As the highest temperature, is recorded here 52 degrees centigrade which is also the highest temperature in India. People called "Titlagarh" as "Tatlagarh", in local language Tatla means hot. In Titlagarh water problem is acute. People are buying water throughout the year for drinking and cooking purpose. In the month of May and June the rate of water increase three times, from Rs 2 per Dabba to Rs.8 per Dabba (container). This is the picture of urban areas, but in rural areas the problem is worse, where the tubewells all are becoming dry but people have no money to buy water. Due to the water problem some villagers are migrating to other places.

In Uttranchal women are suffering a lot in every village where water problem is severe. Natural sources are drying up which adds the kilometres for women everyday to quench the thirst of their family as well as animals.

Women are the major part of the workforce in Garhwal. They work from early morning to late evening to serve the family. They do all household work from cooking to cleaning and washing clothes and soiled utensils as well as look after their children and animals. Women also collect the water required for cooking, cleaning, washing, bathing and drinking both for human beings and animals.

During the survey in Jaunsar area of district Tehri Garhwal, in villages such as Nagthat, Duena, Vishoi, Gadol, Jandoh, Chi tar, Chichrad and Gangoa, it was observed that water in the region is mostly acidic in nature. The water problem in Chi tar and Gangoa villages is very severe, where men and women carry water on mules from 8-10 Km to the village. Because of the poor water quality, most of the villagers in the regions are suffering from many diseases related to skin and teeth. Natural resources of water in the area are very few and they are also disappearing very fast. During the survey, Smt. Nisha Devi of Chi tar village explained that they are not getting enough water for their animals so they take their animals to the spring about 2-3 kms away.

In Bundelkhand, women have no work but to collect drinking water on their heads from long distance. The grim situation of water may be best illustrated by one Bundelkhandi saying which roughly translated as "let the husband die but the earthen pot of water should not be broken".

The scenario is worst in Patha in Chitrakut district where women have to travel a long distance to collect water for drinking. Half of the time of women is spent to collect water, which affects their health and the well-being of their children. The paucity of time due to water crisis aggravates the domestic problem.

Instead of solving the water crisis, attempts are being made to create a disastrous situation in the region. Banda city entirely depends on the Ken river. If Ken is linked with Betwa, then it will not affect only Banda, but would also jeopardize the survival of farmers who depend on Ken.

Even in Delhi the water scenario is no better, being worst in Delhi slums. For example Sanjay colony slum of New Delhi has population about 15,000-20,000 with about 4500 households in the locality. Majority of the population is self-employed and are engaged in making daris, mats and other clothes for sale. In this area people collect water from different sources depending on the availability such as DJB tanker, MCD pipe water supply and from Sulabh International. DJB tanker comes daily but it has no fixed time for water distribution. The water that comes from MCD pipe water has fixed time for water supply but it only comes for 1-2 hr in the evening (around 4.30 p.m.). At MCD pipe line people made bore and fetch water from it. If the people don't get water from the above sources they are forced to get it from Sulabh International near Kalkaji temple for which they have pay @ Rs. 2 for 20 litre or so.

The Water crisis is same in West Bengal. In all the districts, the water commons have ceased to exist, and have become open-access resources, with hardly anyone responsible to take care of the resources. In North Bengal, some women reported they had opinions regarding the use of the water body, but their importance in management decisions is cipher. The absence of the community from the management of the water resources is indeed a tragedy, because now the resources are at the mercy of either the market or government officials.

Punjab; the name stands for abundance of water, but the present situation of water resources in the state is highly critical. The ground water availability is drastically hampered. The village ponds are drying day by day. Women in the villages desperately need water. Near Talwandi Sabo, for some villages, the source for drinking water is about 8 km away. Near Jajjal due to contaminated water, women are suffering from a number of diseases including cancer. There have been several deaths attributed to polluted water.

For Maharashtra, water is an abiding concern. In many villages women have to walk more than 3 kilometres everyday to fetch two huge vessels of water illegally from a government reservoir. They have to make at least three trips everyday. The state government do not send tankers to the villagers. At some places, women spend Rs 5 for two canes of water. Images of women carrying the pots of water, walking miles and miles for one single pot are common in the state of Maharashtra. Women in Maharashtra have carried the water burden both as a result of scarcity and abundance. Drought displacement due to dams and irrigation have contributed to increasing water burden of women. Women in Nandurbar district of North Maharashtra share their woes "forget about getting safe drinking water from wells, we spend most of our time locating streams and springs that quench our thrust". Many Women came as brides, their hair have gone dry, but the search for water has not ended. Karnataka is facing the worst kind of water crisis. In Bangalore, only 35% of the city gets water on daily basis, the rest on alternative days. In addition to the scarcity, erratic water supply is another problem. In Samadhanagar area, water generally comes in the morning at 11 A.M or in the middle of the night. Both these timings make it very difficult for women to collect water as they leave early in the morning to go to work. In Doddanagar slums in the city, women and children who are also breadwinners of the family spend 3-4 hours filling water, losing their wages. In Hosapalya locality women get severe joint pain in their shoulders, hips and knees due to carrying water pits from water sources outside their colony. In Peenya industrial area, many street fights occur among the women over water. Social conflict and tension is high due to water crisis.

In brief, at an estimate about 150 Million-Woman Days and Rs 10 Billion are lost in fetching water.

5

Pakistan and India in Dam Building Race in Interpreting the Indus Waters Treaty

In Kashmir's Neelum Valley, part of which is controlled by India and part by Pakistan, a high-stakes engineering race is taking shape. The rival countries are building hydroelectric power plants on the Neelum River, an Indus River tributary that has long been a source of agricultural and geopolitical strife.

Now a half-century old treaty, the Indus Waters Treaty (IWT), that governs water relations in the shared river basin is under stress as never before. Depending on how the treaty is interpreted in an ongoing legal case, the first side to finish its dam-either India's Kishanganga project or Pakistan's Neelum-Jhelum project-could gain a plum prize: priority rights on the Neelum.

With water near the top of Pakistan's foreign policy priorities and with so many other flash points in the region pivoting on the water issue -Kashmir, terrorism, Afghanistan- there is every indication that the countries are entering a tumultuous period in the treaty's history.

Signed in 1960 to allocate the basin's water, the IWT is widely cited as a model of exemplary cooperation in an often fractious bilateral relationship. But because of India's development plans, there is reason to believe that old amity is being supplanted by mistrust and suspicion. Discord over water pits India's drive for electrical power against Pakistan's vast irrigation needs and vulnerable geopolitical position on the river system.

The legal skirmishing is just beginning. Pakistan filed a 'dispute' in May 2010 against the Kishanganga project-the third and highest category of contention in the treaty's language. A seven-member international arbitration panel is being assembled to hear the case, the first to be taken to such a level. The ruling isn't expected for several years. Depending on how the panel decides, the existence of the Kishanganga project could become the latest escalation for political tensions in the subcontinent.

The case marks the second time in the last five years that upper-level conflict resolution procedures have been invoked. The 450-megawatt Baglihar hydropower plant was the first case to be resolved by a neutral expert, who ruled in favor of India in the key issue of spillway design. The current dispute is the first to be heard by an arbitration panel-India's hydroelectric ambitions seem to guarantee that it will not be the last.

Robert Wirsing, a professor at Georgetown University's School of Foreign Service in Qatar who studies South Asian water issues, says India is considering building 33 dams on parts of the Indus and its tributaries granted to Pakistan. India is allowed to use a small portion of the rivers for storage projects, but the distrust between the countries and the scale of development leave much to worry about, he said.

"Most [dams] are in the planning stage," Wirsing told Circle of Blue, "and some will never be built. But that's a lot of stuff up there. And that's the problem."

"There is a comforting notion," he added, "that this was a really good treaty, and in my judgment it is. It's a phenomenal piece of work. But it's unrealistic because the Indians haven't really gotten started [building dams]. And they have now started big time."

An Agreement Borne from Division

The new dams being built in a contested region on the Neelum incorporate technically complex, wide-bore tunnels that are several dozen kilometers long. Both are estimated to be six to eight years from completion. In the meantime, the wrangling for the river is being litigated under the conflict resolution mechanisms stipulated by the IWT.

The treaty's genesis dates to partition. When the British Raj left India in 1947 and Pakistan was sliced from its western provinces, division of the Indus basin waters was not well considered in the rush to leave. This was a major problem as it left Pakistan at India's mercy for irrigation deliveries during a time of deep animosity. For years after partition, troops from both countries were garrisoned at canal headworks along the border. The irrigation system they watched with eye and gun is the largest such agricultural scheme in the world, roughly 30 million hectares total-60 percent of which lies in Pakistan.

A compromise called the Standstill Agreement was enacted in the fall of 1947, keeping water allocations as they were before partition. When the agreement expired on March 31, 1948, India promptly withheld water deliveries to Pakistan on two main irrigation canals the very next day.

Several interim agreements were signed without a satisfactory conclusion. Further negotiations were stalling when David Lilienthal, a former chairman of the Tennessee Valley Authority, wrote an article in Collier's in 1951 suggesting the problem could be solved through technical and economic evaluations. Lilienthal recommended that the World Bank play a role as a neutral facilitator. Lilienthal's friend, Eugene Black, president of the World Bank at the time, read the article and decided to give it a try.

At the time, the World Bank was a relatively young institution, less than a decade old, and feared that perpetual conflict between two of its principal clients would endanger its lending programs in the region, Salman M. A. Salman, a Word Bank water law expert, told Circle of Blue.

Negotiators focused on key disagreements about allocations, technical specifications, and financing. The deal that emerged granted India primary use of the eastern rivers of the basin (Beas, Ravi, and Sutlej) and Pakistan the same rights to the western rivers (Chenab, Indus and Jhelum). Both sides were also permitted nonconsumptive rights to the other country's three rivers-Pakistan was allotted agricultural use on the Ravi, while India was given restricted storage capacity for hydropower development on all three Pakistan rivers, minding that large amounts of water are not retained or redirected. Storage restrictions were crucial for Pakistan to feel secure that India would not be able to manipulate river flows.

The allocations meant that water rights and land use patterns were thrown out of historical balance. To move its new water sources to the fields in Punjab and Sindh provinces, Pakistan would need to build two mega-dams, five barrages, and eight linking canals-at a total cost of US$1 billion 1960 dollars.

The money to reconstruct the canal system came from several sources. India paid $174 million and Pakistan offered a symbolic token, but the lion's share came from the United States and a group of five other Western countries in the form of grants and loans.

With one particularly long and pointed thorn removed, peace, it seemed, now had a chance.

At a news conference in Washington D.C. preceding the signing ceremony in Karachi in September 1960, President Dwight Eisenhower remarked that it was "one bright spot...in a very depressing world picture."

Hungry for Energy

The question now is whether or not the treaty will hold.

India, like a child without vitamins, lacks sufficient energy resources to grow at the pace the country desires. The peak electricity supply-125,000 megawatts-fell 12 percent short of demand in 2005 and 2006. Electrical capacity must grow 10 percent annually to keep up with demand, according to a study by the Asian Development Bank. These figures reflect just those with electrical access; nearly 40 percent of Indian homes, some 400 million people, do not have reliable electricity. As India grows, extending grid coverage will be a priority. But India has already fallen behind on its Power-for-All Plan, which would add 78,000 MW by 2012.

In India, hydropower generates 32,000 MW and comprises a quarter of the nation's energy capacity. The country has the potential for 84,000 MW, but only one-fifth of that has been developed. The most promising sites, however, are located in contested regions-in the northeast, where there is a border dispute with China over Arunachal Pradesh, and in Jammu and Kashmir, through which the Indus flows.

Kashmir presents conflicting pressures on both the domestic and international fronts, says Uttam Sinha, a research fellow at the Institute for Defense Studies and Analysis, a hawkish Indian think tank funded by India's Ministry of Defense.

Kashmiris demand that the Indian government build more dams to speed up local development, but those dams come at the expense of relations with Pakistan, Sinha told Circle of Blue.

Many in Jammu and Kashmir (JK) feel that their interests are superseded by Pakistan's under the IWT. The Chief Minister of Jammu and Kashmir says that the state was not fully compensated by the national government for economic losses created by the IWT. In October, the JK Legislature passed a bill to tax water used to generate power. The burden will fall mainly on the National Hydroelectric Power Corporation, India's national utility.

The Race is On

Pakistan's 969-MW Neelum-Jhelum project (NJP) is 160 kilometers downstream from the Kishanganga project and is located on a tributary of a river granted to Pakistan under the IWT. A 28-kilometer tunnel will divert water from the Neelum to the NJP dam's powerhouse. The engineering firm that won the US$1.5 billion contract, China Ghazoba Group of Companies, has slowed down construction because of inefficient tunnel-boring machines, according to Pakistani media reports. The project will be completed in 2018, two years behind schedule, at the current pace.

This has drawn much ire from Pakistani officials because

India may gain priority rights on the Neelum with the Kishanganga project, with current target date of 2016.

The relevant section of the IWT, paragraph 15, clause iii, which allows India to divert waters from tributaries of the Jhelum to another tributary only to the extent that it does not adversely effect an existing use in Pakistan.

If Pakistan's NJP is first to the line, it can establish a pre-existing use on the river and claim that India's planned diversion will cause it undue harm, said Neda Zawahri, a political science professor at Cleveland State University, in an interview with Circle of Blue.

Pakistan argues that the Kishanganga project will reduce flows by 15 percent to 20 percent and limit the NJP's power-generating potential, resulting in an annual loss of US$400 million.

A dispute has already been registered under the IWT. Stephen Schwebel, a former president of the International Court of Justice, was selected in October to lead the seven-member arbitration panel.

Historically, conflicts have been worked out by the Permanent Indus Commission, a bilateral body. For example, disagreements over the design of Salal Dam were settled this way in the 1970s.

The Baglihar Dam controversy in 2005 was taken to a second level of adjudication, which is mediation by a neutral expert. Pakistan objected that the dam did not meet the treaty's design specifications for spillways, intakes, and gates. In its rebuttal, India claimed that new designs were needed to deal with siltation problems.

The World Bank-appointed expert Raymond Lafitte, a Swiss engineer, ruled in favor of India on three of six objections. Robert Wirsing, the Georgetown professor, thinks Lafitte missed an opportunity to hit on a solution that would balance technical considerations with the spirit of the treaty.

"His concern was that this be a good dam," Wirsing told Circle of Blue. "Of course, that ran right up against the Pakistani feeling that what was important was the treaty and the treaty's purpose, which was conflict prevention."

John Briscoe, a former World Bank water adviser and now a professor at Harvard, argues that the ruling reinterpreted the treaty to mean that the physical limitations no longer applied in light of modern technical standards, removing Pakistan's main protection against India meddling with the river flows.

Resolution of the Kishanganga dispute will take several years. In the meantime, debate will continue about how well the Indus Waters Treaty can stand up to new circumstances.

Cleveland State professor Zawahri thinks both sides still benefit from the agreement: "As long as they continue to use the conflict resolution mechanisms available in the treaty, the treaty will survive. So I don't see this dispute as the end of the Indus Waters Treaty. On the contrary, both states have an interest in maintaining it."

Wirsing is less optimistic: "If this panel decides that India's Kishanganga project is okay and that Pakistan has to swallow this one too, that will, I think, drain the Pakistanis of any lingering enthusiasm for this treaty and its prospects for defending them against dams planned in India."

WATER CONSERVATION BY DAMS AND THEIR UTILIZATION

Dams as means of storing large quantities of water have been constructed for the past m ore than a century in different parts of the worked. During the 20th century, a very large number of dams were built in the USA, China, Russia, India, Europe and other parts of the world. Many of these were multi-purpose projects providing irrigation, hydropower, flood control and other benefits to the society. The vast network of irrigation canals in India provided a security against severe water shortages and famines of the past.

Coupled with the adaptation of modem farming practices with high yielding varieties of seeds, fertilizers etc., a sort of Green Revolution took place in the irrigated areas of the country and sustained food production with the population growth. Hydropower provided a significant part of power requirements in Europe, USA and India. Drinking water requirements for several large cities and parts of rural areas were also met by these newly created storages. Large dam projects like the Bhakra, Nagarjunasagar, Tungabhadra, Hirakud, Beas. Ramganga, Sharavathi and hundreds of other medium irrigation projects provided the immediate requirements of water and power in the early decades of the country's independence. The Bhakra and the Nagarjunasagar have performed specially well and supported the increase in agricultural production over a vast area. In south India, the dams built on the Cauvery River in the early part of this century have sustained agricultural production (specially rice) for more than half a century and these structures (Krishnarajasagar and Mettur Dams) are revered by the farmers and the people of this area. In south India, hydropower from storage dams has been the main stay of the power requirements of the states of Karnataka and Kerala for the last several decades.

Cost Aspects

The large dam projects constructed prior to 1975 in India and many of the developing countries were cost-effective to some extent. After the world oil crisis in the mid 70s, with the increase in fuel costs for operating construction machinery and in the manufacturing costs of cement and steel (which are energy intensive), the costs of construction of large dam projects with their canal systems etc. also increased significantly. The costs of land acquisition for these projects (both submerged and canal lands) also rose sharply. The costs per hectare of irrigation, which was about Rs. 8,000 prior to 1975. Rose to about Rs. 80.000 in the 1990s. The result of these as well as other factors like delays in construction, brought down the cost-effectiveness of new projects to near unacceptable levels. Indirect social benefits and support to food production (though at higher costs) necessitated the continuation of execution of these projects towards their completion.

Due to faulty planning, some of the mega-projects which could give benefits on stage-wise completion were not executed with such a thinking in mind. Huge public investments were tied up without the people getting any benefit for unduly long periods. The environmental and displacement aspects had to be addressed in a proper and satisfactory manner for which the machinery available with the executing agencies was inadequate. The stage-wise benefits which could be given to the people were not given effect to despite precedents of getting such benefits elsewhere.

Policies Needed for the Future

All mega-dam projects should be thoroughly examined for cost benefits by independent authorities and feasibility of satisfactory rehabilitation of those affected and feasibility of mitigation of environmental impacts. If after all the studies the project appears to be feasible, it should be split up into several stages so that the benefits to the community start accruing with a minimum of investment. If during the stage-wise execution of the project, any of the environmental or rehabilitation aspects cannot be resolved satisfactorily to all concerned, the project needs to be reviewed before proceeding further. It is also necessary that those getting affected by the project should be made stakeholders not only in the execution of the project but also in their I management all through the operational life of the project Part of the benefits from the project should accrue to the affected people on a continuous basis throughout the life of the project.

Community Participation

As stated above, it is imperative that the community getting displaced from any dam project should form a partner in the dam venture, not only during construction but also throughout the life of the dam and its operation. They should have a share of the benefits from the project in terms of land or other permanent assets in the project area as well as annual financial returns from the project (revenue from power, water etc.). The execution and management of these projects should not be done by government departments but by a corporation with representatives of various disciplines like jam builders, environment specialists, representatives of the displaced and the beneficiaries. Such a setup should be made before starting the project and agreement reached with the displaced by assuring them financial incentives as stated above. This will be somewhat similar to any marketable venture in me private sector. The government can plan, regulate the taking up of such dam ventures and monitor their operation subsequently. Such dam ventures for hydroelectric projects seem attractive since they have good returns over their long life.

Where large scale transfer of water over long distances to water-scarece areas are involved, such ventures may not profitable, and public investment may become necessary in the national interest. The Peninsular Rivers Linking Scheme in India contemplates long-distance large-scale water transfers from surplus areas to water-scarce areas, and falls in this category.

Other Solutions

Major dams are not required in many cases for meeting the water requirements of communities. Small or medium dams/ barrages can meet the drinking water needs of towns and urban areas. These should be encouraged 'wherever "needed and feasible. However, the catchment areas of these medium dam projects should be declared protected areas and should be so maintained by catchment area treatment, watershed management and treatment of industrial effluents. The management should be in the hands of a multi-disciplinary empowered Authority consisting of representatives of the municipal, forest and water supply agencies, along with reputed NGOs/experts. Adequate funds should be made available to the authority to fulfil its obligations effectively.

Recent Trends

For augmenting the increasing water requirements of cities and rural areas, Rain Water Harvesting using rooftops of large buildings and open premises appear feasible for many cities. A start is being made in a number of cities in India and it appears that a significant requirement of the cities' needs can be met during the rainy season at very economical costs. In Chennai, the scheme is already in operation with some success. Other cities like Bangalore, Hyderabad, New Delhi etc. are also planning to take up this scheme in a similar way. Large consumers of water can meet a good percentage of their requirements through this clean means. In areas, where recharging of ground water is needed, the harvesting or rainwater for this purpose appears a dire necessity. In parts of western India, water harvesting has been tried for rural areas along with watershed management and has had appreciable success unlike mega-dam projects which take a long time to give benefits; rainwater harvesting fulfills immediate augmentation of water. This is specially needed for urban and industrial users. It is also cost-effective.

Tank Irrigation

Tanks are small reservoirs built across the slopes of valleys to collect natural flows during the rainy season. In southern India, thousands of tanks dot the landscape. These tanks have been the sources of water for centuries, but most of them have lost their storage capacities due to silting and other causes. Even so, these tanks irrigate well over two million hectares in the states of Tamil Nadu and Kamataka. The renovation of these tanks to their original or higher capacity can provide much needed water for the village communities and also recharge the wells in their areas. Large-scale community participation can be generated in their renovation and maintenance by suitable funding and rewards. In this region, these tanks can supplement the existing dams for meeting the water requirements to a considerable extent. Schemes for renovation of these thousands of tanks need to be taken up in a phased manner. An institutional setup like a Tank Development Board backed with adequate finance can initiate this program with the active participation of the village— communities. Piece-meal attempts made by the existing government departments at renovation of a few tanks here and there in recent years have not had any large-scale impact. A well-drawn out program to renovate and maintain such large number of tanks in a period of a few years is needed.

Fish Production

Although large dams impede migration of certain varieties of fish, the lakes formed by the dams increase fish production enormously and provide livelihood to thousands of fishermen. In general, high production of fish has been observed in reservoirs where commercial fishing has been encouraged. The water quality in reservoirs is adequate for survival and growth of fish. The vast areas and volumes of water in the reservoirs provide additional habitats for aquatic life. In Indonesia, fishery development in two reservoirs provided livelihood to 7,500 families and produced 10,000 tonnes of fish during the year 1992. Revenues exceeded those of rice harvest from farmlands submerged. Further, it is said that 21,000 additional jobs were created for fish production, marketing etc. by extending the scheme to several reservoirs in the country.

In the Gobind Sagar Lake of Bhakra Dam in India, 1,500 families get their livelihood from fisheries in the reservoir. Many other dam reservoirs in India provide jobs for thousands of fishermen. Properly designed fish passages can help migration of fishes affected by construction of dams. This will be discussed later while describing requirements for new dams.

Future Requirements

Irrigation currently accounts for 70 of all water withdrawals in the world and is likely to be still the major consumer over the next 2-3 decades. Irrigation grew very fast between 1950 and 1975 (from 95 to 220 million hectare), but subsequently the growth has been much slower due to a variety of reasons including the utilisation all easily available sources and the higher costs of new irrigation projects. Future trends indicate that the increase in irrigated area will come through better management of water to some extent and by new projects.

Urban Water Requirements

Urbanisation is taking place rapidly in the developing countries of the world. In 1998, 39 of the world's population was urban and it is expected that the figure will reach 57% by 2020 and 70 % by the year 2050. In southern and western India, urbanisation is occurring rapidly and the demand for water for domestic and industrial use is increasing sharply. The requirements of more dams of medium and small storage will be mainly for meeting the municipal and industrial uses. It is estimated that well over 500 medium dams or barrages on small streams and rivers will be required to meet the water supplies for urban centres in the country. Fortunately, these dams barrages do not submerge areas more than those occurring during floods as they need small storages to meet the dry season water supply requirements.

Industrial requirements may be met to some extent by recycled water. There is already a water-saving trend in various water-intensive industries all over the world. Cooling water for thermal power plants is a substantial requirement and is being met through recycled water in many cases.

Rural Water Supplies for Drinking and Sanitation

International agencies have proposed 55 litres per person per day as the basic human requirement for drinking, sanitation, bathing etc. In the year 1990, based on this figure, over a billion people were below this line, mainly in development countries. Rural water supply requirements in developing countries are mostly met by ground water pumping through borewells etc. Ground water is also being used extensively for irrigation and may reach shortage levels in many parts of the world in the next couple of decades.

In developing countries, rural sanitation programmes are being taken up on a large scale and the requirements of water for this sector will also be considerable. The rural requirements for drinking and sanitation may in due course encroach into the irrigation supplies, thus resulting in requirements of additional storage. Recharging of ground water on a large scale has to be taken up in the same way as other development projects.

Small Hydroelectric Schemes

There is need to take up these schemes in large numbers as in China. Rural communities can meet their power requirements for water pumping from these schemes, as captive power plants for their own use. These schemes can be taken up wherever irrigation canals or small streams flow nearby the villages. Similarly, greater use of solar energy for meeting the water pumping requirements of rural areas is called for.

Changes Needed in Dam Projects and Water Management

Since quite a number of new dam projects are likely to be taken up in developing countries, certain changes need to be incorporated in the light of experience gained with existing dams. There is need for changes in dam designs:

1. Dam projects involving large-scale submergence of forests with bio-diversity (which cannot be replaced) may not be taken up. There are instances of abandonment of execution of such projects after the project plans were prepared (Bodhghat in Madhya Pradesh and Silent Valley in Kerala-both in India).
2. In some of the ongoing dam projects, there is need to review and plan them into stages which can be completed early to give benefits to the people. These are lingering on and are having difficulty in carrying out rehabilitation measures. Some of them do not have the financial resources to complete them in a reasonable time so that they are economical and cost-effective and such projects may have to be truncated ones or modified into run-off-the-river schemes etc.
3. Fish passages should be properly designed based on recent experiences and research in this field.
4. Devices for passage of silt should be incorporated in the designs. A number of recent dams built in the Himalayan regions in India have incorporated silt trapping and flushing tunnels in addition to under-sluices for silt removal.
5. Desilting of existing dams at a rate at which river conditions are not adversely affected should be taken up. Such measures have been tried successfully for many dams in China.

6. Pumped storage schemes should be considered near the existing dams for augmenting peak power requirements.

Integrated Land and Water Resources Management

This is needed with respect to land and water for sustainable development. The catchment areas of all dams (small or big) should be protected from environmental degradation by carrying out measures to prevent soil erosion and sustained growth of vegetation. District level authorities consisting of representatives of local administration, forests, water supply, pollution control boards and NGOs should be set up to monitor and implement the various measures so that the water supply sources are well protected. In India, there are institutions called Water and Land Management Institutes (WALMIS) in each state, and these should also be associated with the catchment area maintenance. Pollution of surface and ground water resources by industrial effluents etc. should be prevented by enforcing the control measures.

INDIA RE-THINKING INDUS WATER TREATY

"Many of the wars of the 20th century were about oil, but wars of the 21st century will be over water", said Dr Isamil Serageldin, former Vice President of the World Bank. Water is surpassing oil as the world's scarcest critical resource as water has no substitute. There's an increasing feeling in the world that everyone has a basic right to a minimum 13 gallons of water a day for basic human health. Today, the world stands divided between water haves and have-nots and Pakistan is facing critical water issues. Water management and distribution has always been an important but cumbersome process in Pakistan being a semi-arid country and its economy based mainly on agriculture and related industry.

The positive thing is that Pakistan has the largest contiguous supply-based canal irrigation system in the world. In Pakistan, the muddy plains of the Indus basin cover approximately 25 percent of the land area of Pakistan. Whereas in India, the basin includes only 9.8 percent of the total geographical area of the country. On negative side, the aqua environment of Pakistan has been shrinking since last two decades as the World Bank had put the country in the category of "water-stressed" in 2000. The availability of water in Pakistan has been declining over the past few decades from 5000 cubic meters per capita 60 years ago to 1200 cubic meters per capita in 2010.

Unfortunately, Pakistan's water problem is not new, as soon after independence, the country faced water problems due to blockage of its water in canals by India. Political boundary between Pakistan and India was drawn right across the Indus Basin making the country the lower riparian to India. The headwaters went to Indian side leaving Pakistan vulnerable as India got the physical capacity to cut-off vital irrigation water. Adding insult to injury, India started demanding proprietary rights on the water of Punjab Rivers, denying Pakistan its due share as a lower riparian.

INDUS WATER TREATY (IWT) 1960

Negotiations commenced between Pakistan and India in 1951 under the World Bank and resultantly the famous Indus Waters Treaty (IWT) was signed on September 19, 1960. It was the partition of waters like land in 1947. Pakistan got the rights of the waters of the three western rivers, i.e., Indus, Jhelum, and Chenab, while the three eastern rivers, i.e., Beas, Sutluj, and Ravi went in total jurisdiction of India. India was not allowed to build storages on the western rivers except to a very limited extent and also restrictions were imposed on the extension of irrigation development in India. The permanent Indus Commission was appointed for both states. International financial assistance was given to Pakistan for the development of irrigation works utilizing the waters of western rivers.

Strain & Stress on IWT and Violations by India: There is no denying the fact that the IWT survived in the midst of wars and border clashes between the two states but the Indian projects on Pakistani rivers created stress and strain as India could either reduce water flows to Pakistan or cause floods by releasing the stored-waters. There are numerous water disputes between the two, e.g., Wular Barrage, Kishanganga Project, Baglihar Dam, etc. Salal Dam was started by India without informing Pakistan, in violation of the IWT. Though an agreement was reached between the two countries, yet there is no guarantee that India would not do the same in future. Now India has got the leverage to hold water for 25-26 days which can cause acute shortage of water for winter crops in Pakistan. This, besides causing electricity shortage, can greatly affect wheat crop in the Punjab. According to Dr John Briscoe, Professor of the Environmental Engineering and Environmental Health at Harvard University and former Senior Water Advisor to the World Bank on the Baglihar case, "in case of Baghliar, Pakistan's vulnerability was driven home when India chose to fill Baglihar exactly at the time when it would impose maximum harm on farmers in downstream Pakistan. Following Baglihar is a veritable caravan of Indian projects, i.e., Kishanganga, Sawalkot, Pakuldul, Bursar, Dal Huste, Gyspa…The cumulative live storage will be large, giving India an unquestioned capacity to have major impact on the timing of flows."

Implications for Pakistan: Water flows in river Chenab declined to about 6000 cusecs from a 10 year average of 10000 cusecs, mainly because of construction of over a dozen Hydro-electric Projects (HEPs) upstream by India. To fill Baglihar Dam, India had consistently obstructed River Chenab's flow. Resultantly, Pakistan received lesser water when it should have been receiving a minimum of 55,000 cusecs per day. In order to achieve the required growth targets in agriculture, Pakistan needs an estimated 277 MAF in 2025. Otherwise, the shortage of surface water will result in drought and more dependency on ground water for irrigation; hence water table will go down causing water constraints to the population. Indian water regulation capability has increased as with the completion of Salal Dam, India has enhanced its water regulation capability over river Chenab by 6-7 times. After completion of Baglihar Dam, India will be able to stop the flow of water in the river for 30-40 days as compared to previous capability of only 8-10 days. Kishanganga HEP will also enhance Indian storage capability over river Jhelum with a stoppage capability of 14 days. Also, Wullar Barrage will further enhance Indian storage capability in river Jhelum for additional 30 days. So, depending upon the degree of water regulation capability, India can create three types of effects:

- Drying up of rivers-related canal
- Flooding of rivers
- Fluctuate discharge of rivers

Possible Impacts on Global Security: Since water security has become a principal concern for sustainable development, so availability of freshwater is one of the greatest challenges that the world is going to face in the near future. As water shortages are growing, the result could be a series of disasters and confrontations leading to regional crises. Nowhere else on earth are the prospect of water wars more serious than in South Asia, where two of the world's greatest river systems crisscross the international boundaries of the world's largest and most densely-populated countries being:

- Indus River System (IRS)
- Ganges-Brahmaputra-Meghna (GBM)

Water issues are likely to continue as a major source of conflict between India and Pakistan in coming decades as forecasted by many analysts. As populations rise, levels of economic development increase and the adverse effects of climate change become more extreme, the South Asian region will struggle to meet its growing demand while managing dwindling water supplies and the trans-boundary rivers, especially those in the IRS and GBM basins. These disputes could prove to be dangerous for world security since war over water between two nuclear armed states, i.e., Pakistan and India, would be dangerous. The possibility of such a war can not be ruled out since water poses a survival issue there is no substitute of this commodity.

INDIA RE-THINKING IWT

Indians consider IWT generous to Pakistan and Pakistan thinks it discriminatory right from its inception. At official levels, there is no such demand by the Govt. of India/Indus Water

Commission India and so is the case with Pakistan as there is no such demand from the Govt. of Pakistan/Indus Water Commission Pakistan. But at non-governmental level, intellectuals/academia in India have started asking for re-visiting/ re-thinking the IWT and probably they are making a case for the future. Brahma Chellaney, a Professor of Strategic Studies at the New Delhi-based Centre for Policy Research, said that "Pakistan's reopening of the water-sharing agreement could backfire, as it might prompt India to rethink a treaty that was extremely generous to Pakistan. There was no treaty in the world which had been so generous on the part of the upper riparian to the lower riparian state. India was starving its own northern regions and reserving four-fifths of the water for Pakistan. If Pakistan played this dangerous game, they would make India review its generosity."

IDSA Report: Institute for Defence Studies and Analyses (IDSA) had published its book/task force report in 2010 titled *"Water Security for India—The External Dynamics"* in which they have given reasons and plans for re-visiting the IWT. According to the report, "...with Pakistan, given some stringent provisions in the IWT that thwart India's plans of developing projects on the western rivers, a 'modification' of the provisions of the treaty should be called for. Whether it is done through re-negotiations or through establishing an Indus-II Treaty, modifications of the provisions are crucial in case of the western rivers.

Under the draft provisions of the International Law Commission 'Responsibility of States for Internationally Wrongful Acts, 2001', India can consider the abrogation of the treaty...Pakistan aids and abets terrorist actions from its soil. India should quantify the damage it has sustained over the decades because of Pakistani support to terrorism and seek as a first step suitable compensation. If Pakistan does not comply, India can possibly threaten to walk out of various bilateral agreements including the IWT." Pakistan is using water propaganda to get international attention on Kashmir so India should "talk" to Pakistan but not "negotiate". The talks should be about "water needs" and not "water rights".

Five Constituencies/Point of Views in India on Re-thinking the IWT: According to the same IDSA report, there are five constituencies that ask for revision or a re-think. "The first constituency seeks to evolve an Indus-II under the provisions of Article VII and Article XII of the IWT for an integrated or joint development of the Indus water basin. Indus-II should be fed into the current peace process as a means both for defusing current political strains over Indus-I and managing adverse impact of climate change."

"The second constituency while understanding the merits of a new hydrologic relationship on the Indus does not see any viability of Indus-II and contends that a totally new treaty has to be negotiated. The IWT was a partitioning treaty, like the partitioning of the land. How can cooperation be built on that basis?"

"The third constituency is the domestic pressure group in [Indian occupied] Jammu & Kashmir which feels that the IWT has restricted the state's overall development by not allowing it the usage of "its" rivers, i.e., Jhelum, Chenab and Indus. It has been calling for a complete review of the treaty. The [Indian occupied] Jammu & Kashmir government has been contending that in spite of having an untapped hydro-electric potential of 15,000 MW, the state continues to suffer from acute power shortage and related agro-economic underdevelopment."

"The fourth constituency springs into action when the political climate between India and Pakistan becomes acrimonious. While war over water is not an option, this group suggests strong-arm tactics in dealing with Pakistan and using water as a coercive tool and a bargaining instrument in the larger politico-strategic objectives of India."

"There is a fifth constituency that argues that any attempt to review the treaty, can be done only after India exploits the potential already permissible under the treaty. Only a crying child, it is argued, gets the mother's milk. This constituency argues that first India should fully exploit the existing potential and then cry for more. Any attempt otherwise to review the treaty may not be seen as logical. The IWT is a product of its time and could be fruitfully modified and renegotiated to bring it more in line with contemporary international watercourse law, the Helsinki rules, and emerging concerns with water quality, environmental sustainability, climate change, and principles of equitable sharing."

Pakistan's serious projected shortages, India's trend of damming and diverting waters and global warming's expected depletion of water in the IRS are a source of increasing tensions between Pakistan and India. Based on supply and demand projections, India faces its own water scarcity, which would provide India an excuse to store or divert river water that would otherwise reach Pakistan. Water shortages would pressure the Pakistani government to increase its share of water drawn from the Indus system under the treaty as Pakistan is heavily reliant on the Indus and has few alternative water supply sources unlike India. In this environment, renegotiation of the IWT may become an important diplomatic issue between India and Pakistan. With India, water issue will be far more political and strategic than just water. India has also started propagating that Tibet's water is for humanity, not for China alone. But they (Indians) forget that the Indus-Ganges basins are also for humanity, not for India alone.

THE WAY FORWARD

As for as the existing treaty is concerned and keeping pros and cons in mind, there is no need to revisit/review/rethink the IWT. Due to India's continuous hegemonic attitude, Pakistan would not be in a better position to have any revision in its favour. Instead, Pakistan should continue lobbying that India has been violating the IWT and India should be compelled to abide by the IWT in its true letter and spirit. Also, Pakistan should engage with India within the context of the IWT in a comprehensive way. International lobbying should be intensified on the point, i.e., water being the "lifeline" issue for Pakistan and this could trigger war.

Pakistan should be calling for a sophisticated forecasting system, accurately estimating how much water flows into the

IRS, as almost 90% of the water in the Upper Indus River Basin comes from remote glaciers of Himalaya and Karakorum mountain ranges, which border Pakistan, China and India. This region is so remote that the authorities in Pakistan do not know the exact weather conditions there. This system will also help in alleviating droughts in the country. The water forecasting system could ultimately help Pakistan in optimizing water allocation at national level by working out how much water is used for irrigation, industry, and domestic purposes.

Internally, water management in Pakistan has been poor. So, keeping in view the dwindling water resources, water must be made part of new "security agenda."

PAKISTAN AND WATER: NEW PRESSURES ON GLOBAL SECURITY AND HUMAN HEALTH

PRESSURES ON THE WATER OF the Indus River, the major water source for the more than 180 million persons living in Pakistan, are increasing, with serious implications for the health of the population. Rural Pakistanis (more than half the population) use irrigation water from the river for domestic purposes, even though it is unfit for drinking and a major cause of stunting and diarrhea. Diarrhea causes 21.6% of infant mortality in rural Pakistan. In Karachi, a megacity of approximately 18 million people, it is estimated that more than 30 000 people, 20 000 of whom are children, die every year because of unsafe water. Control of river flow is still a major challenge for the country, which was tragically demonstrated during recent flooding that affected 20 million people and was described by the secretary general of the United Nations as the worst disaster he had ever seen.

Beyond the direct effect on human health, disputes over the flow of the Indus may erupt into a military conflict between India and Pakistan, endangering the lives and security of millions. The future of water flow in the Indus is also threatened by regional environmental changes. Public health professionals must be fully engaged in the development of this crucial resource for the country and the health of its population.

PAKISTAN AND THE INDUS RIVER

Pakistan was created in 1947 with the partitioning of British India, becoming the first Islamic republic. With one of the fastest growing populations in the world, Pakistan had a population of 180.8 million in 2009 and is projected to reach 208 million by 2020. Approximately 20% of the population lives below the international poverty line of US $1.25 a day. Health and social indicators have lagged behind those of other South Asian countries whose economic conditions are poorer than Pakistan's.

The strategic importance of Pakistan has gone through important shifts, first with the Pakistan–India conflict that began after the 1947 partition, then with the Cold War's denouement, and now with the war on terror. The geopolitical importance of Pakistan, which shares borders with Iran, India, China, and Afghanistan, also intensified when it became a nuclear power in 1998.

The majority of the people in Pakistan live near the Indus River, the longest river in the country, and the 21st largest river in the world in annual flow. The snows and glaciers of Tibet, India, and Pakistan feed the river. Beginning in the Himalayas, the Indus courses the entire length of Pakistan—a total of 1976 miles—and empties into the Arabian Sea near Pakistan's major port, Karachi. As much as 65% of agricultural land in Pakistan is irrigated by water from the Indus, which accounts for approximately 90% of the country's food and fiber production.

THE INDUS WATERS TREATY

During the early years after partition, disagreements over the flow of the Indus River led to the danger of military conflict; by 1951, the two sides were no longer meeting, and the situation seemed intractable. India's control of the headwaters of the Indus gave it the power to turn fertile Pakistan into a desert. With the conflict over Kashmir and the trauma of partition still in vivid memory, the threat of a "water" war became imminent.

David Lilienthal, a former chairman of the Tennessee Valley Authority and the US Atomic Energy Commission, visited the region in 1951 to write a series of articles for *Collier's*magazine. Working behind the scenes with the US Department of State and the World Bank, he engaged the governments of Indian and Pakistan in negotiations that lasted nine years. Those negotiations led to the Indus Waters Treaty, signed in 1960. This agreement has been faithfully implemented and upheld by both India and Pakistan and has been the longest-running accord ever between the two countries. The treaty gives India exclusive use of all of the waters of the Eastern Rivers and their tributaries before the points where the rivers enter Pakistan. Similarly, Pakistan has exclusive use of the Western Rivers. Pakistan also received a one-time financial compensation for the loss of water from the Eastern Rivers.

Continuing tensions between India and Pakistan, however, have begun to erode confidence in the treaty. India has greater bargaining power over Pakistan because the upper stream is in its territory, and Pakistan's water rights under the treaty are hard to enforce. Critics of the treaty suggest that benefits have gone to major players and not to those most in need. For Kashmir, where only 40% of cultivated land is irrigated, the result has been limited economic development. One quarter of the people of Kashmir lack electricity, and 55% lack safe drinking water. Kashmir also remains at the heart of the political tensions between India and Pakistan.

India's plan to build a dam on a tributary of the Indus within its borders has created new tensions. The construction of the dam would give India even more control over the flow of the river. The collapse of a dam could cause a disaster in the Northern Areas of Pakistan, and India's history with dam failure is considerable. Ongoing political confrontation between India and Pakistan makes the future of the Indus Waters Treaty uncertain. Even worse, war—globally the worst threat to public health—appears increasingly likely to break out over Indian–Pakistani water issues. Rapidly changing issues related to water quality and access to water for basic human needs have given a new direction to global security discussions. UN Deputy Secretary General Asha-Rose Migiro said,

Projections are that by the year 2050, water accessibility for human consumption will have dropped by 40 percent. Probably the next major conflict will be about water.

NEW PRESSURES ON THE RIVER

Intensification of water use in Pakistan threatens the quality of water in the Indus. Rapid population growth over the past half century has intensified the pressure on agriculture and the need for irrigation water. The management of the flow has historically been inefficient because of poor water storage capacity, seepage, and inadequate maintenance of reservoirs. Heavy irrigation and seepage have overwhelmed the drainage of irrigated land, leading to accumulation of salts on the surface of the soil and rendering large tracts of land unfit for agricultural production. These inefficiencies have prevented Pakistan from attaining food self-sufficiency.

Environmental degradation of the Indus River and other wetlands in Pakistan has created additional health risks for the population. Water pollution in the Indus comes from a number of sources, including return flow from agriculture, which adds sodium nitrates, phosphates, and pesticides to the river. Additionally, untreated or incompletely treated sewage from cities along the Indus is discharged into the river. The river also receives a wide range of industrial waste: organic matter and ions such as sodium, potassium, calcium, magnesium, carbonates, bicarbonates, and chloride as well as inorganic wastes such as fluoride, silica, and cyanide. Finally, thermal power plants along the Indus cause sudden increases in surface water temperature that harm marine life.

Little research has been carried out to date on the effect of river pollution on human health in Pakistan, but the problem should not be underestimated. Much of the population along the Indus depends on the river for drinking water, and boiling does not remove polluting chemicals. Water pollution in the Indus River has reduced the species diversity of fish and decreased the supply of subsistence food for many who live near the river. In parts of the lower Indus delta, mangroves that were once abundant with marine life and an important source of food for coastal populations have almost disappear because of the toxic effect of polluted water that flow into this ecosystem.

Cities near the river are major water users. Karachi needs enormous quantities of water for both human and industrial use. The Indus River to the east and the Hub River to the west are the main water sources for Karachi. Water management in the city is a serious problem; one quarter of the population has no piped water, and as much as a quarter of the city water is wasted in faulty pipes.

Sewage management has been chaotic in Karachi for many years. The sewage system established by the British during colonial days has been overwhelmed and is in a poor state of repair. Open sewers, raw sewage overflowing into streets, and contamination of water lines with sewage are all common in Karachi. The city has annual outbreaks of cholera. Newspaper reports document thousands of hospitalizations attributable to sewage lines breaking and merging into water lines. Half of middle-class children in Karachi have intestinal parasites.

Also dependent on the Indus are Lahore (population six million) and Faisalabad (population five million). The groundwater table in Lahore is falling at a rate of 30 centimeters per year in the central part of the city because of heavy water use by the growing urban population.

Regional climate change also threatens the future of the Indus water flow and the millions of people who depend on it. The recent fast pace of glacier melt and warmer temperatures may lead to a serious diminution of river flow. One of the suspected reasons for the rapid melting of these glaciers is settling of aerosolized soot and particles on the icy surface. This "Asian brown cloud," caused by the burning of fossil fuels and biomass by the more than one billion people who live on the subcontinent, can be seen from outer space. As the cloud settles on the white glacial ice, light and heat are absorbed rather than reflected, melting the ice. Even a small decrease in the flow in the rivers fed by these glaciers (the Indus and Ganges) would have huge consequences for agricultural production and human life.

NEW DIRECTIONS FOR HEALTH DIPLOMACY

Health has emerged as a global security issue, and the water needs of human populations have become part of that issue. After the partitioning of British India, Pakistan and India began sharing the Indus River, but the contentious relations between the countries have already sparked two wars and water issues could cause further conflict. New pressures on water in Pakistan include intensification of use to meet the rapidly growing needs of agriculture and industry, environmental degradation of the river, and increasing use by cities.

These new problems will have serious public health consequences for people living in the region and must be added to the agenda of health diplomacy. Improved management of the Indus River could improve the health of the people of Pakistan. Public health has an important role in achieving this goal and in global diplomacy to safeguard water supplies and human health.

6

Indus Water: Treaty, Conflicts and Disputes

In a world burdened by burgeoning populations and faced by declining water resources, water is likely to trigger conflict. For India and Pakistan, too, fed as they are by the common Indus river watershed, water is a serious issue.

The Indus river, having its source in Indian Kashmir and flowing through Pakistan, is the primary freshwater source for the latter. Agriculture being the mainstay of the economy in both countries, their dependence on the Indus and its tributaries is implicit and any problems with the flow therein can have serious consequences for both. In recent years, the water levels in the river system have been affected adversely by increasing populations, industrialisation and consequent ecological changes. The problem, posing an existential threat, apparently is more serious for Pakistan.

The Indus Water Treaty addressing the sharing of waters of the Indus between India and Pakistan assumes a crucial role. Concluded after prolonged negotiations and facilitated under the aegis of the World Bank, it is the world's most generous water-sharing pact, both in terms of the sharing ratio as well as the total quantum of waters reserved for the lower riparian state. On September 19, the treaty signed in 1960 in Karachi enters its 55th year, surviving hostility, conflicts, and wars between two nuclear-armed rivals.

MOST GENEROUS

Some disputes notwithstanding, the treaty is considered one of the world's most successful trans-boundary water accords, as it addresses specific water allocation issues and provides unique design requirements for run-of-theriver dams, which ensure the steady flow of water and guarantee hydroelectricity.

The agreement also provides a mechanism for consultation and arbitration should questions, disagreements, or disputes arise.

The resolving of issues perceived by Pakistan regarding the construction of the Baglihar Dam and Kishanganga hydroelectric project within the framework of the deal bears ample testimony to its inherent strength.

However, for the past decade or so, Pakistan has been demanding a bigger share of water from rivers that flow from India, by objecting to the run-of-the-river hydroelectricity projects under construction on the western rivers, and by accusing India of diverting/storing water entitled to Pakistan.

PAK OBJECTIONS

During the recent inconclusive talks between the Indus Commissions at Lahore, Pakistan has raised the disputed issues under the provisions of the treaty. It has objected to design technicalities such as "deep gated spillway, excessive pondage and height of freeboard" in the construction of the Ratle (850 megawatt), Pikkal Dul (1,000 MW), Miyar (120 MW), and Lower Kalnai (48 MW) hydroelectricity projects on the Chenab river. Pakistan has accordingly asked for changes in the design of these projects.

It has reservations, again, on our developing of Kishanganga Dam on the Neelum river, even though an international arbitrator has recognised India's right to go ahead with the project as long as the water level in the reservoir is not below minimum (dead storage level in technical terms) and the flow in the river is at least 9 cumsecs (318 cusecs).

India Adhered

In response, India has maintained that it has all along adhered to the treaty and has never deprived Pakistan of its legitimate share of water, and has no intention of doing so. However, to look at Pakistan's requirements, there will be another round of talks in New Delhi after about two months, after Pakistan has made two visits to Miyar and Kishanganga to witness first-hand the constraints and justifications put forward by India.

It is clear to Pakistan that instead of going into unending and costly international arbitrations, it should find a middle path.

Must Appreciate

Pakistan must appreciate that the provisions of the treaty, while allocating the western rivers to Pakistan, permit a limited use of those by India, as they pass through the Indian territory, for drinking water, existing agriculture use, limited expansion, a storage of no more than 3.6 MAF (million acre feet), and generation of hydroelectricity through run-of-the-river projects.

These permissive provisions,, are hemmed in with stringent conditions and restrictions to ensure that Pakistan stands protected from the possibilities of stoppage of flows or harmful flooding.

India has been trying to utilise the permissive provisions to the full, and Pakistan has been attempting to apply the restrictive provisions stringently.

Pakistan will be well advised to understand the Indian perspective and resolve issues, if any, bilaterally under the provisions of the treaty.

Fortunately, a mechanism exists under the accord to carry out consultations and research on behalf of both countries and to remove misconceptions and anxieties. Article 7 of the Indus Water Treaty mentions 'Future Cooperation', which, inter alia, discusses efforts in the future to optimise the potential of the Indus river system jointly. Very little attention has been paid to this aspect, so far.

Simple Solution

Therefore, a simple solution is to form a joint study group of experts who should function as a part of the mechanism available within the purview of the Indus Water Treaty on bilateral basis.

This group should carry out consultations and research on various current issues to optimise the availability/utilisation of water for various economic purposes and to further India-Pakistan relations. The study group may also consider building hydroelectricity projects with large dams on the western rivers with assured discharge to Pakistan to offset natural calamities because of floods.

The provisions of the treaty will continue to remain the cornerstone of the watersharing between India and Pakistan; and both countries will operate in a spirit of constructive cooperation. Thus, a regional approach is required in maintaining the prosperity and dominance of the mighty Indus.

TURNING WATER CHALLENGES INTO OPPORTUNITIES

Water is vital in South Asia, where most countries are still largely agrarian. As such, water is inherently political – its socio-ecological flows are implicated in competition by economies, individuals and nations, while its distributional regimes have the capacity to alter lives and livelihoods. Competing water-use for agriculture, industry, and domestic purposes have led water to become an increasingly scarce resource with limited and threatened supply. In 2012, a total of 1023.8 billion cubic meters of water was withdrawn in the eight SAARC nations (including agricultural, industrial, domestic use, as well as desalination plants), out of a total 1982.0 billion cubic metres of renewable internal freshwater sources available (including river flows, rainfall and groundwater). Climate change, volatile rainfall patterns, groundwater depletion and the inefficient usage have precipitated a resource shortage, verging on a crisis in the region. Water disputes amongst the SAARC member nations, then, primarily centre on India's access to rivers and its competition with Nepal, Pakistan and Bangladesh for water 'rights'. Despite the various disputes for river water, there have been efforts at regional cooperation.

The Indus Water Treaty (1960) granted India rights over the eastern rivers (Sutlej, Beas and Ravi) and Pakistan the rights over the western rivers (the Indus, Jhelum and Chenab). Despite the treaty, there have been several disputes: Pakistan objected to the construction of the Kishenganga Dam, terming it a clear violation by India of the Indus Water Treaty, while contesting four more dams proposed by India on the Chenab. A second round of talks in August 2014 yielded no compromise.

Since the Kosi River Agreement between Nepal and India to manage flooding in 1954, talks between the two have stalled. As a result of mismanaged flood control, poor communication, and lack of cooperative maintenance, a dam neglected for decades by both led to the catastrophic flood in 2008, destroying 300,000 homes, 800,000 acres of cropland and displacing over 3 million individuals. More recently Nepal and India have agreed to expedite the 17-year-stalled Pancheshwar project, to generate 6,720 MW of hydropower along with increased irrigation facilities. Nepal has also cleared a GMR Company proposal to build a 900 MW Upper Karnali hydroelectric power plant as part of a scheme aimed at exporting electricity to India.

Despite the 1972 Joint River Commission for Water Management, tensions between India and Bangladesh on sharing resources came to a head in a dispute over the Teesta River. The 1996 comprehensive river pact established a 30-year water-sharing arrangement between the two countries. This was set to change in September 2011 when India's Prime Minister, Manmohan Singh, was to sign a pact with his Bangladesh counterpart for access and use of the Teesta waters. However, the Chief Minister of West Bengal, Mamata Banerjee, refused to approve the treaty, fearing that loss of higher volume of water to the lower riparian would cause problems in her state, especially during drier months. The Tipaimukh hydroelectric project in India is another similar source of contention. While it is expected to control floods in Assam's

Barak valley and generate electricity for states in northeast India, farmers in Bangladesh fear it would reduce the water flow to their land, thus damaging rice crops that depend on seasonal flooding of these trans-boundary rivers during every monsoon. However, there has been a decision between the two countries to conduct a joint Environmental Impact Assessment of the project.

While SAARC initiatives have not addressed water management, storage and sharing, they have focused efforts on disaster management – both short-term (in terms of response) and long-term (primarily combating the effects of climate change). The SAARC Disaster Management Centre (SDMC) mandate serves all eight members of SAARC by providing policy advice and facilitating capacity building services. This includes strategic learning, research, training, system development and exchange of information for effective disaster risk reduction and management in South Asia.

The SDMC initiative stressed priorities for action on integrating disaster risk reduction, climate change adaption and a sustainable development agenda; increasing knowledge management (South Asia Disaster Knowledge Network (SADKN)) as an effective tool for networking, information sharing and knowledge transfer; and facilitating regional cooperation for trans-boundary disasters.

A multilateral forum like SAARC gives members the invaluable opportunity to develop bilateral cooperation on protection of water sources from pollution, degradation or denudation; dealing with drainage in the Indus Basin; addressing the issue of arsenic-poisoned aquifers in India and Bangladesh; and flood management, to name a few. Apart from sharing of river water, a major cause for dispute has been the construction of large hydro-electric projects which divert shared river water. The upcoming SAARC summit can encourage joint water management solutions and joint hydroelectric projects. Greater focus on watershed management and storage in Nepal would generate hydro and irrigation benefits there and flood control benefits in Bihar. Water storage in northeast India could provide hydropower, flood control and dry season water augmentation in Bangladesh; similar prospects exist between Afghanistan and Pakistan.

Cross-border management of water resources could help control flooding across countries sharing a basin while simultaneously enhancing the availability of water. Improved inland water transport linkages and trade facilitation could have multiple benefits, particularly to enhance regional trade. All SAARC member need to operationalize the declaration of the 17th Summit in 2013, which emphasized water sanitation, availability and access to drinking water.

COLONIAL CONFLICTS OVER RIVER WATERS

Under colonial influence, water was diverted from its role in the survival economy and nature's economy and was transformed into a source of revenue and taxes, or as an input to commodity production for the generation of profits. The introduction of market forces in the water economy of the country created new conflicts over water resources between the market and survival economies.

The Salt Economy and Water Conflicts

On 5 April 1930 Mahatma Gandhi launched the national noncooperation movement with the campaign for the production and distribution of salt at Dandi beach in Gujarat, violating the Salt Law of the British that had guaranteed their monopoly in the production and distribution of salt. Salt is a vital resource for the survival of both human and animal life specially in tropical countries like India. It remained a common resource till the British monopolised its production and distribution to transform it into a source of revenue. The growth imperative compelled the expansion of the salt industry, as monopolised by the British, at the cost of diversion of resources from essential economic activities like food production. Further, in order to increase revenue the British government raised the salt tax in 1923 through the Indian Finance Bill of the Viceroy. This triggered off strong protests all over the country since a basic resource like salt was being denied to the people in order to increase revenue. The anguish of Gandhi on this appropriation of a common resource was clear when he said,

They even tax our salt-a necessity of life, only less necessary than air and water. It ought to be free as they are.... Nature bestows it on us and we may not use it. There is salt beside the sea and they forbid us to gather it's

The production of salt in certain pockets like Rajasthan and in the coastal areas as well as its distribution in all parts of the country had been a part of the living history of the Indian civilisation. Salt is one of those commodities which cannot be produced everywhere notwithstanding the self-sufficiency of the village economies. The demand for salt from all parts of the country led to the establishment of salt industries wherever it was possible to extract salt from saline water. All along the coastline except in Bengal, salt was manufactured by digging hollows in the ground and allowing the saline water to evaporate.

The Sambhar Lake in Rajasthan was a major inland source of salt for the whole of Central India. The manufacture and trade of this essential commodity and the possibility of a high margin of profits in case of monopoly in production, led to the East India Company securing the entire lake. In 1870 the British government forced a treaty on the States of Jodhpur and Jaipur through which it acquired the right of not only manufacturing and selling salt but also levying a duty on it. The peculiarity of the Sambhar Lake is that there is no rock salt bed in the geological formation of the area. The salt granules in the great salt marsh of Kutch are carried north-east by the trade winds in the summer and deposited in the catchment of the Sambhar Lake. In the monsoons the salt granules are dissolved and the solution is carried into the lake by a large number of streams. the largest of which is Rupnagar. Through the quick evaporation of water from the lake. millions of tons of salt get deposited in the Sambhar Lake. According to the British estimates of that period. 46 million people in India depended on supplied from this lake. This made the control of this 90 sq miles lake economically valuable for the growth of the salt industry.

Though the British salt industry in India grew by more than 33 per cent in the first twenty years of its existence, it was not content with only monopoly in production and distribution. To enhance the profits and growth of the industry, the British had maximised the inflow of water into the Sambhar Lake by denying the more basic uses of water for irrigation and drinking. Rupnagar, the largest stream feeding the lake, was the main source of water for the State of Kishengarh whose most important economic activity was agriculture which depended solely on the water of Rupnagar for irrigation. Thus the British attempt to increase the inflow of water into the lake came into direct conflict with the survival needs of the people in Kishengarh.

In 1900, a famine year, Kishengarh wanted to store some water by constructing an embankment tank on Rupnagar. The salt authorities strongly opposed this use of water for drinking and irrigation by the people. The Finance and Commerce Department of the then Government of India promptly accorded higher priority to the interest of the salt industry as opposed to the water needs for the survival of the people of Kishengarh. In a note dated 13 July 1901 the Department issued the following statement:

In view of the way in which the manufacture of salt depends on a sufficient supply of water in the lake and the precariousness of the supply, the Govt. of India consider that it is most inadvisable that anything should be done in the shape of constructing new reservoirs, irrigation works, or of extending any existing works on any of the feeder streams of the lake, either in the British territory or in native states which will be likely to diminish supply....

The Government of India desires that in future the Salt Commissioner may be consulted before any of the existing works' in British territory or the native states are enlarged, strengthened or improved.

In 1906 the villages of Kishengarh faced a severe drought. In sheer desperation to ensure a minimum supply of water for the biological survival of human and animal life, the people built an earthen dam which the British promptly destroyed. In the same year the rulers of Kishengarh pleaded for permission to construct low masonry weirs across Rupnagar and to sink some wells. The Salt Commissioner made sure that these projects could not be undertaken. It is this undisclosed destruction of agricultural ecosystems in the catchment of the Sambhar Lake that made possible and visible the growth of the salt industry there. By 1922 the prosperous and populated Kishengarh was desolate. Large areas of cultivable land became waste and wells could no longer be used. Another desperate attempt by the kingdom of Kishengarh to construct four irrigation tanks was postponed for twenty-four years, thus ensuring the total destruction of the local agricultural economy.

This was the general pattern of destruction of the survival base of the people in all regions of the country where the salt monopoly led to economic growth for British interests. This monopoly forced the people to give up the production of a basic resource like salt, which was being produced by them with simple technologies that required no capital input. The control made people totally dependent on the British supply, to be bought at a price determined by British interests. It was this exploitation by the British through the denial of a basic need as well as the associated destruction of other related resources that led to non-violent violation of the Salt Law as an assertion of the people's right to vital natural resources for survival. As a mode of protest it spread throughout the country with people breaking the Salt Law in large numbers. Its impact, both immediate and long-term was immense. By 5 March 1931 the British government was compelled to retrace its steps and issued a notification that people could produce salt for their own use.

WATER CONFLICTS IN THE KRISHNA BASIN

The east flowing krishna river originates in the mahadev range of the western ghats, north of the hill station of Mahabaleshwar in Maharashtra, and after flowing over a distance of about 1,40(1 km it meets the Bay of Bengal, south of Vijayawada. In between its origin at 1,337 metres above the MSL and its delta, the river fows across the entire width of the Indian peninsula through the states of Maharashtra, Karnataka and Andhra Pradesh.

The Krishna river is joined in its course by a large number of tributaries, big and small, draining a total basin area of about 256,000 sq km of which the share of the three riparian states of Maharashtra, Karnataka and Andhra Pradesh is 26.8 per cent, 43.8 per cent and 29.4 per cent, respectively. The basin drains a length of approximately 700 km of the Western Ghats which is the predominant source of water of the river. As the river flows about 135 km from its origin near Mahabaleshwar Hills, it is joined by the Koyna river flowing from the western side of the same hill. Further along its course. it is joined by tributaries like Varna, Panchaganga and Dodhganga draining about 150 km of the Western Ghats. As the river emerges from the eastern slopes of the Western Ghats, it is joined by Ghataprabha and Malaprabha from the south at a distance of approximately 500 km from the origin.

After traversing the Deccan proper the east flowing Krishna then enters the alluvial lands and at a distance of about 800 km from the source, just before it enters Andhra Pradesh, a major tributary Bhima, draining the Western Ghats, north of Mahabaleshwar joins it from the north. Near Kurnool the river is joined by another major tributary, Tungabhadra from the south, draining a major section of the Western Ghats in Karnataka. Within a short distance from this confluence, the river enters the Naliamali Ranges characterised by peep gorges. At this place the Srisailam Dam and further downstream the Nagarjunasagar Dam have been constructed. At this point the major water sources of the Western Ghats have all been united. Tributaries like Dindi, Musi, Palleru and Muneru draining the dry north-eastern parts of the basin join the river between Srisailam ad Vijayawada but do not add much water. Below Vijayawada, where the Krishna is blocked by the barrage constructed during the British period, the river spreads out into the delta and below the last major village Nagailanka it joins the Bay of Bengal in three branches, thus ending the long eastward journey of the waters of the Western Ghats.

Since water flow creates an interconnectedness within the basin, each intervention in land and water use, depending on its scale, can become the source of conflicts. The mining of iron ore at Kudremukh and Manganese ore in Sandur in the upper catchments of Tungabhadra has seriously affected the stability of the catchment and has led to severe soil erosion and silting of the Tungabhadra reservoir, thus conflicting with irrigation needs. The Krishna river system has a large number of small, medium and major dams starting from Dhom which is located within 5 km of its origin.

This storage and diversion of water from the original river course has destroyed the fishing economy which was dominant on both banks of the river as well as the indigenous irrigation system that existed throughout the course of the river. Further, large dams have also generated conflicts by creating waterlogging in the command areas. The hydroelectric power generation from the river water has come into conflict with irrigation needs both in terms of the spatial and temporal characteristics of water storage and distribution. The maximisation of power generation from Koyna demands that the water of the Krishna basin, draining into Bay of Bengal, be diverted to the Arabian Sea.

Industrial uses of the river system are a major source of conflict. For example, the pulp based industries on Tungabhadra have polluted the river and destroyed the fishing economy 20 km downstream. Moreover, the large-scale cultivation of pulpwood species like Eucalyptus in this part of the basin has impaired the groundwater recharge potential.

In the Krishna basin comprising mostly of arid and semi-arid regions water management had reached a high level of sophistication, both for surface as well as groundwater utilisation. An aerial view of the basin reveals a network of a large number of tanks, some pre-historic, others constructed by the local people or the rulers at different times in history. In general the technology used for all these tanks involved the construction of an earthen embankment at the exit of a natural water collection point that is a result of topography.

These tanks were used for surface irrigation of approximately 500 acres of land as well as for enhancing ground water recharge to support the wells. These tanks formed a network so that water did not drain out easily and was conserved at the site. To some extent indigenous water management techniques also included the diversion of streams to irrigate land by canals. The total number of tanks in the basin may be around 30,000. By arresting the scanty rainfall, these tanks actually provided a cushioning effect against variations in rainfall which is common in the basin. This decentralised water conservation system met both drinking water and agricultural needs. There was no major long distance transfer of water and the local cropping pattern evolved in accordance with the local water endowment.

The needs of the Vijayanagar Empire led to the first major intervention in the natural water flow. In the sixteenth century, specially during the reign of King Krishnadevaraya, there were many attempts to divert the water of Tungabhadra through seven canals in the Bellary district, these are now known as the Vijayanagar Canals. The canals provided water for irrigation as well as satisfied the needs of the large army stationed in the capital city of Hampi. The interests of the Vijayanagar rulers were not limited to canals. Understanding the crucial role of tanks in food production as well as in providing drinking water supply, the kingdom undertook a systematic programme of tank construction. The Daroji tank and the Vyasayaraya Samudram in Cuddapah district are the result of this programme.

The first large-scale intervention in the natural flow of water in the Krishna river basin was seen in the late nineteenth century. It was motivated both by the irrigation needs of export crops like cotton and groundnut, as well as for transporting these products easily to major ports like Madras.

The Krishna delta canal system based on the Vijayawada barrage was constructed in 1855 The Nira Canal in Maharashtra was constructed in 1835 to irrigate about 150,000 acres and the Kurnool Cuddapah Canal was constructed in 1886 to irrigate 100,000 acres. With the passage of time. an increasing number of government aided large and medium projects came up and today the Krishna river has numerous dams including the Dhom Dam which is at a distance of 5 km from its source. Midstream, we find the Alamatti and Narayanpur Dams of the Upper Krishna Project while further downstream Srisailam and Nagarjunsugar Dams generate electricity and divert water for irrigation. The tributaries have also been used extensively in this respect.

The Koyna Dam is situated 58 km below the origin of the river. The Tunga river is impounded at Gajanur and Bhadra at Lakavalli. The Tunga and Bhadra meet and the Tungabhadra Dam is located 265 km from the origin. In Ghataprabha the reservoir at Hidkal in Karnataka is the major irrigation project while Malaprabha is impounded at the peacock gorge near Manoli. The spread of water-intensive cultivation throughout the basin has dramatically altered the water balance, leading to major conflicts between water for cash crop cultivation and staple food production on the one hand, and between irrigation and drinking water needs on the other. The case of sugarcane cultivation in Maharashtra and grapes in Hyderabad are two instances of over-exploitation of water resources in the basin for cash crop production and a consequent destabilisation of the water cycle, leading to water scarcity in large parts of the basin.

Dams for irrigation and/or power are also a source of conflict between the traditional rights of people to land and water and the rights of the state to displace and uproot them for building river valley projects as in the case of Srisailam Dam. Large dams require massive submergence areas, and hence necessitate the displacement of large numbers of people. Big dams also allow large diversions of water. Major diversions from the river basin as in the case of the Telugu-Ganga Canal taking off from Srisailam Dam, affect the riparian rights of the states and have generated unresolvable inter-state conflicts.

FUNDAMENTAL WATER ISSUES BETWEEN PAKISTAN AND INDIA

There is growing feeling in Pakistan that while India is increasingly building dams on its western rivers, it is simultaneously engaged in activities aimed at stopping Pakistan, the lower riparian, from building storage dams on Pakistani rivers. In the case of its upper riparian neighbour, Nepal, India has even deployed heavy artillery to partially destroy dams which were being constructed by the Nepalese. India's water strategy thus boils down to construction of more and more dams on cross-boundary rivers inside its own territory while obstructing dams in lower- riparian neighbours and destroying those in upper-riparian Nepal.

Honorary vice-president of the International Commission on Large Dams (ICOLD), Asif H. Kazi in his column titled "Misusing the Indus Treaty" argues that: "Pakistan's farmlands have been deprived of the uses of the waters of three eastern rivers, Ravi, Beas and Sutlej. The flows of these rivers were allocated to India under the 1960 Indus Waters Treaty. Authorities on the subject accept that when rivers and canals in Pakistan's demarcated area were classified as Pakistan's assets under the Partition Act, 1947, it meant only one thing: that these rivers and canals were to continue to receive water in the same way as before. Under the treaty, Pakistan was to enjoy the unrestricted use of the Indus, the Jhelum and the Chenab. However, exceptions were inserted as annexure which allowed India to develop and use certain specified quantities of water of the three western rivers as well".

Indian storage limits on the western rivers, which add up to 3.6 MAF (million acre feet). However, India deliberately followed a pattern of filling water behind Baglihar Dam constructed on the Chenab River by impounding flows in the low-flow month of September, a clear breach of the treaty which prescribes the filling period as being from June 21 to Aug 31 (Ibid).

Obviously, the foregoing was not the intent of the Indus Waters Treaty. And it is precisely for this reason that Pakistan has been insisting that India adopt well- known dam design features, especially for the outlets, which can easily ensure that the reservoir operators would not be able to manipulate flows of the western rivers at their own sweet will. India is opposing this using as an excuse the need for the prolongation of the reservoirs' lifespan through sediment flushing (Ibid).

BACKDROP: THE INDUS WATERS TREATY (IWT)

Analysts are of the opinion that, "the highly sensitive and charged water issues between Pakistan and India have emerged out of the way the 1947 partition lines were drawn. A seemingly minor change, but one with far-reaching consequences, was introduced in the partition map, in violation of all principles laid down by the British government. It came about at the very last minute when, upon the insistence of the Indian leaders, the partition award turned over to India three vital districts that were originally allocated to Pakistan, with the sole objective of providing India with access to Kashmir. The three remaining western rivers on which Pakistan now relies upon all originate in or pass through Kashmir before entering Pakistan. In other words, India, after having obtained the waters of the three eastern rivers through Indus Waters Treaty, is now trying to take control of three western rivers as well".

Momin Iftikhar provides further detail: "The Indus Waters Treaty (IWT) signed in Karachi on September 19, 1960, by India's Prime Minister Jawaharlal Nehru, Pakistan's President Muhammad Ayub Khan and Mr W.A.B. Illif of the World Bank has shown a remarkable endurance and resilience in withstanding the jolts of the Indo-Pak turbulent relations. The treaty allocates the water of the three western rivers of the Indus Basin (Indus, Jhelum and Chenab) to Pakistan, while the eastern rivers (Ravi and Sutlej) have been assigned to India for utilisation. The treaty allows India to tap the hydroelectric potential of the Pakistan specific rivers; with the important proviso that generation of power should not interfere with the timings and the quantity of flow of waters into Pakistan".

In his column titled "Tackling the Kishanganga knot" Iftikhar held the view that: "If India and Pakistan had normal and trustful relations, with a credible monitoring mechanism in place, this would not have been too demanding a task to accomplish within the parameters provided by the IWT. However, with emerging water shortages for agriculture in Pakistan, and the sensitivity of timings to the flow of water in the rivers that feed the defense-oriented canals and sustains the capacity for the generation of hydroelectric power, it is easier said than done" (Ibid).

CONSTRUCTION OF KISHANGANGA HYDRO – ELECTRICITY PROJECT (KHEP)

The water sharing environment in South Asia is fast deteriorating. The Pakistani frustration at Indian inflexibility was evident when it referred the matter of Baghliar Dam on River Chenab to the World Bank in January 2005. The verdict by a neutral expert, appointed by the bank ultimately settled the issue in February 2007. The decision accommodated both the parties and each country felt that its respective stance had been addressed and vindicated. The problem did not end there; within four years, the two countries are back for arbitration over the water issue and the bone of contention this time is construction by India of the Kishanganga Storage-cum-Hydroelectric Power Project on River Neelum (Indians call it Kishanganga), which is a major tributary of River Jhelum. Iftikhar (2011) points out that: "The matter is sensitive because not only the dam will curtail the flow of water for agriculture, but Pakistan is also constructing the Neelum-Jhelum Hydroelectric Project on River Neelum, downstream of Kishanganga Project."

Pakistan's fundamental objection to Kishanganga is that it involves diverting the water of Neelum River through a 21km long tunnel towards the Wullar Lake to generate 330MW power. This is manifestly not allowed by the IWT. Iftikhar indicates: "This diversion is against the provisions of the IWT and has not only serious consequence for the 969MW power generation capability of Neelum- Jhelum Hydrolectrical Project, but will also reduce the water supply for agriculture in the areas of Azad Kashmir, which are dependent on the Neelum River flow. It is estimated that the diversion of water towards Wullar Lake will reduce flow into Pakistan by 27 percent (Ibid).

According to the available data, it is estimated that, "the dry spell is likely to extend to eight months per year. The lack of water is going to have an adverse impact on the agriculture in over thousands of acres in Azad Kashmir, which are dependent upon the flow of River Neelum, besides causing damage to the environmental aspects of flora and fauna nurtured by the rivers flow in the Neelum Valley" (Ibid).

Kazi (2011) supports the view that, "the proposed Kishenganga project violates the treaty in a most glaring way. Firstly, the hydroelectric plant is not located on the Kishenganga but way off the channel at the end of a long tunnel that discharges into another tributary. And, secondly, the recipient tributary ultimately outfalls upstream of the Wullar Lake, and this completely changes the patterns of the flows of both Kishenganga and Jhelum Rivers."

The International Court of Arbitration's Decision

In response to Pakistan's appeal for 'interim measures' against the dam which may inhibit the restoration of the river flow to its natural channel, "The International Court of Arbitration (ICA) barred India from any permanent works on the controversial Kishanganga hydro-electricity project (KHEP) on River Neelum at Gurez in occupied Kashmir".

Farhatullah Babar, Spokesman for President Asif Ali Zardari, said that, "The arbitration court took the decision on an appeal filed by Pakistan that India was diverting the flow of the river and violating Indus Water Treaty (IWT) between the two countries" (Ibid).

The court order said: "India shall not proceed with the construction of any permanent works on or above the Kishanganga/Neelum River bed at the Gurez site that may inhibit the restoration of the flow of the river to its natural channel. Pakistan and India shall arrange for periodic joint inspections of the dam site at Gurez in order to monitor the implementation of the court's order" (Ibid).

Irfan Raza reports that, "Islamabad had submitted its version in the World Bank's arbitration court in July (2011). The major contention was that under the law India cannot divert the route of River Neelum. Pakistan fears that the Kishanganga dam would rob it of 15 per cent water share – a violation of the Indus Water Treaty. Islamabad accused Delhi of trying to divert the water of

Neelumriver in order to harm Pakistan's Neelum-Jhelum hydro-electricity project (Ibid).

In its request Pakistan had required: "A stop work order; An order that any steps India has taken or may take in respect of the KHEP are taken at its own risk without prejudice to the possibility that the court may order that the works may not be continued, be modified or dismantled, that India be ordered to inform the court and Pakistan of any imminent and actual developments on the Kishanganga Dam that may adversely affect the restoring of the status quo ante or that may jeopardise Pakistan's rights and interests under the treaty; Any further relief the court considered necessary" (Ibid).

Indian Response

Indian experts denied the allegations raised by the Pakistani Government on building Kishanganga Dam. Former Secretary, Water Resources, Ramaswamy R Iyer in his column titled "Pakistan: Water on the Boil Again" writes: " So far as one knows, India has not built any storage, not even the 3.6 MAF permitted by the Treaty, nor does it intend to cause harm to Pakistan by diverting Indus waters. In any case, there is such a thing as the Permanent Indus Commission. How can India store or divert waters to the detriment of Pakistan under the watchful eyes of the Indus Commissioner for Pakistan" ?

On violations of the provisions of the Indus Treaty by India, Iyer elaborates that, "The Treaty envisages and permits Indian projects on the western rivers, and so the projects in themselves cannot be violations of the Treaty. They can be violations of the Treaty if they deviate from certain restrictive provisions, but that will be questioned by the Indus Commissioner for Pakistan. The questions may be resolved within the Commission, or become differences and get referred to a Neutral Expert (as happened in the Baglihar case), or may be in the nature of disputes to be referred to a Court of Arbitration (as has now happened in the Kishenganga case)".

Vibha Sharma in a column titled "India confident of winning Kishanganga dispute" writes: "India today termed as "favourable" the International Court of Arbitration (ICA) order last week which prevents the country from undertaking permanent works above the riverbed level at the Gurez site of the Kishanganga hydropower project.

The final orders are expected either in 2012-end or in early 2013".

Water Resources Minister Pawan Bansal asserting that "the stay was merely an interim legal position and in no way signified any "loss of position" for India, as was being projected by Pakistan. Bansal told The Tribune that "the neighbouring country had raised two issues-stopping the work and dismantling the construction already done -and the court did not agree to either of its two contentions" (Ibid).

"India can go ahead with construction of powerhouses, tunneling works, coffer dams, temporary bypass tunnel and concretisation under the riverbed for the dam. The only thing we cannot do is go above the surface of the river bed, which is not a problem since we would only be able to complete these works by 2012- end and 2013 beginning, by when the court will give its final decision," Bansal said (Ibid).

For now, India is compiling a rejoinder to emphasize its point before the International Court of Justice. "The Hague-based ICA has directed India to submit a report on environmental hazards to the ecosystem due to this project" (Ibid).

Former Secretary, Water Resources, Ramaswamy R Iyer also maintained that "the ruling was neither a win nor a loss for either country. It is just a temporary stay. India can still continue with related works except constructing the dam" he said (Ibid).

However, taking into account political and environmental consequences of the project, Sharma is of the view that "there appears to be some amount of skepticism with an expert saying that investments could go waste if the final award goes against India, which in other words also means that the power problem in Kashmir will continue."India will be taking a risk by carrying out with other works till the final ruling," said the water resources expert, who did not wish to be quoted" (Ibid).

Confidence Building Measures

Daily *The Telegraph* reports that "Ahead of another round of Indo-Pak water talks scheduled in mid-September (2011), the Jammu and Kashmir government quietly abandoned the controversy-ridden plan to construct a concrete barrage where the Jhelum meets the Wullarlake in north Kashmir". Thakur, Sankarshan (2011) believes that: "It's a small move with big implications: a persistent irritant in bilateral ties, the dumping of the barrage could prove a significant confidence-building measure between India and Pakistan". Giving further details Thakur writes that "Work on the venture, christened the Tulbul Navigation Project by New Delhi but better known as the Wullar barrage, was stopped two years after it commenced in 1984 upon strong objections from Pakistan which argued the lock-cum-control barrage would not only deprive it of water but could also be used as a "natural weapon" against it" (Ibid).

The Jammu and Kashmir minister for irrigation and flood control, Taj Mohiuddin, confirmed that "the state government had resorted to alternative measures to prevent flooding in the Jhelum's upper catchments and ensure navigability in the river" (Ibid). "We have given up the barrage project in favour of temporary rubber dams, which can work as effectively," Mohiuddin told The Telegraph. "Why should we want to erect a huge concrete structure when modern technology allows us to solve problems with more flexible methods" (Ibid)?

He did say the barrage had become "an unnecessary source of tension and suspicions" between the neighbours. "We had not been able to move on the project, it was stalled, this new rubber damming technique can probably help us a win-win way out," he said (Ibid). Mohiuddin appeared convinced that "the new initiative would address reservations that Pakistan has had with the erection of a concrete barrage" (Ibid).

Role of Media

Zahra (2011) argues that the "Paucity of direct communication between the two states has increased the role of the media. The two nuclear neighbours are caught in a warp where the status quo in bi-lateral relations vacillates between improvement and deterioration but does not sway beyond a certain point — either way — so as to achieve anything decisive."

This part of the study glimpse at the role of the media on the water issues between Pakistan and India during 2011. Excerpts from the editorials and news reports of two leading newspapers from each country i.e. daily *Dawn* and *The Nation* from Pakistan and *The Tribune* and *The Kashmir Times* from India have been included.

Pakistani Media

An elite Pakistani newspaper daily *Dawn* in its editorial captioned "Controversial Project" expressed concerns on the Kishanganga hydropower project being constructed by India. The paper reads: "A series of disputes on hydropower generation projects initiated by India has given rise to concerns that New Delhi is trying to control the river water and thus `strangulate` Pakistan`s agriculture and economy. Many experts also believe that, given the situation, a future war over water between India and Pakistan cannot be ruled out" ('Controversial Projects', 2011).

Dawn extends its comments by saying that: "Repeated Indian attempts in the past to find loopholes and technical flaws in the 50-year-old water treaty that can be used to New Delhi`s advantage have hardly been helpful in easing tensions over water-sharing between the two neighbours" (Ibid).

In its course of discussion the paper writes, "We will have primarily ourselves to blame in case of such an eventuality. Successive governments in Islamabad have failed to raise and resolve crucial water issues, including this one, that have arisen from time to time with India to the peril of Pakistan's agriculture and economy. While Islamabad must vigorously pursue the case at international forums to protect its economic interests, India should remember that the failure to satisfy Pakistani concerns will only delay the realisation of the dream of a prosperous South Asia whose various parts are at peace with one another" (Ibid).

Another leading English language Pakistani newspaper *The Nation* criticizes Indian policy on water sharing. In its news report *The Nation* reads, "The Treaty has in great detail covered a just distribution of water of rivers flowing from India to Pakistan. Under the Treaty India in no case can hold the water or hamper the flow of water during various seasons to Pakistan" ('Pakistan likely to win', 2011).

The paper further writes, "The Kishanganga project is a part of the India move to build a series of water reservoirs on all the three major rivers including river Chenab to utilize water at the upstream for the purposes of irrigation and power generation depriving a huge agricultural lands of waters which have been irrigating from these sources for centuries" (Ibid).

Commenting on the World Court of Arbitration's decision that stayed India's construction of a dam across the Neelum at Kishenganga, *The Nation* in its editorial "Kishanganga stayed" reads: "This stay order is not a final injunction, though it is the first sign that Pakistan is taking India's constant violations of the Indus Waters Treaty (IWT) with some seriousness.

Earlier this year, in bilateral secretary-level talks, Pakistan had conceded acceptance of a revised Indian design of the Wuller Barrage, something which only encouraged Indian ambitions in this direction, and which furthered its ambitions to turn Pakistan into a barren wasteland, by using its illegal occupation of Kashmir to stop Pakistan's water from getting to it".

The Nation suggests the Pakistani government to follow a two-pronged strategy. "First, to pursue this case with full vigour, and ensure that the stay is confirmed; second, to utilize this breathing space to start building irrigation-cum- generation projects on the Indus, and thus rid itself of this charge which is justified only because certain pro-Indian lobbies have been working against the Kalabagh Dam.

. The stay order, when confirmed, will also provide a useful precedent which will help stop Indian depredations on the Indus. However, a permanent solution will involve a settlement of the Kashmir issue. It would mean a general Indo-Pak settlement, ridding us of threat of water projects in Held Kashmir" (Ibid).

Indian Media

Daily *The Tribune* is published from Chandigarh. In news report it provides details about Pakistan's stance in the ICA. The paper writes, "Pakistan has moved the Court of Arbitration asking it to direct India to stop work at the 330-MW Kishenganga hydropower project in Jammu and Kashmir. The project is likely to be completed by 2015. A seven-judge Bench has started arbitration proceedings from January 14 this year in the Hague".

The report further reads, "Incidentally, this is the first case referred for international arbitration under the provisions of the Indus Water Treaty, 1960. Earlier, India and Pakistan had sought the services of a neutral expert appointed by the World Bank to resolve their differences over the Baglihar Dam under construction on the Chenab. The Bench – comprising Justice Stephen M Schwebel (head), Justice Sir Franklin Beman, Prof Howard S Wheater, Justice Bruno Simma, Jan Paulsson, Justice Peter Tomka and Lucius Caflisch – has three neutral umpires, including the head of the Bench, and four arbitrators nominated by India and Pakistan. Noted lawyer and expert on International law Shankar Das and legal luminary Fali s Nariman, both of whom had argued India's case in the Baglihar dam issue, are representing India" (Ibid).

Another newspaper *The Kashmir Times* from Jammu published a news report on the Nimoo-Bazgo hydropower project being built by India on the Indus River. It reads, "Pakistan wants to raise objections to the project, saying it allegedly violates the Indus waters treaty. The decision to approach the ICJ on the Nimoo- Bazgo project was made after Pakistani officials made their first visit to the project site and concluded it was allegedly in "total violation" of the Indus waters treaty of 1960, a senior unnamed member of Pakistan's Indus Waters Commission told the media. The unnamed official claimed India would be able to complete the Nimoo- Bazgo project by July 2012 and thus "suffocate" the water flow in the Indus. The design of its gated spillways and the depth of the dam allegedly breach the Indus waters treaty. The Pakistani side has raised five objections to the design of the project" (Ibid).

INDO-PAK WATER DISPUTES: TIME FOR FRESH APPROACHES

Unfortunately, South Asian countries, particularly India and Pakistan, have both faced challenges in water management and proper river basin management. The consequence of this has been a severe water crisis, which has a bearing on both ground and surface water. A cursory glance at the data on fresh water availability per person, per year reveals this vulnerability. South Asia's renewable freshwater resources are about 1,200 cubic meters per capita. In comparison, a large number of countries have between 2,500 – 15,000 cubic meters per capita. Some like Canada and Norway have over 70,000 cubic meters per capita.

The difficulties in managing surface water are especially complex in South Asia. River basins— the ultimate source of all water used in households, agriculture and industry (like hydropower companies), as well as the receptors of most wastewater—often transgress international borders. Since actions upstream can lead to disruption of the natural flow of rivers, water pollution, diversion of the waters with the occasional threat of even blocking the flow of water, water sharing can often lead to political tensions and acrimony, as has happened in the case of India and Pakistan. The lower riparian countries become especially vulnerable. Effective river basin management therefore necessitates that water users take into account the relationships, interaction and impact that their actions have on others, especially those downstream.

INDO-PAK WATER DISPUTE: THE ORIGINS

The Indo-Pak dispute on the Indus basin has drawn immense attention in South Asia and across the world, largely due to the nature of the tense political relationship between the two countries. This attention has grown more intense in recent years, in the aftermath of the Mumbai attacks on 26 November 2008, which had kindled fears of a nuclear war. Analysts began exploring, not only the sources of the tension between the two nuclear states but also areas which had the potential for increased cooperation and thereby reduce the possibility of a war at any point in the future. Water is one such area, especially the Indus basin.

The system of rivers in the Indus basin comprises 2,000 miles of the river Indus and its five tributaries from the East — Jhelum, Chenab, Ravi, Beas and Sutlej, with an aggregate length of 2,800 miles. Most of the upper reaches of the Indus basin lie in India. All these rivers combine in Mithankot in Pakistan and flow into the Arabian Sea near Karachi.

The Indus system of rivers has been used for irrigation ever since civilization took root in the area. The water disputes too date back to the pre-partition era, when there were significant inter-state differences between Punjab, Sind, Bahawalpur and Bikaner. After Pakistan was created in 1947, this inter-state dispute amongst the four states became an international water dispute between the two newly formed nation states. The issues around water sharing were now between West Punjab of Pakistan and East Punjab of India. Lands on the West (which are today part of Pakistan) are fertile and the British, wanting to take advantage of the fact, developed the Indus Basin irrigation system. On the other hand, the land in Haryana and the East Punjab (which is today part of India) was not considered particularly fertile. At the time of Partition, Sir Cyril Radcliffe, who was entrusted with the task of boundary demarcation, drew a line across the Indus, dividing not just the land, but the waters and the integrated Indus canal system. Thus, at Independence, the newly formed states had the onerous responsibility of finding a proper mechanism to share and jointly manage the irrigation system for the future.

Over the years, India built its irrigation system which could serve the needs of Himachal Pradesh, Punjab, Haryana and Rajasthan. On the other side, the fact that the source of the rivers of the Indus basin were in India resulted in fear of droughts and famine in Pakistan. In fact, until the signing of the Indus Water Treaty (IWT) in Karachi on 19 September 1960, significant disagreements persisted between the two countries. To quote a defining example, although the Inter-Dominion Conference was held in May 1948, and an agreement between the two countries was signed, wherein India assured Pakistan of not withdrawing water delivery, without allowing time for Pakistan to develop alternate sources, Pakistan communicated its dissatisfaction with the ground situation. On 16 June 1949, Pakistan sent a note to India which called for a conference to resolve the "equitable apportionment of all common water" and suggested giving the World Court jurisdiction on the application of either party. But India categorically objected to third party involvement and instead suggested that judges from each side be allowed to narrow the disputes first.

In August 1951, Eugene Black, President of the World Bank, invited prime ministers of both the countries to Washington and they finally agreed on an outline of essential principles and arrived at a common understanding that neither side will reduce the river water supplies for existing uses.

The World Bank then came out with its own proposal which suggested division of the western tributaries to Pakistan, and the eastern tributaries to India, besides a proposal of continued deliveries to Pakistan during transition period of ten years. India accepted the proposal while Pakistan gave its qualified acceptance on March 25, 1954. Later when the World Bank arranged an international Indus Basin Development Fund and raised $893 million, the Indus Water Treaty was finally signed by both the countries on 19 September 1960.

The World Bank effectively brokered a settlement on the dispute arising out of water sharing of Indus River and it continues to play a significant role whenever the two countries are unable to resolve issues bilaterally in this area.

FACTORS LEADING TO THE INDUS WATER TREATY

Under the Treaty, India was given an exclusive right of three eastern rivers – Sutlej, Beas and Ravi, while Pakistan was given the right of three western rivers – Indus, Chenab and Jhelum. The tributaries of these rivers are also considered their part under the treaty. One school of thought believes that the treaty has been a success. B.G. Verghese, senior Indian journalist, and one of the key proponents of this argument states that,

The Treaty has worked well and withstood wars and tensions, though some on both sides feel it is unfair to them. However, the fact is that the IWT enabled both sides to get on with the responsibility of settling refugees following the Partition and lay the foundations for the Green Revolution that followed. Pakistan built Tarbela and Mangla and India Bhakra- Nangal and Pong.

Pakistan has important reservations on the treaty.

PAKISTANI APPREHENSIONS ON THE IWT

In Pakistan, some political leaders, certain sections of the Pakistani press and militant groups have made water sharing an emotive issue. The argument that IWT is a success has not convinced them and they emphasize that Pakistan is the lower riparian and a predominantly agrarian economy and voice fears that India can block Pakistan's rightful water share by building dams. An important concern expressed by some analysts in Pakistan in this regard is that while the Treaty includes provisions on a minimum supply of water, it does not address the question of the distribution of water and neither does it foresee demographic developments within each country which change the demand for water. Therefore, while it protected usage at the time, it did not safeguard each country's interest in the future since it did not take into consideration the increase or decrease in requirements that may occur. However, most of the disputes that have arisen between the two countries whether on Baglihar, Kishanganga or Wullar barrage have involved the issue of flow to the lower riparian.

In 2010, Pakistan lodged a complaint with The Hague's Permanent Court of Arbitration (CoA) on India's plans to build a dam on the Kishanganga river (Neelum in Pakistan), as part of a run- of-the-river hydroelectric project, claiming that it was a violation of the Treaty. Pakistan is building the Neelum-Jhelum hydroelectric project downstream. In 2011, after visiting both projects, the CoA put a stay order that prevented India from constructing a permanent structure which could affect the flow of water downstream to Pakistan. Recently on September 1, 2012, CoA concluded a two-week hearing, the verdict of which is expected within a period of six months. Importantly, the Pakistan press reported that India was set to receive $700 million as carbon credits for ten years against seven hydropower projects built on Pakistan's share of rivers under the IWT – the Indus, Chenab and Jhelum. This raised fears in Pakistan that it might grant legitimacy to projects such as the Kishanganga on the Indian side.

Notably, the earlier disputed projects too were related to the construction of dams. One was the construction of Salal Dam on the Chenab in 1978, the first ever dispute after the signing of IWT, the other being the Wullar Barrage / Tulbul Navigation Project which began in 1987. While the resolution of Salal Dam dispute is considered as a case of successful water conflict resolution between India and Pakistan, the Tulbul navigation project on the Jhelum still remains unresolved. Yet another dispute was related to Baglihar Dam on the Chenab River, which was resolved only after a neutral expert from the World Bank was appointed. In his verdict of February 12, 2007,16 the arbitrator accepted some of the objections raised by Pakistan relating to the design of the dam, diversion of water and power generation scheme. The decision was largely perceived as a balanced one.

The fear of water deprivation has become a major source of bilateral dispute. In the recent past, India's Ministry of External Affairs (MEA) has cited evidence to show that certain sections of Pakistan's polity have been falsely stating that New Delhi is deliberately depriving Islamabad of its share of water guaranteed under the Indus Water Treaty, and is bent upon destroying Pakistan's agrarian economy. The militant fringe in Pakistan's polity took up the Indus waters as a 'lifeline' issue in 2009-10, when Lashkar-e-Tayyeba chief Hafiz Saeed, paraded the streets of Muzaffarabad, Rawalakot, Lahore and Faisalabad with placards saying, "Water must flow or else blood will flow".

Amidst such statements, there were many voices of sanity in Pakistan. Significantly, the same MEA document points out that there are many voices in the Pakistani establishment who have unequivocally stated that India is not violating the IWT in any way and that water shortages in Pakistan are a result of domestic policy failures and not some sinister Indian strategy.

The document, while citing Indus Water Commissioner Sayyed Jamaat Ali Shah, states that many Pakistan officials themselves agree that all hydro-electric projects built by India are in total conformity with the IWT, and have only been initiated after obtaining necessary permissions.

In a counter to Saeed's argument, Shah Mehmood Qureshi, a former foreign minister of Pakistan, has clearly stated that India was not stealing water. Rather, Pakistan was wasting thirty-five million acre feet (MAF) of water, and if there were seasonal variations this was only because of the natural hydrological cycle. Qureshi's argument is validated when one examines the real reasons for Pakistan's water crisis.

REASONS FOR THE WATER CRISIS IN PAKISTAN

According to Pakistan's *Economic Survey* (2011-12), the agrarian economy is heavily dependent on river water provided by melting glaciers. The survey also highlighted that during the period 2011-12, the availability of water for both *kharif* and *rabi* crops was respectively 10 percent and 19.2 percent less than normal. Also water availability for Rabi crop was 15 percent less than 2010-11.

This *Economic Survey* also highlighted the excessive wastage of water from the irrigation system due to the improper lining of waterways. As a consequence, the agriculture, livestock and fisheries sectors were adversely affected. According to the World Bank and Needs Assessment Report, 2011, the total damages caused to these sectors were $1,840 million while reconstruction costs were estimated to be about $305.6 million. Damages to agriculture, livestock and fisheries sectors accounted for 49.33 percent of total damages of all the sectors during that period.

Pakistan has one of the world's largest glacial reserves in the Karakoram-Hindukush-Himalaya ranges supplying fresh water to the Indus River System, the world's largest irrigation system.

Fears of this supply getting affected by climate change have been voiced since the 1990s. With global average temperatures rising, it was feared that glaciers would be melting at an alarming rate. However, a separate study found that Karakoram glaciers and ice caps, as a whole, were losing mass less quickly than once feared, offering some respite to the effected region. This fact was noted by the National Plan of Pakistan 2012-13.

The same National Plan mentioned that the Integrated Irrigation Network of Indus Basin is under serious threat of water logging, hydro-salinity, adverse effects of pollution and contamination of surface and ground water. Consequently, the Plan suggests that an overall environmental management plan and process for approval and implementation be put in place. Hence, one can infer that more than anything else, it is inadequate water policies and loopholes in the regulations for management of water systems, that are acknowledged as the causes of the water crisis in Pakistan. Its impacts on various sectors including agriculture and allied activities have also been documented.

The Pakistan Economic Survey 2010-11, categorically acknowledges that water related issues are a serious threat in Pakistan. It states that, 'the existing water resources in the country are under threat due to untreated discharge of municipal and industrial wastes to rivers and other surface water bodies. The majority of the population of Pakistan is exposed to the hazard of unsafe and polluted drinking water.' These issues are testimony to the limitations of existing water management policies and regulations in Pakistan.

WATER CRISIS IN INDIA

Like Pakistan, India too faces acute water shortage. This has been stated in various government documents, including the Draft Water Policy of India -2012, which listed several causes of the precarious water situation in India. The policy document states that water stress in large parts of India can be attributed to population growth, urbanization and changing lifestyles, improper addressing of water governance, mismanagement of water resources, and the threat of climate change. Many of these are also leading to salinity of both groundwater and surface water.

Interestingly, it also highlights that while multi-disciplinary water resources projects are planned and implemented, they suffer from problems of fragmentation and ignore optimum utilization, environmental sustainability and holistic benefits to the people. These issues, besides others raised in this draft make many of the earlier National Water Policies inconsequential.

When we move from the broader national scenario and look specifically at water quality of Indus basin on the Indian side, we find that several studies have been conducted to test the quality of water. One such physico-chemical water quality analysis was conducted in Harike Wetland, a site at the confluence of the two rivers–Sutlej and Beas. The study revealed the deterioration in water quality towards Sutlej River resulting from untreated effluents and municipal wastes from townships and industries situated on its banks. A gradual increase in temperature, Electrolytic Conductivity, high proportion of Total Dissolved Solids, Alkalinity, Hardness, High levels of Calcium and Magnesium were observed in Harike waters. Thus, both long-term water security in the region and more immediate local concerns, offer compelling reasons for India and Pakistan to cooperate.

Room for cooperation between both countries

As aforementioned, there have been many concerns raised by Pakistan on Indus Water Treaty and there is room for further negotiations. Citing Article XII of IWT, B.G. Verghese, an India based expert on water issues, has proposed Indus II that will be largely based on the foundation of Indus. Some on the Pakistan side, like F.S. Ajjazuddin, have articulated that the conflict is too important to be left to the two commissioners to discuss and refer to an arbitrator (in this case the Word Bank). He proposes the setting up a Joint Commission, whose structure is based on the belief that water resources are a common asset and that neither country owns them. Each country should see itself as a trustee of the resource for future generations. Rather than having two Commissioners from each country sit across the table and negotiate, the Joint Commission will be different in the sense that it would function as one body looking at the interests of both Pakistan and India.

But the crux of the matter is beyond this Treaty and is the water crisis faced by both the countries. The crisis cannot be attributed to any provisions of the IWT but is largely related to the mismanagement of water resources in general by each country and Indus River Basin in particular. Both these countries found themselves in such a crisis due to common factors like population growth, urbanization and ineffective polices dealing with these factors in order to tackle the water crisis. The fear of the melting glaciers of the Himalayas is adding to the woes of the existing water stress.

Therefore, at the first instance what these countries need is, to deal with their current water management problems and then create spaces for cooperation wherever possible, including those that can help deal with climate change. Thinking of Indus II or even abrogation of the same cannot guarantee any solution to the existing water crisis these two countries are trapped in.

The first step by each country should be to recognize the water problems of not only its own people but those of its neighbor, for the simple reason that these issues transcend national territories or borders drawn by states. Action or inaction of either country would impact the situation in the other country and more so in Pakistan, which is a lower riparian country. Even if the existing treaty were to be abrogated, Pakistan will still continue to have normal lower riparian rights over the rivers flowing into its territory under international law.

The next step would be for India to allay Pakistan's fears with regard to the Indus Treaty. In April 2012, India's Indus Water Commissioner G. Aranganathan, speaking to *Time*, had clarified that "there was no question of interrupting or reducing Pakistan's water supply". He had said that India was not preventing the flow of water to Pakistan. After filling the reservoirs in the initial stages—of the Tulbul navigation project on the Jhelum—the waters would only be used for running the turbines. Such clarifications can build confidence and it is important for India to continue to take further steps to address Pakistani concerns.

Pakistan on its part must acknowledge that the Indus Treaty is an example of successful conflict resolution between the two rival countries, which have otherwise fought three wars after independence and have locked horns on various issues over the years. Therefore, it is time that both countries end their shrill and clichéd stances that restrict fresh approaches in dealing with challenges as existential as water scarcity.

Building on the stability of the IWT both nations should go beyond just conflict resolution over Indus water sharing and develop partnerships in the water sector by setting up institutional mechanisms and building joint capacity to tackle the water problem.

The current institutional mechanism in the two countries is similar in many respects and it will not be difficult to bring the relevant levels of administration to partner with their counterparts in the other country. Both Central and State Governments in these countries have been entrusted with the responsibilities of development, conservation and management of water.

Like India, it is the Federal Government in Pakistan which is responsible for the overall policy formulation in this area. Besides, it provides technical assistance to the states/provinces on irrigation, multipurpose projects, groundwater exploitation and exploration, flood control, water logging and so on. Furthermore it is the State/provincial Government which has the responsibility of using and controlling this precious resource.

A partnership between the governments of two Punjabs can go a long way in ensuring that the common problems are viewed from a holistic perspective and not from a standpoint of suspicion and uncertainty. While this may seem like a difficult proposal to push, given the history of the bitter and violent partition along this part of the border, the fact also remains that the two Punjabs share common climatic conditions, similar water management practices, non- stringent water policies and water intensive crop cultivation. Once both sides come to an agreement that they could each benefit from the others' innovations and practices in dealing with water scarcity; and are transparent about developments, this process can become a template for cooperation in other areas of mutual interest.

The improved bilateral relations in recent months provide an opportune moment for this cooperation to take shape.

Addressing the water management issues in the Indus river basin on both sides of the border can improve the status of water availability and water quality in both countries and bring India and Pakistan closer to achieving the MDGs.

At a political level, the water issue is important for the politically dominant province of Pakistani Punjab and finding synergies may be a way of reaching out to those sections of the population who have apprehensions with regard to India's stand on water and are in some senses the driving force behind the continuing hostility.

By driving home the point that policy failures and not India is responsible for the water crisis, Pakistan can begin to concretely address its water security problem.

The purely technical and juridical aspects of the water issue can be augmented by focusing also on greater interaction and enhanced dialogue between important stakeholders on both sides, some of whom include farmers, researchers and students of various water and agricultural universities.

Some of the possible areas of cooperation are discussed below.

CONDUCTING JOINT STUDIES ON RECEDING GLACIERS BY BOTH COUNTRIES

Various independent studies have been conducted on receding Himalayan glaciers by agencies worldwide.

Appreciating the source of the problem, both the countries could cooperate on conducting research on the specific impacts of the receding glaciers.

This would help these countries to come up with solutions on River Basin Management, instead of harping on the provisions in the treaty itself.

Once the fundamental problem of water stress is taken care of through joint efforts, the problems in the Treaty will become immaterial.

Greater interactions between farmers groups of both countries

On 7-8 May 2012, when a business delegation from India visited Lahore to participate in the second Aman ki Asha Indo-Pak Economic Conference, the idea of exporting farm produce to Pakistan was seriously discussed.

One of the farmers, Rattan Singh Randhawa, who was part of the Indian delegation, echoed the sentiments of many when he said that: "In a village only those neighbors, who exchange household goods or farm equipment with each other, have good relations.

It is the same with nations." Frequent interactions of a similar nature will thus not only strengthen Indo-Pak trade ties, but also give a fillip to cooperation between the agricultural sectors of both countries. Further, if there are more exchanges for farmers of both countries such as those facilitated by the Two Punjab Centre which is part of the Centre for Research in Rural and Industrial Development (CRRID) Chandigarh and Aman Ki Asha, it would contribute towards improved relations in other areas as farmers can more easily arrive at consensus on shared issues and problems.

Finding common ground in combating desertification

India and Pakistan can also join hands for fighting environmental degradation in their shared desert region along the border. Desertification can easily lead to agricultural losses resulting in food shortages.

This phenomenon is already visible in both India and Pakistan. With collaboration, both countries can protect agricultural lands vulnerable to desertification through water conservation measures and modern irrigation techniques.

Both countries have already shown interest in protecting communities and farming operations that lie on the desert's fringes. For example in the case of Pakistan, a collaborative project between Pakistan's Integrated Rural Awareness and Development Organization and the One-UN Joint Program on Environment aims to build check dams, rehabilitate ponds in the area of Nagar Parkar, and construct earthen embankments to help store water and promote conservation. Similarly, in Rajasthan's Churu district, the Bhoruka Charitable Trust, an Indian NGO, is encouraging villagers to build and renovate water tanks, ponds, and dug-wells to preserve potable water.

Efforts of both countries in the Thar Desert can be shared as best practices and this sharing could go a long way as a confidence building measure.

Effectively utilizing the SAARC platform

There should be more emphasis towards greater interaction and cooperation within South Asian Association for Regional Cooperation (SAARC) countries on issues like water management and agricultural growth.

The SAARC, from its very inception has focused on regional cooperation in the spheres of agriculture and rural development. The Technical Committee on Agriculture and Rural Development (TC-ARD) conducted a number of meetings on the application of statistics on agricultural research, exchange of scientific and technical information and so on.

It has also deliberated on various demand-driven areas such as 'Water Resources Management' and 'Water for Agriculture' in SAARC countries.

More concerted action in these areas using the space provided by the regional body can contribute to improving bilateral relations.

Greater collaboration between the two Punjabs

In this context, a substantial start could be made by accelerating cooperation between the two Punjabs. The two Punjabs share a similar culture and face similar problems. They can be a good starting point for collaboration on the problem of water shortage. The two premier agricultural institutions of the region, the Punjab Agricultural University, Ludhiana and the University of Faisalabad in Punjab province of Pakistan can collaborate. Training can be provided to Pakistani students on understanding the hydrological data, water management techniques, restoration of water bodies, watershed management practices, and improving the quality of groundwater, and restoring the water tables through rainwater harvesting. The two countries can learn from each other in the policy sphere as well.

"For example in 2009, India promulgated the Sub-Soil Water Preservation Act and discouraged its farmers from planting a nursery before 10 May and sowing before 10 June each year, thus bringing down the irrigational requirements of canal water and maximizing the use of monsoon rains. This actually helped in raising water levels in the Indian Punjab". Such knowledge can easily be disseminated between farmers across the border. There is limited awareness in India about the innovative techniques being used by the farmers in Pakistan, however, we believe that similar knowledge can be offered by them to the Indian side as well.

7

Water and Energy: A Flashpoint in Pakistan-India Relations

Water resources are tied to the trajectory of economic growth in an intricate way. They are linked to food production, energy security and climate issues. In fact, in many ways, the entire gamut of future human security challenges hinges on how water resources are to be managed. A number of reports often indicate that the 'water bubbles' which sustained much of the growth in the past are in many parts of the world 'bursting'. Clearly water scarcity has serious consequences not only for human well-being but also for regional security and stability.

INDUS BASIN

Of the many river systems in the world, the mighty Indus with its tributaries is of striking and unmatched importance. The Indus basin has the largest irrigated area on any one river system. It is comprised of the main river Indus and its major tributaries: the Kabul, Swat, and Khurram from the west and the Jhelum, Chenab, Ravi, Beas, and Sutlej from the east. There are three distinct physical features of the basin that must be noted. First, the Greater Himalayan ranges, with their lofty peaks, snow, and glaciers form a natural storehouse from which the rivers draw perennial supplies of water. The impact of climate change on the glaciers is therefore critical to the future flows in the rivers.

Second, given the physiography of the Lesser Himalayas and the Shivalik hills or range, they have great potential as a source for development of hydroelectricity. This is because the rivers of the Indus system receive all their waters only in the upper parts of their mountainous catchments and have maximum flow when emerging from the foothills.

Third, the basin also covers Tibet from where the Indus and Sutlej originate and Afghanistan from where the Kabul begins. China is or provides the ultra-upper riparian (river banks) and, given the capacity and capability it has to harness or divert the waters of the Indus and Sutlej, China can change the hydrological dynamics of the basin. Comparatively, Afghanistan is less significant as an upper riparian given the political instability in that country, but it remains an important aspect of this basin system. A Study on the Hydroelectric Schemes by the Central Electricity Authority of India suggests that the Indus basin has a potential capacity of 19,988 MW at 60% load factor, which is the highest in India. In Pakistan, hydropower is the second largest source of electricity, contributing 33.1% of total power generation. While Pakistan's hydroelectric generation potential is estimated to be 46,000 MW, only 14% has been exploited. Unlike India, Pakistan is a one-river-basin country and all of its hydroelectric power projects come from the Indus.

Table : Indus Basin

Total Basin Area	**1170838 km^2**
Annual Available Waters	224 billion metric^3
Country	Basin Area (Km^2)
Pakistan	632,954
India	374,887
China	86,432
Afghanistan	76,542

INDIA AND PAKISTAN: WATER SHARING AND HISTORICAL PAINS

Water issues between India and Pakistan are historically constructed, emotionally charged, and politically divisive.

Although water is technically not a 'core issue' between the two, differences over the use of the rivers in recent years have the potential to derail any peacemaking efforts. It is not too difficult to imagine why. With an exponential growth in population and with agriculture as the pivot of economy, demand for water for irrigation and electricity generation is straining the distributive arrangements that were settled by the Indus Water Treaty (IWT) in 1960. The distributive arrangements refer to the distribution and utilization of the six rivers in the Indus basin: Indus, Jhelum, Chenab, Ravi, Sutlej, and Beas.

The partition of the rivers was an inevitable outcome of the partition of undivided India in 1947, as the political boundary was drawn right across the Indus basin. The partition changed the entire hydrography of the subcontinent—from being one political unit to two riparian states. The water issue therefore was no longer a domestic one. After eight years of discussion and negotiation, the IWT was signed. Water sharing was precisely designed to deescalate the tension over sharing the rivers for irrigation and hydropower.. That the treaty has survived hostility over the past 50 years deserves cheers, but only two cheers. The fact that the "fairness" of the treaty is today being questioned, from both sides, suggests that the distinction and separation between the 'functional' and 'political' aspects of the IWT have come under stress.

It is often said that an international treaty that gives one party all that it wants cannot be a good treaty. The IWT, like many treaties, was a compromise with both sides conceding from their earlier intractable positions. The treaty, at least in letter, settled the water sharing issue, but the perception remains unsettled. Therefore it is important to revisit the claims and counter assertions raised during the period of negotiations between 1952 to 1960 to understand how the water debate is framed today, with its impact on energy generation in both states tomorrow.

Before the IWT was signed, both India and Pakistan were unable to agree on the technical aspects of allocation or the distribution of water. The World Bank as a consultative actor worked on evolving a sharing formula that kept aside questions of historic rights or allocations. The idea was how best to utilize the waters of the Indus basin through joint development. While India agreed to a new framework of allocation, Pakistan felt strongly that its share of waters should be based on pre-partition distribution, taking into account its current and future water needs. Pakistan relentlessly articulated its lower riparian vulnerability, fearing that its part of divided Punjab could turn into a desert. In order to give traction to the negotiating process and a decisive push towards final settlement, the World Bank proposed the partitioning of the Indus river system into three eastern rivers (Sutlej, Beas and Ravi) to India and three western rivers (Indus, Jhelum and Chenab) to Pakistan. Importantly, canals and storage dams were to be constructed to divert waters from the western rivers and replace the eastern rivers supply lost by Pakistan.

As mentioned earlier, a settled treaty does not necessarily mean that differences in perceptions have been settled. There is probably no other issue that sparks misperception and mistrust as water does, and, in the context of India and Pakistan, emotions dangerously run high. In spite of the fact that the IWT genuinely safeguards Pakistan's riparian concerns, angst and anger continues to reverberate in Pakistan even today. There is a deep feeling that the partition of the Indus basin gave a certain physical capacity to India to cut-off vital irrigation water to Pakistan. As a lower riparian, Pakistan continues to link water as a lifeline issue and questions the fairness of the treaty. This finds active space in Pakistani politics, and its linkage to the Kashmir issue implies that any future peaceful settlement with India would have to still consider water distribution of the Indus system. For Pakistan water issues remain an unfinished business. For India, the treaty is done and dusted, and any grievances have to be addressed through the Permanent Indus Commission (PIC), a mechanism developed under the IWT to resolve disputes.

Another question frequently asked on the division of the rivers, is why India allowed the western rivers to go exclusively to Pakistan except for certain nominal and specified uses by

India? Often India's magnanimity and generosity are projected while answering this. It is possible that India did not want to be seen as an unconcerned and unreasonable upper riparian. India also paid about 62 million pounds sterling for new construction works in Pakistan, while the World Bank and the US along with other aid-giving countries mobilized the rest. Goodwill aside, India was equally pragmatic in its approach to sharing the rivers. It needed exclusive rights over the eastern rivers for the construction of the Bhakra Nangal dam and the Rajasthan Canal, both of which were crucial to India's development programs. Otherwise, Pakistan could have raised lower riparian restrictions and thwarted India's plans. Ramaswamy Lyer, former Secretary to the Government of India in the Ministry of Water Resources says that "...the price paid for this was a substantial sacrifice of rights over the western rivers. The difficulties that this would lead to in due course, and the discontent that this would cause in Jammu & Kashmir, were perhaps not anticipated."

CURRENT DYNAMICS OF WATER, ENERGY AND SECURITY

Judging by recent political statements from Pakistan, water issues are being pitched politically and couched increasingly in the language of security vis-à-vis India. Pakistan's motivations are not too difficult to decipher. First, in order to keep the enmity with India as its foremost policy issue, water becomes the existential driver. It pays political dividends for the Pakistani establishment to focus its lens on India being the upper riparian "aggressor", "stealing" the waters of the Indus system, and a country with "malevolent" intentions. So when President Asif Ali Zardari's article in *The Washington Post* on January 28, 2009 warned: "The water crisis in Pakistan is directly linked to relations with India. Its resolution could prevent an environmental catastrophe in South Asia, but failure to do so could fuel the fires of discontent that may lead to extremism and terrorism", or when Sardar Aseff Ali, a former Foreign Minister and presently the Prime Minister's adviser on education, says that "water is a sensitive issue and if India continues to deny Pakistan its due share, it can lead to a war between the two countries," the purpose is to whip up anti-Indian sentiments.

Water is an emotive issue. It is a mobilizing factor and, unfortunately, even those who argue for cordial existence with India are unlikely to take an objective view. More importantly, by aggressively accusing India of "stealing" the waters, the current establishment is trying to absolve itself of its questionable water management policies and the inter-provincial water dispute between Punjab and Sindh. Projecting water as a flashpoint directly benefits the political-military class by drawing international attention. Pakistan's articulation of its lower riparian concerns tends to get a sympathetic international audience. Not surprisingly, water experts like John Briscoe, who is currently Gordon McKay Professor of Environmental Engineering at Harvard University, speak more from the lower riparian perspective, often but not intentionally ignoring the upper riparian accommodation. Briscoe's article "War and Peace on the Indus" published in South Asian Idea puts the onus on India, being the regional hegemon, to show restraint on the Indus basin, ignoring the fact that India has been far more accommodating than any upper riparian in the world. Clearly, Pakistan wants to re-frame a new set of lower-upper riparian dynamics by articulating its 'water rights' under the provisions of the treaty and asking India for explanation. It is an effort to put India on the defensive.

The way ahead

Notwithstanding the bellicose tones and the projecting of water as a flashpoint, there is far greater value to sharing the benefits of water, and that needs to be structured in the bilateral relations. Both India and Pakistan are in need of energy. For Pakistan hydropower is its second largest source of electricity. In spite of the hydrological gradient that favors rapid flow of waters, particularly in the northern region, hydropower generation in Pakistan has been hampered by administrative problems, aging infrastructure, and significant inter-provincial rivalry. Dams and storages for multipurpose uses are politically sensitive in Pakistan and tend to easily become polarized. For example, the 3,500 MW Kalabagh dam, though an engineering marvel, has created a deep social rift. Punjab, seen as a preferred state, advocates large dams and is a prime beneficiary of projects like Kalabagh, but for provinces like Khyber-Pakhtoonkhwa (earlier North West Frontier Province) it is a bane since large pieces of the land would be submerged. Sindh equally fears being deprived of its share of water. This goes to prove that the Inter-Provincial Agreement of 1991 on water sharing has completely failed. It is ironic that the concerns raised by Pakistan on the Baglihar and Kishanganga projects with India are quite identical to those raised by Sind on the Kalabagh dam. Pakistan needs multipurpose reservoirs for hydroelectric power generation, as it ensures the availability of energy on a sustainable basis and at affordable prices.

India has a much higher ratio of storage to water flow as compared to Pakistan on the Indus basin. Estimates suggest that while Pakistan has only achieved 11% storage capacity, India on its allocated eastern rivers has accomplished 52% and is utilizing almost 80% of hydroelectricity potential. In comparison Pakistan has only managed to harness 5,200 MW against a potential of 38,000 MW on the rivers. The planning commission and implementing bodies for some strange reasons have delayed the development of hydropower. This has only given India the 'priority' advantage, as the IWT stipulates that the country which first completes its project on a river will get complete rights of that river.

Jammu-Kashmir is a key factor in the water debate. The population at the time of the treaty was 3.5 million, which now has grown three-fold. The demand for irrigation and electricity is critical to the agricultural sector. In spite of its vast hydroelectric power potential, which varies from a high estimate of 15,000 MW to a low of 7,487 MW, the state of Jammu-Kashmir remains industrially backward. The people and leadership in Jammu-Kashmir are largely critical of the IWT. They feel that the restrictions placed on the use of water resources by the Treaty have become a hamper to economic development. The IWT gives a virtual veto to Pakistan to scuttle proposals for harnessing the hydroelectric power potential of the western rivers. The restrictive provisions under the Treaty allow for only 10% of hydroelectric potential in Jammu-Kashmir and 40% of cultivable land.

Remarkably, the means to overcome some of the predicted water woes and the energy crisis between India and Pakistan are farsightedly laid out in the IWT itself. Article VII is about 'Future Cooperation' and opens up a range of possibilities through "optimum development of the rivers" by "mutual agreement to the fullest possible extent." It relates to "installing hydrological observation stations" and "carrying out such new drainage works as may be required...." It also states "...the two parties may, by mutual agreement, co-operate in undertaking engineering works on the rivers." However, if such engineering work "affects the other party materially, it shall notify the other party of its plans and shall supply such data relating to the work as may be available...." Keeping in mind the 'optimum development,' new dams should be selected in ways that take into account the 'health of the rivers,' which includes ecological considerations, sediment loads, and flow regimes. Often the social and ecological costs are not fully considered. A completely new orientation to dams needs to be developed involving greater public participation.

In order to energize riparian relations, continued dialogue is crucial. The public discourse on water issues between India and Pakistan, and by association the development of energy and power, is far too narrow and is largely based on misconception. In spite of the detailed permissive and restrictive provisions of the treaty, water figures and facts have tended to be shrouded in secrecy. Transparency will help in clearing the air and will allow for shared benefits on the waters, building ideas of 'water peace' rather than 'water wars.' The negotiators to the treaty were visionary and had initially approached the dispute through joint development. 50 years of the IWT have not seen such synchronization, but the next 50 years should. The thrust should be the sharing of data and joint research on climate change mitigation, and joint development of the vast hydroelectric and irrigation potential of the western rivers for mutual benefit. There is much sense and sensibility in the IWT that cannot be easily dismissed. Three cheers to it!

UPSTREAM COUNTRIES AND THE NEED FOR ENERGY

Downstream countries depend on upstream countries for water for irrigation purposes, but for the upstream countries, lack of cooperation when it comes to water management is an energy concern. As exporters of water to downstream countries for irrigation, who on their side are rich in oil and gas, Tajikistan and Kyrgyzstan on the other hand are struggling to meet their energy needs for electricity, especially in the cold winter months. They have tried to cope by arranging barter deals with their western neighbors, trading summer water releases and hydropower for coal and gas for fall and winter use. However, as downstream nations began to charge for oil and natural gas imports, the two countries began to alter their hydroelectric facilities' water flows, increasingly hoarding it in the growing months for winter release to generate electricity rather than pay ever rising energy import bills, raising political tensions with their downstream neighbors.

Kyrgyzstan and the Kambarata-2 hydroelectric Plan

In recent years, Kyrgyzstan has been cut short in not having enough power for the winter. Barter arrangements with neighboring countries have also broken down. The responsible intergovernmental bodies for water management is the Ministry of Energy and the Ministry of Natural Resources and the government has embarked on reforms to improve management and transparency in the water and energy sector, that gives hope that workable solutions may be feasible. In 1998, Kyrgyzstan and Uzbekistan signed an agreement to manage the Syr Darya water basin. This agreement governed the Toktogol complex, which permitted Kyrgyzstan to generate electricity. To prevent damaging water releases, a number of barter agreements were created to ship natural gas and coal to Kyrgyzstan in the winter. But these barter agreements were not followed and Kyrgyzstan sought to charge the downstream nations the full use of the water, which caused protests from the downstream countries. The barter agreements could never tackle the core question of water allocation and how to pay for the aging Soviet era dam and irrigation system. There remains a fundamental disagreement over the pricing of water versus other natural resources, which were sold in the region for full market value. Leaders of different countries were also suspicious of each other and did not trust the water agreements, which were promoted by international agencies like the World Bank.

Kyrgyzstan's parliament in 2001 passed a law on water pricing to the downstream countries, maintaining that water was property of the Kyrgyz state. The law also stipulated that downstream countries should pay for the maintenance of the dam and canal system. Uzbekistan and Kazakhstan objected saying it violated international law, and Kyrgyzstan eventually backed down from insisting that downstream countries pay for the full price of the river water. In 2008, Kazakhstan, Tajikistan and Kyrgyzstan signed a new set of barter agreements on supplies of water, oil and coal. The influence of the agreement was limited since Uzbekistan opted out. To complicate matters, Uzbekistan and Kazakhstan pulled out of the regional electrical grid in 2009.

In 2007, Kyrgyzstan resumed construction of the Kambarata-2 project, abandoned in the 1990s. The project was able to draw on a $300 million loan from Russia to help revive the country's economy and infrastructure. The first unit of the Kambarata-2 hydroelectric project will allow Kyrgyzstan to produce an additional 500 million to 700 million kilowatt hours per year of electricity. The country currently generates about 14 billion kilowatt-hours annually, and the increase in power production is destined for export to Russia and China. Kyrgyzstan's ambitions to control the flow of its rivers in order to generate more hydroelectric power are of particular concern to Uzbekistan, its immediate neighbor to the west and the most populous post-Soviet republic in Central Asia. Uzbekistan relies on rivers that originate or pass through Kyrgyzstan and its other mountainous neighbor, Tajikistan, to irrigate its arid cotton fields and farmland.

The Kambarata project is only the first of several projects planned along the Naryn River, which rises in the Tien Shan Mountains and is dammed at Toktogul, the largest reservoir in

Kyrgyzstan, before running on to merge with another river to become the Syr Darya. The power plant has received critique from people inside Kyrgyzstan, especially energy experts who argue that the Kambarata dams are too expensive. Instead, Kyrgyzstan must look into developing its coal industry. Both Kyrgyzstan and Tajikistan, however, lack public debate over how water resources must be managed, as leaders make these decisions without the interference of public opinion.

Tajikistan and the Rogun Dam Controversy

Tajikistan is also suffering from chronic mismanagement of water resources. This is especially evident during the winter months, when the country faces electricity shortages and severe cold and darkness. In Tajikistan, the Ministry of Melioration and Water Resource as well as the Ministry of Energy and Industry are the responsible intergovernmental bodies for water management. However, the government and the Tajik Central Bank have come under international scrutiny after the International Monetary Fund (IMF) scandal. The IMF demanded that Tajikistan repay nearly $48 million after it accused the Tajik Central Bank of not providing accurate information about the country's financial state. This led to investors being more cautious about investing in hydroelectric projects. These projects have been a source of tension with Uzbekistan because it claims water supplies will be severely reduced.

One of the more controversial dam projects is the building of the Rogun Dam. Construction of this project began in 1976, but was frozen after the collapse of the Soviet Union. In February 2007 Tajikistan, with support from Russia announced the plan to complete the dam. This would allow the Tajik Republic to overcome its energy crisis through increasing electricity production as well as decrease its dependence on energy imports from Uzbekistan. It is also seen as contributing to the stabilization of Afghanistan through electricity exports. However, Uzbekistan is sternly against any new construction arguing that it will devastate their water intensive economy. Further, they warn against potential environmental damage, particularly to the Aral

Sea. Tajikistan sees this opposition to reflect fears that the project will decrease Uzbekistan's leverage over Tajikistan. Energy security is important to both parties, on the one side Uzbekistan wants to retain its leverage and on the other side Tajikistan is seeking greater energy independence.

Downstream Countries and the Need for Irrigation

Uzbekistan is the largest consumer of water resources in the region, which is used for agriculture. Uzbek farmers have been using the water flows from Amu Darya and Syr Darya to irrigate their water-intensive cotton fields since ancient times. Recently there has been an inconsistent supply of water. The year of 2000 and 2001 marked the most severe water-shortage in Uzbekistan recorded over the last two decades devastating their economy. The country is moving away from a highly centralized water management structure to a decentralized system. However, these efforts have not been completely successful. The Main Water Management Department (MWMD) under the Ministry of Agriculture and Water Resources is responsible for the development and management of irrigation and drainage infrastructure. There is ten Basin Irrigation System Authorities (BISAs) responsible for the management of inter-farm irrigation and drainage systems, financed from the state budget. However, the sector is facing financial crisis and is unable to make the necessary investments in the deteriorating sector. In 2000, Uzbekistan gave Water Users Association (WUAs) a management role over irrigation systems to address the hierarchical management of the sector. One of the last institutional reforms was in 2003, changing from an administrative territorial-water management to hydrologic basin water management. Yet, these WUAs have internal problems stemming from favoritism and their role in resolving conflicts and imposing sanctions.

Turkmenistan faces many of the same problems as its downstream neighbor Uzbekistan stemming from a high dependency on water intensive cotton production. The water sector in Turkmenistan is represented by a complex governance system comprising a number of ministries and institutions. The key specialized governmental ministries responsible for water resource management and protection are the Ministry of Water Resources and the Ministry of Nature Protection, but very often authorities share joint responsibilities and functions. In addition to the complicated management structure, there is a lack of interaction and coordination among the ministries and institutions of the water sector.

Considerable efforts have been made in the recent years to modernize the existing infrastructure; still a lot has yet to be implemented. Because functions of water resource management are divided between a number of government agencies, priorities and objectives of these authorities are sometimes different. This makes coordination between them quite complicated. The mismanagement of scarce water resources has severe consequences for the agricultural sector.

As agriculture in Turkmenistan is almost totally dependent on irrigation, proper management of the region's water resources is essential for this industry. One of the major challenges for the management of water in Turkmenistan is that increasing food production is one of the major goals of Turkmenistan's national agricultural policy. This means that irrigation development and agricultural intensification have to be achieved in a general context of limited water resources, creating a need for a more efficient water management system.

Turkmenistan and Uzbekistan have developed a higher dependency on cotton production than Kazakhstan. However, Kazakhstan is also very dependent on irrigation for its agricultural sector which consumes over 70 percent of total supply in the country. A significant problem is that a large amount of the water is lost through inefficient use, leakage due to old infrastructure and pollution. These problems for the most part do not stem from supply shortages but from poor water management. All around the country, almost half the pumps and public taps are turned off permanently because they are worn out or sub-standard. The intergovernmental bodies responsible for water resources management are like the other downstream countries fragmented, under-funded and poorly governed, and budget and staffing cuts has had a dramatic effect on the ability of the authorities to manage water.

The Government of Kazakhstan has embarked on a water resources management project aimed at strengthening the water management organizations within the country by instituting the practice of Integrated Water Resource Management (IWRM).

Aral Sea Crisis

If there is a particular issue that puts a face on the ill-planned Soviet development policies of the past it is the Aral Sea, one of the worst man-made environmental disasters in the world. The crisis first began in the 1950s when the Syr Darya and Amu Darya rivers, which feed the Aral Sea, were diverted as part of the Soviet Union's grand agricultural scheme. Large areas were set aside for cotton production, which meant more water for irrigation and less to replenish the Aral Sea, since it was regarded as expendable. At one point the Aral Sea was the fourth-largest landlocked body of water in the world, occupying an area of about 66,000km and a volume of 1,062 km· Now it has split into two separate bodies: Little Aral Sea, which is in Kazakhstan, and Big Aral Sea, which is in Uzbekistan.

The grand scheme is now in disrepair and continued mismanagement is not addressing the waste of water resources. Further contributing to the Aral Sea's demise is the ongoing usage of the poor agricultural practices from the Soviet Union era. Currently over 80 percent of the land used for crop growing is saline, which requires more water to be used to flood the fields in preparation for the spring planting season.

This water then goes back downstream and is recycled again, further adding to the water and soil's high salt concentration. These poor agricultural practices are mostly done by the downstream states and will only continue due to their high population growth rates and the need to produce large amounts of food. These states are also resistant to diversifying their agricultural sectors to include less water-intensive crops, as they feel any changes to this system will negatively affect their economies.

Climate change is projected to have a negative effect on the crisis, as increasing temperatures and natural evaporation rates are causing the flow of the source rivers to decrease, which means even less water is available to replenish the Aral Sea. A decrease in rainy days has led the coastline to recede and speed up the rate of desiccation, thus exposing toxic salts on the seabed that are from the excessive use of fertilizers and pesticides.

These salts are being carried by dust storms and causing high rates of tuberculosis, anemia, hepatitis, respiratory and eye diseases, and throat cancer for the area's inhabitants. These dust storms are the result of the Aral Sea no longer providing the moisture block needed to prevent these winds from occurring. Also being affected is the livelihood of those who once depended on the Aral Sea as a source of income. Most of the fishing and shipping industry jobs that existed because of the Aral Sea have since been lost and the Sea's high salinity level has led to the extinction of various types of flora and fauna once native to the area.

Efforts to Save the Aral Sea

In 1993, the five heads of state came together to create the International Fund for saving the Aral Sea (IFAS), an organization designed to facilitate regional cooperation in order to address this crisis. IFAS was also created to attract funds from the five states needed to carry out projects and inform the international community about the crisis and gain its support in addressing it. Since its inception, IFAS has partaken in a number of projects, such as the 1993-1997 Aral Sea Basin Programme.

This project's four main objectives focused on stabilizing and rehabilitating the surrounding area, developing better water management strategies, and increasing the ability for regional and national organizations to advance their projects. Another key initiative was the 1998 and 2002 Water and Environment Management Project.

IFAS, in collaboration with the World Bank, attempted to create both a regional and individual strategy with the help of a group of neutral experts. Although this initiative's first two attempts were unsuccessful, there have been discussions on reviving it in order to achieve the goals it set out to do.

Since 1992 Kazakhstan has been attempting to save the Little Aral Sea by building a dam in order to preserve it and bring it back to its former levels. For many years the dam's poor planning and the usage of sand for building material caused it to breach a number of times. But international support from the World Bank helped fund the building of the Kokaralsk Dam, which was completed in 2005. In just a few years the sea level has risen, salinity has been reduced, and fish species have flourished, which has revived the area's fishing industry.

Although some attempts were successful in addressing the Aral Sea crisis, not all have met the same result, especially those by the international community. Analyst Erika Weinthal criticized the international community for responding to the Aral Sea as either a water crisis (World Bank, UNDP, UNEP) or as a water/energy crisis (USAID) but not as a crisis of agriculture. The five states and the international community have rejected any dramatic reform to the agricultural sector in the downstream countries. This move alone could have had the most impact on this crisis, but the political power of the cotton producers is too entrenched to allow this necessary change to finally occur.

The need to modify these agricultural practices due to its effects on the Aral Sea is even more evident now that Uzbekistan's Big Aral Sea is splitting into the Big Aral East and Big Aral West. It is apparent a complete overhaul of the agricultural sector cannot occur with how much these states economically depend on it, but they, along with the international community, need to find a balance between economic needs and the environment before it leads to more problems.

The case of the Aral Sea is one, if not the best, example of the effect that lack of cooperation is having on the region and the disregard the Soviet planners had for the environment while organizing their "grand" scheme. It is interesting to note that once the Aral Sea problem was first realized, the Soviet Union's plan to address it included diverting water from Siberia into the Aral Sea instead of the Arctic. But this would have led to yet another problem and continued the cycle of mistreating nature for human gains. Even though various attempts have been made by the Central Asian states and the international community to save and revive it, the Aral Sea will never return to its former state and will forever be a constant reminder to the region of its Soviet Union legacy.

HYDROGEOLOGY

Hydrogeology (*hydro-* meaning water, and *-geology* meaning the study of the Earth) is the area of geology that deals with the distribution and movement of ground-water in the soil and rocks of the Earth's crust, (commonly in aquifers). The term geohydrology is often used interchangeably. Some make the minor distinction between a hydrologist or engineer applying themselves to geology (geohydrology), and a geologist applying themselves to hydrology (hydrogeology).

Hydrogeology is an interdisciplinary subject; it can be difficult to account fully for the chemical, physical, biological and even legal interactions between soil, water, nature and society. The study of the interaction between ground-water movement and geology can be quite complex. Ground-water does not always flow in the subsurface down-hill following the surface topography; ground-water follows pressure gradients (flow from high pressure to low) often following fractures and conduits in circuitous paths. Taking into account the interplay of the different facets of a multi-component system often requires knowledge in several diverse fields at both the experimental and theoretical levels. The following is a more traditional introduction to the methods and nomenclature of saturated subsurface hydrology, or simply hydrogeology.

Hydrogeology in Relation to other Fields

Hydrogeology, as stated above, is a branch of the earth sciences dealing with the flow of water through aquifers and other shallow porous media (typically less than 450 m or 1,500 ft below the land surface.) The very shallow flow of water in the subsurface (the upper 3 m or 10 ft) is pertinent to the fields of soil science, agriculture and civil engineering, as well as to hydrogeology.

The general flow of fluids (water, hydrocarbons, geothermal fluids, etc.) in deeper formations is also a concern of geologists, geophysicists and petroleum geologists. Ground-water is a slow-moving, viscous fluid (with a Reynolds number less than unity); many of the empirically derived laws of ground-water flow can be alternately derived in fluid mechanics from the special case of Stokes flow (viscosity and pressure terms, but no inertial term).

The mathematical relationships used to describe the flow of water through porous media are the diffusion and Laplace equations, which have applications in many diverse fields. Steady ground-water flow (Laplace equation) has been simulated using electrical, elastic and heat conduction analogies. Transient ground-water flow is analogous to the diffusion of heat in a solid, therefore some solutions to hydrological problems have been adapted from heat transfer literature. Traditionally, the movement of ground-water has been studied separately from surface water, climatology, and even the chemical and microbiological aspects of hydrogeology (the processes are uncoupled). As the field of hydrogeology matures, the strong interactions between ground-water, surface water, water chemistry, soil moisture and even climate are becoming more clear.

For example: Aquifer drawdown or overdrafting and the pumping of fossil water increases the total amount of water within the hydrosphere subject to transpiration and evaporation processes, thereby causing accretion in water vapour and cloud cover, the primary absorbers of infrared radiation in the earth's atmosphere. Adding water to the system has a forcing effect on the whole earth system. An accurate estimate of the climatic forcing effect due to this hydrogeological fact is yet to be quantified.

Definitions and Material Properties

One of the main tasks a hydrogeologist typically performs is the prediction of future behaviour of an aquifer system, based on analysis of past and present observations. Some hypothetical, but characteristic questions asked would be:

- Can the aquifer support another subdivision?
- Will the river dry up if the farmer doubles his irrigation?
- Did the chemicals from the dry cleaning facility travel through the aquifer to my well and make me sick?
- Will the plume of effluent leaving my neighbor's septic system flow to my drinking water well?

Most of these questions can be addressed through simulation of the hydrologic system (using numerical models or analytic equations). Accurate simulation of the aquifer system requires knowledge of the aquifer properties and boundary conditions. Therefore a common task of the hydrogeologist is determining aquifer properties using aquifer tests.

In order to further characterize aquifers and aquitards some primary and derived physical properties are introduced below. Aquifers are broadly classified as being either confined or unconfined (water table aquifers), and either saturated or unsaturated; the type of aquifer affects what properties control the flow of water in that medium (e.g., the release of water from storage for confined aquifers is related to the storativity, while it is related to the specific yield for unconfined aquifers).

Hydraulic Head

Changes in hydraulic head (h) are the driving force which causes water to move from one place to another. It is composed of pressure head ($\o$) and elevation head (z). The head gradient is the change in hydraulic head per length of flowpath, and appears in Darcy's law as being proportional to the discharge.

Hydraulic head is a directly measurable property that can take on any value (because of the arbitrary datum involved in the z term); ϕ can be measured with a pressure transducer (this value can be negative, e.g., suction, but is positive in saturated aquifers), and z can be measured relative to a surveyed datum (typically the top of the well casing). Commonly, in wells tapping unconfined aquifers the water level in a well is used as a proxy for hydraulic head, assuming there is no vertical gradient of pressure. Often only *changes* in hydraulic head through time are needed, so the constant elevation head term can be left out.

A record of hydraulic head through time at a well is a hydrograph or, the changes in hydraulic head recorded during the pumping of a well in a test are called drawdown.

Porosity

Porosity (n) is a directly measurable aquifer property; it is a fraction between 0 and 1 indicating the amount of pore space between unconsolidated soil particles or within a fractured rock. Typically, the majority of ground-water (and anything dissolved in it) moves through the porosity available to flow (sometimes called effective porosity). Permeability is an expression of the connectedness of the pores. For instance, an unfractured rock unit may have a high *porosity* (it has lots of *holes* between its constituent grains), but a low *permeability* (none of the pores are connected). An example of this phenomenon is pumice, which, when in its unfractured state, can make a poor aquifer.

Porosity does not directly affect the distribution of hydraulic head in an aquifer, but it has a very strong effect on the migration of dissolved contaminants, since it affects ground-water flow velocities through an inversely proportional relationship.

Water Content

Water content is also a directly measurable property; it is the fraction of the total rock which is filled with liquid water. This is also a fraction between 0 and 1, but it must also be less than or equal to the total porosity. The water content is very important in vadose zone hydrology, where the hydraulic conductivity is a strongly nonlinear function of water content; this complicates the solution of the unsaturated ground-water flow equation.

Hydraulic Conductivity

Hydraulic conductivity (K) and transmissivity (T) are indirect aquifer properties (they cannot be measured directly). T is the K integrated over the vertical thickness (b) of the aquifer ($T=Kb$

when K is constant over the entire thickness). These properties are measures of an aquifer's ability to transmit water. Intrinsic permeability is a secondary medium property which does not depend on the viscosity and density of the fluid (K and T are specific to water); it is used more in the petroleum industry.

Specific Storage and Specific Yield

Specific storage (S_s) and its depth-integrated equivalent, storativity ($S=S_s b$), are indirect aquifer properties (they cannot be measured directly); they indicate the amount of ground-water released from storage due to a unit depressurization of a confined aquifer. They are fractions between 0 and 1.

Specific yield (S_y) is also a ratio between 0 and 1 (S_y d" porosity) and indicates the amount of water released due to drainage from lowering the water table in an unconfined aquifer.

The value for specific yield is less than the value for porosity because some water will remain in the medium even after drainage due to molecular forces. Often the porosity or effective porosity is used as an upper bound to the specific yield. Typically S_y is orders of magnitude larger than S_s.

Contaminant Transport Properties

Often we are interested in how the moving ground-water water will move dissolved contaminants around (the sub-field of contaminant hydrogeology).

The contaminants can be man-made (e.g., petroleum products, nitrate or Chromium) or naturally occurring (e.g., arsenic, salinity). Besides needing to understand where the ground-water is flowing, based on the other hydrologic properties discussed above, there are additional aquifer properties which affect how dissolved contaminants move with ground-water.

Hydrodynamic Dispersion

Hydrodynamic dispersivity is an empirical factor which quantifies how much contaminants stray away from the path of the ground-water which is carrying it. Some of the contaminants will be "behind" or "ahead" the mean ground-water, giving rise to a longitudinal dispersivity, and some will be "to the sides of" the pure advective ground-water flow, leading to a transverse dispersivity.

Dispersion in ground-water is due to the fact that each water "particle", passing beyond a soil particle, must choose where to go, whether left or right or up or down, so that the water "particles" (and their solute) are gradually spread in all directions around the mean path.

This is the "microscopic" mechanism, on the scale of soil particles. More important, on long distances, can be the macroscopic inhomogeneities of the aquifer, which can have regions of larger or smaller permeability, so that some water can find a preferential path in one direction, some other in a different direction, so that the contaminant can be spread in a completely irregular way, like in a (three-dimensional) delta of a river.

Dispersivity is actually a factor which represents our *lack of information* about the system we are simulating. There are many small details about the aquifer which are being averaged when using a macroscopic approach (e.g., tiny beds of gravel and clay in sand aquifers), they manifest themselves as an *apparent* dispersivity. Because of this, α is often claimed to be dependent on the length scale of the problem — the dispersivity found for transport through 1 m^3 of aquifer is different than that for transport through 1 cm^3 of the same aquifer material.

Molecular Diffusion

Diffusion is a fundamental physical phenomenon, by which Einstein explained Brownian motion, which describes the random thermal movement of molecules and small particles in gases and liquids. It is an important phenomenon for small distances (it is essential for the achievement of thermodinamic equilibria), but, as the time necessary to cover a distance by diffusion is proportional to the square of the distance itself, it is ineffective for spreading a solute over macroscopic distances. The diffusion coefficient, D, is typically quite small, and its effect can often be considered negligible (unless ground-water flow velocities are extremely low, as they are in clay aquitards).

It is important not to confuse diffusion with dispersion, as the former is a physical phenomenon and the latter is an empirical factor which is cast into a similar form as diffusion, because we already know how to solve that problem.

Retardation by Adsorption

The retardation factor is another very important feature that make the motion of the contaminant to deviate from the average ground-water motion. It is analogous to the retardation factor of chromatography.

Unlike diffusion and dispersion, which simply spread the contaminant, the retardation factor changes its *global average velocity*, so that it can be much slower than that of water. This is due to a chemico-physical effect: the adsorption to the soil, which holds the contaminant back and does not allow it to progress until the quantity corresponding to the chemical adsorption equilibrium has been adsorbed. This effect is particularly important for less soluble contaminants, which thus can move even hundreds or thousands times slower than water. The effect of this phenomenon is that only more soluble species can cover long distances. The retardation factor depends on the chemical nature of both the contaminant and the aquifer.

BAGLIHAR HYDROELECTRIC PLANT - ISSUE BETWEEN PAKISTAN AND INDIA

The Indus Waters Treaty (IWT), between Pakistan and India, was signed in 1960, following stoppage of water by India (upper riparian) to Pakistan (lower riparian) in 1948. Each country was allocated three rivers for almost exclusive use with some exceptions. Amongst the exceptions, India was allowed construction of Run-of-River (ROR) Power Plants on rivers allocated to Pakistan.

In 1992, India proposed to construct a run of river Baglihar Hydroelectric Power Plant, on the River Chenab, which is one of the rivers allocated to Pakistan. Within three months, Pakistan objected that the design of the free board (empty space over the full reservoir level) and the pondage (operational storage) enabled

India to store more water than permissible under the designed criteria given in the IWT. Pakistan also objected to the location of power tunnels and the sluice spillway, which allowed India capability to exercise control over waters of River Chenab. The Permanent Indus Commission, created under the IWT, could not resolve the issues. In the mean time, in the year 2000, India unilaterally started implementation of the project. Thus on Pakistan's request a Neutral Expert (N.E) was appointed in 2005 through the good offices of the World Bank.The Neutral Expert determined, on 12 February 2007, that modifications were needed in the design of free board, power tunnels and pondage but allowed India to retain the sluice spillway. Pakistan was aggrieved that the N.E misinterpreted the IWT in respect of the sluice spillway, therefore, it approached the Court of Arbitration (CoA) in the subsequent case of Kishenganga Hydro Electric Project. The CoA ruled in favor of Pakistan. Now it is to be seen whether India complies to this decision in future plants!

NATURAL, HISTORIC, ECONOMIC, REGIONAL, AND POLITICAL FRAMEWORK

The Baglihar Hydro Electric Plant (BHP) with 900 MW capacity is located on River Chenab in the territory disputed by India and Pakistan, namely Jammu and Kashmir, about 147 km from line of control between Pakistan and Jammu and Kashmir. The River Chenab is one of the tributaries of the Indus. The headwaters of the Indus rise in the glaciers of the Himalaya Hindu Kush (HKH) often called the "water towers". River Indus flows from the Tibetan Plateau in western China and after crossing into the Kashmir region and traversing Pakistan's territory, flows out into the Arabian Sea. The Indus River has six tributaries,, Chenab, Ravi, Sutlej, Jhelum, Beas in the East flowing through Indian and/or Indian held Kashmir and the Kabul River in the West flowing through Afghanistan.

ECONOMIC DEPENDENCE ON WATER

Pakistan has world's largest contiguous canal irrigation system dependent solely on waters of Indus Basin shared with

India and Afghanistan. About 64% of it's population depends upon agriculture. Water is a critical input for agriculture to meet food and fiber requirements, drinking water, sanitation, industry, environment, etc of Pakistan. Agriculture contribute about 21-23% of GDP. 80% of rural work force engaged in agriculture. It is responsible for 60 to 70% exports of the country. The country has over 60,000 MW hydroelectric power generation capacity which can produce electricity at a fraction of the cost of generation of power from fossil fuels. Water is truly the life line of Pakistan.

Political Environments

The Indian Sub-Continent was partitioned in two independent countries, Pakistan and India in August 1947 ending the British colonial rule. The partition took place in an atmosphere of animosity, as Indian Congress Party was not in favor of partition, and resulted in ethnic/communal riots killing millions of people in one of the largest migration of people in the history of the world.

Since Partition, Pakistan and India have a checkered relationship history. The countries have fought three major wars besides many border skirmishes. Reports of border clashes appear quite frequently. The major bone of contention between the two countries is the issue of the disputed territory of Jammu and Kashmir, part of which is occupied by India and the rest is the Independent Azad Kashmir— an autonomous administrative territory of Pakistan. The UN had 1948 passed a resolution that a plebiscite be held in the area to decide accession of Jammu & Kashmir to India or Pakistan. However, this could not be done for 66 years because of India's unwillingness to comply with the UN Resolution. At some times it appeared that the two governments were making political efforts to come closer, but it was found impossible for them to make any compromises on their stances on the Kashmir issue. Added to that had been fanatic terrorist activities on both sides and fanning of negative sentiments by some political parties, organizations and some factions of media. Tension, blame throwing and mistrust continues through with amplitudes varying with time.

HISTORICAL BACKGROUND OF INDUS WATERS TREATY (IWT)

The new geographic boundaries after the partition in 1947 cut across the Indus Basin boundaries. As Indus river and its tributaries, Jhelum, Chenab, Ravi, Sutlej and Beas were flowing through Indian territory or Indian held Kashmir, India became the upper riparian and Pakistan became the lower riparian. All the upstream control structures on the rivers fell on the Indian side of the divide. The Boundary Commission for partition had proceeded in good faith that the pre-partition arrangement for of sharing of water will be continued by the two new governments. However, just one day after the Arbitral Tribunal for settling issues arising out of partition between Pakistan and India ceased to exist, on 1 April 1948, India cut off the supplies of water to Pakistan in every canal flowing from the Indian Territory. This affected 1.7 million acres of land, cattle and other livestock and endangered millions of human beings dependent on the waters of these canal systems. Mutual Trust (whatever was left of it after the bloody partition in 1947) was a major casualty!

Following this episode, efforts were made by the governments of the two countries to come to some mutual agreement for sustainable water sharing arrangements but to no avail. Eventually, a third party, the World Bank, became involved and 12 years later Indus Waters Treaty was signed in 1960 under the aegis of the World Bank.

The process of evolution of the Treaty entailed initial attempts to harness the potential of Indus Basin through mutual cooperation for managing the shared water resources, but the only feasible settlement was found to be division of waters. Pakistan was unwilling to allow means of control of flow of waters to India in the wake of the incidence of stoppage of water flowing to Pakistan in 1948, while India wanted sovereignty over waters flowing through its territory. Fortunately, it was possible to exclusively allocate three rivers, each, to divide the water between the two countries to overcome the impasse. India was allocated Sutlej, Ravi and Beas Rivers (called the Eastern Rivers) and Pakistan was allocated Indus, Chenab and Jhelum Rivers (called the Western Rivers). Consequently, Pakistan had to divert waters of the Western Rivers to the command areas of the three Eastern Rivers which were feeding vast tracts of agriculture land in Pakistan.

SALIENT FEATURES OF THE INDUS WATERS TREATY

India was allowed some use of waters of the Western Rivers for domestic, non-consumptive, agricultural uses and generation of power based on Run-of-River (ROR) Power Plants as well as storages quantified in the Treaty. Likewise Pakistan was also allowed some limited use of water of Eastern Rivers for domestic and Agriculture uses (but not for power generation). Design and operational criteria was laid down in respect of ROR, storage based power plants and other hydraulic infrastructure allowed under the Treaty so as to ensure that India would "let flow" waters of Western Rivers without any "interference" beyond the exceptions allowed under the Treaty.

Specific river-wise ceilings were given in the IWT for the categories of General, Power and Flood Storages and that which is incidental to a barrage on Jhelum Main and Chenab Main Rivers. The Treaty also envisaged that if either Party plans to construct any engineering work which would cause interference with the waters of any of the Rivers then it will inform the other party giving it due chance to evaluate impacts. In respect of new RoR projects by India on Western Rivers, it envisaged that India shall provide prescribed information six months in advance of the beginning of construction of river works connected with the Plant and Pakistan was allowed three months, from the receipt of information, to communicate objections, if any.

A Permanent Indus Commission was formed under the Treaty with two Commissioners, one from each country to "serve as the regular channel of communication on all matters relating to the implementation of the Treaty". It's functions inter-alia included, "to make every effort to settle promptly, in accordance with the provisions of Article IX (1) [of the Treaty], any question arising thereunder". The Treaty also provided a mechanism for

Settlement of Differences and Disputes. Briefly, in simple words, it envisaged that the Permanent Commission shall first try to resolve "question" arising of interpretation of Treaty or breach of Treaty. If the Permanent Commission fails to resolve the matter, it can be referred to a Neutral Expert for engineering issues (called Points of Difference") or a Court of Arbitration (CoA) for legal matters (called Dispute") appointed in accordance with the provisions of the Treaty.

Except for the issue on Wullar Barrage (a barrage over river Jhelum), no other issue has arisen so far with regards to storages. The Wullar Barrage called Tulbul Navigation Project in India, was justified by India as a navigation project.

This envisaged a barrage on the outflow point of Wullar Lake on river Jhelum, a Western River. The storage incidental to the barrage was 320,000 MAF of water as against specific restriction of 10,000 MAF in the Treaty. The work on the project has been suspended since 1987.

Most of the post Treaty issues relate to Run of River Plants (RoR) constructed (or proposed) by India. The Treaty did not envisage any ceiling for the number or capacities of the projects as long as those met the design criteria/ restrictions laid down in the Treaty.

Issues/ objections raised by Pakistan on RoR projects had mainly been that India was not strictly adhering to the design and operational criteria/restrictions laid down in the IWT. On the other hand, India had rejected Pakistan's stance and started projects unilaterally, without settling the issues.

The Issue of Baglihar Hydroelectric Project (BHP)

Information about the Baglihar Dam, on the River Chenab, was communicated by India to Pakistan in 1992. Pakistan had objected to the design of the Baglihar Hydroelectric Plant within the period of three months prescribed in the IWT.

The essence of the objections was that the project, as designed, would enable India to acquire potential to store excessive water and capability of greater control on waters of Chenab River than permissible according to the design criteria given in the Treaty. Regarding the potential to store, Pakistan objected that the free board (empty space over the full reservoir level) and the pondage (operational storage of water to meet the fluctuations in the discharge of the turbines arising from variations in the daily and weekly loads of the plant) were excessive.

Regarding control on waters, Pakistan's objection was that following the design criteria in the Treaty, the location of power outlets (power intake tunnels) and the orifice spillway (five submerged gates with cill level 32 meters below the full pondage level) provided capability to India to exercise control over waters of Chenab River.

Pakistan's view was that, as per the design criteria in the Treaty, the power outlets can be moved up by a few meters and the orifice spillways could be converted to surface spillway by locating the gates at upper elevation such that their top level was at the surface of water.

This would truncate India's capability to control flow of waters. Pakistan's objections were based on the specific design criteria given in the Treaty meant to minimize India's storage and control on waters of Western Rivers.

The two Commissioners continued exchanging letters and debating the procedure for settlement of Pakistan's objections up to year 2000 (for 8 years) without any success. Many correspondences and meetings ended up in arguing about whether the stage for invoking the clause on settlement of differences and disputes had arrived, items of agenda of the meetings, contents of the minutes of the meetings, completeness of data/project details and other modalities.

Practically, barring exceptions, no substantive discussion of engineering issues took place.

In 2000, to Pakistan's surprise, it was learnt that India had started implementation of the. Efforts were made at Commissioner's and diplomatic levels to prevail on India from going forward on the project without settling the issues but to no avail. It seemed that India interpreted the Treaty that it only envisaged provision of information by India six months in advance of start of construction and receipt of objections by Pakistan in three months, if any. There was no specific provision to settle the issues before start. Commonsense and interpretation in a spirit of good faith would have revealed that the whole purpose of the provision was to settle disputes before start of projects. It was the letter, not the spirit of the Treaty, which was being given over riding importance.

Diplomatic efforts resulted in raising the level of the dialogue at the level of Secretaries of the two Governments dealing with water. This followed by two Secretary Level Talks but couldn't resolve the matter. Meanwhile construction of the project continued.

Worried by 65% completion of construction works of the dam Pakistan finally invoked the clause on Settlement of Differences and Disputes and approached the World Bank for the appointment of a Neutral Expert in 2005. India strongly contested this move and opposed appointment of N.E. contending that the matters be resolved bilaterally. The record, however, was a testimony that bilateral efforts between the upper and lower riparian had been futile, therefore the World Bank appointed a Neutral Expert in 2005.

Proceedings before the Neutral Expert

Both sides pleaded their cases with the support of engineering studies before the Neutral Expert. Location of the gates of the orifice spillway was the most critical and contentious issue. India had justified the location of the orifice spillway, submerged by 32 meters from the full pondage level, on the grounds that it will be used to pass flood waters and also sluice/flush sediments. Pakistan argued that flood waters can be passed through properly designed surface spillways. Sedimentation sluicing/flushing would require lowering of water level by 32 meters but as the Treaty did not allow lowering of water below dead storage level (DSL) for Run of River project except for emergencies, therefore India's justification based on sediment sluicing/flushing was not valid. India in it's submissions to N.E admitted the Treaty restriction regarding DSL and it's intention to fully comply with it. Yet it contended that sediment sluicing/flushing can take place without lowering the level of water below DSL. Pakistan contended that it was contrary tp engineering facts and that location of orifice spillway will unnecessarily allowed India control over 164000 acre feet of water of the Western River (Chenab).

This could be avoided if the criteria laid down in the treaty was followed. Both sides submitted mathematical and physical model studies prepared with the help of world renowned experts/ institutions.

In the final analysis, India failed to establish that sediment sluicing/flushing can be done without lowering the water level below DSL. The N.E, in it's draft Determination, observed that "The calculations done by India in the near field of the dam and the model tests (but with less evidence) are not representative of the reality, —" and, "In particular to expect a cone just upstream of the sluice spillway, with a length 300 or 400 m is illusory – ". The N.E further noted, "a difficulty results from the definition of the Dead Storage contained in the Treaty which states that it cannot be used for operational purposes".

He then went on to make the suggestion that India may draw down water below Dead Storage Level for operational (maintenance) purposes, which would result in justification of orifice spillway. He observed, "This is a suggestion of the NE, conscious that he is beyond the scope of his mandate".

The Neutral Expert, accepted the essence of all the objections by Pakistan but in his final Decision he allowed India to retain the orifice spillway on the grounds that lowering of water below DSL was permissible, wrongly interpreting the Treaty. The design in respect of all the other features of the dam on which Pakistan had objected was, however, modified.

Pakistan felt that since both Pakistan and India as well as the expert lawyers had concurred in their interpretation of the Treaty that water level cannot be lowered below DSL except for emergencies, the Neutral Expert had overstepped his jurisdiction by indulging in legal interpretation in allowing draw down of water below DSL for foreseeable phenomenon and also deviated from the procedure set for the resolution of the matter. Therefore, Pakistan recorded it's dissent to the Decision of the N.E in respect of the location of the orifice spillway.

Subsequently, Pakistan took up the matter of misinterpretation of the Treaty with the Court of Arbitration (CoA) in the subsequent case of Kishenganga Hydro Electric Project where India had included a similarly designed orifice spillway in the plant. The Court of Arbitration (CoA) ruled in favor of Pakistan on 18 February 2013.

Now it is to be seen whether India complies to this decision in future plants on Western Rivers. Since the BHP had already been completed, the decision applies to all subsequent RoR projects. The matter is of great importance to Pakistan because India has planned a large number of RoR projects on the Western Rivers whose cumulative effect can be substantial, specially in the dry years. India plans 170 plants, 31 on Indus, 63 on Jhelum and 76 on Chenab with total capacity of 17207 MW.

Role of Media and Public Perception

In the initial years of the interaction between the two Commissioners, the issue was not on the radar screen of the media. However, as the construction started and the matters were taken up at the Secretary Level, it attracted great attention from the media. Misreporting and media twists picked by lobbies on both the sides polluted the environment. In brief, on the Indian side some public perception was that Pakistan is opposed to the construction of this dam and that the IWT was too onerous for India. On the Pakistan side, a section of the public thought that Pakistan had been passive in agitating the issue, India should not be allowed control of waters of Western Rivers in view of it's past record and that India was trying to get control on waters under the garb of project design necessities. Some Indian lobbies were attributing Pakistan's objections as move to stop construction of dam allowed to India under the Treaty. Upon the announcement of final decision by N.E. various talk shows and fora debate focussed on who won and who lost. Similar was the tenor of follow up by media after the decision of the CoA who overturned Neutral Experts interpretation of the Treaty.

Issues and Stakeholders

Run of River Projects must be constructed by the upper riparian (India) such that India does not acquire capability to control or store water beyond what is genuine in accordance with the criteria and principles envisaged in the Treaty between the parties (Pakistan and India).

The Ministry of Water Resources and Water Receiving Area are the primary stakeholders.

8

Indus Water Treaty and the Mechanism

THE INDUS WATER TREATY 1960

India and Pakistan accepted the rights and obligations of each other on the use of water of Indus Basin through the Indus Water Treaty. On 19 September, 1960, the Indus Water Treaty was signed in Karachi by Prime Minister of India, Jawaharlal Nehru, and the President of Pakistan, Muhammad Ayub Khan and senior vice president of the World Bank, W.A.B. Liff. The treaty was subsequently ratified by two governments and the ratification was exchanged in New Delhi in the January of

1961. The Indus Water Treaty considered a landmark step in promoting trust and understanding between the people of the two countries.

Apart from Indus Water Treaty, three other agreements were signed in 1960. The first agreement was related to the establishment of an Indus Basin Development Fund (IBDF) of $ 894 million. Out of the total, $ 640 was contributed by friendly countries, such as Australia, Canada, West Germany, New Zealand, the United Kingdom and the United States. The IBDF agreement was signed between Pakistan and aforementioned friendly countries. To facilitate the agreement, India also contributed $ 174 million, and $ 80 million was given from the proceeds of the World Bank loan to Pakistan. The fund was mainly collected for the transfer of infrastructure and construction of replacement works on western rivers. The second agreement was signed between Pakistan and the World Bank for a loan of $ 90 million. The last agreement covered a loan of $ 70 million from the US Development Loan Fund.

The Indus Water Treaty addressed both the technical and financial concerns of each side and included a timeline for transition. It was retroactive from 1 April, 1960. The basic aim of the treaty is to increase the amount of water available to the both parties and to distribute the water resources of the Indus Basin equitably to them.

It is indeed a comprehensive treaty in view of its objectives. It is based on the simple distribution of the rivers and not the base of quantity of waters.

This unique division of the Indus system has eradicated the very disturbances and conflicting demands that would have followed the equitable distribution of water. Another unique feature of the treaty is that it is the only international water treaty co-signed by a third party. This third party was the World Bank, which mediated the original dispute over the Indus Basin and assisted the two parties in reaching an agreement. Furthermore, the Indus Basin dispute settlement was not just only an agreement but also tried to change the history of water dispute into history of cooperation and peace.

The Indus Water Treaty was not only a novel and original document to enhance the availability of water between the parties to the treaty (India and Pakistan), but also has conciliated the differences over the rights of water usage. Prior to the treaty, both countries were demanding their water share by interpreting water laws of "absolute rights" and "historic use". The Indus Water Treaty tried to find a better solution that was driven by the principles of water engineering and economics rather than legal principles. The treaty instead of dividing the waters of the rivers, divided the rivers between the two parties, which gave them independent control and regulation of supplies within their territories, subjected to limited use of water of the rivers allocated to the other party. Some of the main principles of the treaty are:

Provisions Regarding Eastern Rivers

1. All the waters of the Eastern Rivers shall be available for unrestricted use in India.
2. Except for domestic and non-consumptive uses, Pakistan shall be under an obligation to let flow, and shall not permit any interference with the waters of the Sutlej main and Ravi main in the reaches where these rivers flow in Pakistan and have not yet finally crossed into Pakistan.
3. All the waters, while flowing in Pakistan, if any, tributary which, in its natural course, joins the Sutlej main or the Ravi main after these rivers have finally crossed into Pakistan shall be available for the unrestricted use of Pakistan.

PROVISIONS REGARDING WESTERN RIVERS

1. Pakistan shall receive for unrestricted use all those waters of the Western Rivers.
2. India shall be under an obligation to let flow all the waters of the Western Rivers, and shall not permit any interference with these waters, except for the following uses, restricted in the case of each of the rivers, The Indus, The Jhelum and The Chenab, to the drainage basin thereof.
   (a) Domestic Use;
   (b) Non-Consumptive Use;
   (c) Agricultural Use; and
   (d) Generation of hydroelectric power.

Provisions Regarding Eastern and Western Rivers

Pakistan shall use its best endeavors to construct and bring into operation a system of works that will accomplish the replacement from the Western Rivers (and other sources of) the water supplies for irrigation canals in Pakistan, which on 15th August, 1947, where dependent water supplies from the eastern rivers.

The use of the natural channels of the rivers for the discharge of flood or other excess waters shall be free and not subject to limitation by either party or neither party shall have any claim against the other in respect of any damage caused by such use.

Each Party declares its limitation to prevent, as far as practicable, undue pollution of the waters and agrees to ensure that, before any sewage or industrial waste, it will be treated, where necessary, in such manner as not materially to affect those uses.

PRINCIPLES OF COOPERATION BETWEEN THE PARTIES

Indus Water Treaty recognises the interests of both the countries in the optimum development of rivers, and to that effect, calls for cooperation and collaboration between the two countries. Article VI and the Article VII of the treaty deal with the "exchange of data" and the clause of "future cooperation".

Further, the Article VII clearly anticipates future cooperation that both the parties did recognize that they have a common interest in the optimum development of the rivers, and to that end, they declare their intention to cooperate, by mutual agreement, to the fullest possible extent. The Article further elaborates on the cooperation in the field of engineering works on the rivers.. However, the Article has encountered a number of problems and challenges from the both sides in term of its interpretation and implementations.

As per the terms and conditions of the treaty, data regarding the daily flow and utilisation of the water of the rivers is to be exchanged regularly. This includes (a) daily (or as observed or estimated less frequently) gauge and discharge data relating to flow of the rivers at all observation sites, (b) daily extractions for or releases from reservoirs, (c) daily withdrawals at the heads of all canals operated by government or by a government agency (hereinafter in this Article called canals), including link canals, (d) daily escapades from all canals, including link canals, and (e) daily deliveries from link canals. The data is to be exchanged on monthly basis, but when "necessary for operational purpose," it shall be exchanged daily or less frequently as may be requested. In addition, if any party "requests the supply of any data relating to the hydrology of the rivers, or to canal or reservoir operation connected with the rivers or to any provisions of this treaty, it shall be furnished."

Dispute resolution mechanism and Permanent Indus Commission

The principle of cooperation advocates that all states in an international watercourse should seek a settlement of the disputes by peaceful means in case states concerned cannot reach agreement by negotiation. The Indus Water Treaty, articulates the mechanism for dispute resolution. The "questions" are to be decided by the Permanent Indus Commission (PIC), "differences" to be settled by Neutral Experts (NE) and "disputes" to be settled by the International Court of Arbitration (ICA). It is important to note that the applicable law for the ICA is to be followed within the framework of Indus Water Treaty itself. Firstly, the case is tried in the institution of PIC, if the Commission fails to settle. The case will be extradited to the Neutral Expert and if the case remains unresolved again, it will be solved in the International Court of Arbitration.

The Indus Water Treaty has established the institution of the Permanent Indus Commission (PIC) under the Article VIII. A Permanent Indus Commission consisting of two commissioners (one appointed by India and another from Pakistan) was to establish and maintain cooperative arrangements for the implementation of the Indus Treaty.

The commissioners should ordinarily be high- ranking engineers, especially competent in the field of hydrology and water use. The basic objectives of the Commission was to promote cooperation between the parties in the development of the waters of the rivers, and in particular, to study matters referred to it for help, resolve questions concerning the interpretation or application of the treaty and to make tours of inspection. The commissioners have to meet regularly once a year in India and Pakistan alternately and submit reports to respective governments before 1st June every year or shall also meet when requested by either commissioner.

On the other hand, there are also some measures of dissatisfaction, which have been noted about the role of the Commission. As some are of the view, the treaty has mandated the Commission with a complex system of dispute settlement and the Commission appears to be heavily biased towards dispute settlement and monitoring system. The unresolved disputes and debates over the share of water of Indus Basin witnesses that the Commission has been ineffectual in its role. It can be understood by revision of disputes after treaty.

PRINCIPLE OF FINANCIAL PROVISION AND INDUS BASIN DEVELOPMENT FUND

With the purpose of maintaining everlasting peace and future development in the Indus Basin, the treaty established the Indus Basin Development Fund. The main objective of this fund was to construct head-works and canals from the Western Rivers and other sources of water for irrigation canals in Pakistan, which, on 15th August, 1947, were dependent on water supplies from the Eastern Rivers. In order to carry out these works, the World Bank had been instrumental in the creation of an Indus Basin Development Fund.

To facilitate the IDBF the financial contribution was made available by friendly countries and the World Bank itself. All these countries agreed to support development in the Indus Basin, which was estimated at about $900 million and India was committed to provide $174 million (£62 million) in 10 installments. In fact, the Indus Water Treaty was a billion dollar investment made possible because of the personal and sustained interest of Eugene Black, who was the moving spirit in its creation.

The programme for construction work in Pakistan included eight link canals that are nearly 400 miles long for transferring water from the Western Rivers to areas formerly dependent on the Eastern Rivers, two storage dams, Mangla on the Jhelum and the Tarbela on the Indus River, 2,500 tube wells and other works to integrate the Western Rivers and canal system. The Indus settlement also envisaged the construction of a storage dam on the Beas River in India which, together with the Bhakra Dam on the Sutlej and the Rajasthan Canal, was meant for irrigation to new areas in India. But these works did not come within the scope of the Indus Basin Development Fund.

In the context of the administration of the Indus Basin, the World Bank played an active and constructive role and therefore, its reputation due to its role in resolving the dispute, granting loans to both countries, has been exceptionally important in this dispute. The World Bank did not have any political power but its ability to bring together several countries with the financial commitment was a generous third-party inducement to the successful resolution of the dispute. The resolution of the dispute implies that the critical role of third party in facilitating the agreement is important in conflict resolution.

However, one quarter of the Pakistan society criticizes the role of the World Bank, on the presumption that the funds allocated by the World bodies were insufficient and indirectly favored India. More notably, the well-known Pakistani water resource expert B. A Malik (2005), is of the view the Bank extended its special favor to India both in granting funds and waters from western rivers. The Bank went out of its way to offer to India $56 million against its needs of $33 million. As against this generosity Pakistan was given only $60 million with which Pakistan could hardly manage to build its link canals only. Moreover, the Bank allowed India to carry its projects by its own indigenous resources, whereas in Pakistan almost all water projects were carried out by foreign consultants, which returned all foreign assistance in the form of services, equipment and supplies.

Furthermore, The World Bank has, inadvertently put Pakistan in a highly precarious situation, it has, in the final analysis of Indus Water Treaty, made it (Pakistan) to surrender its rights on the rivers, which it was, traditionally using for various consumption purposes and other wise, in favour of India. India got the sovereign rights over three rivers. It has, absolutely no obligations to Pakistan, carrying out its present and structuring its future plans on the waters concerned. While as India, in Kashmir retains its upper riparian rights on the western rivers comprising Indus Jhelum and Chenab with specific conditions and some obligations to Pakistan. The conditions to be observed by India are such that can be state of art technology and intelligent or diluted or rendered in effective. Pakistan can, at the most, with its arguments, only delay the inevitable. But this is, only the half of the story—an half, which still has something to rejoice, for Pakistan.

IMPLICATIONS OF THE INDUS WATER TREATY

The Indus Water Treaty has successfully ended a decade-long water dispute, which had been a major cause of tension between the two countries since partition. It was appreciated by the international community and considered as a good example of water conflict management. The immediate result of the treaty was that the Indus Basin became politically and economically viable for two countries. It has opened new ways for independent development of the water of the Indus Basin. Some are also of the view, had the Indus Treaty not been in place, water dispute would have remained a contentious issue in the political arena between the two countries and the subsequent development might have been wholly or partially withheld.

Development of Indus Basin in India

During partition, both India and Pakistan are agricultural economies, water formed an integral part of their economy. There was a dire need to develop good infrastructures to provide irrigation facilities to those agricultural areas which were uncultivated before partition. India, as an upper riparian country wanted to develop its irrigation facilities in these areas and Pakistan as the lower riparian also needed sufficient water supply for its own irrigation and agriculture.

In 1960, by the signing of the treaty, India has been able to expand her irrigation system. The Article III of the treaty facilitates India to unrestricted harness the water from eastern rivers for any purposes. Immediately after the treaty, a major step was taken by India to construct interlinking canal projects from the Ravi, Beas and Sutlej rivers through the diversion of the rivers. The interlinking canal system increased the irrigated command area, which brought a green revolution in the Indus Basin states and made the country self-sufficient in food production. India implemented various other new schemes, such as the Upper Bari Doab Canal, the Sirhind Canal and the Rajasthan Canal system and the gigantic Indra Gandhi Canal Project. The canal system is connected with the Bhakra Nangal, Pong and Harike barrage. The Bhakra and Nangal dams were constructed on the Sutlej River while the Harike barrage has been constructed at the confluence of Beas and Sutlej rivers to provide supply to Rajasthan and Ferozpur feeders.

The Bhakra Nangal project was designed to provide irrigation to some 1.46 million hectares in Punjab, Haryana, Chandigarh and Rajasthan. The construction of the project has enlarged India's irrigation efficiencies which led to the growth of agriculture in Punjab, Haryana and Chandigarh and Rajasthan. From 1960 onward, the project has added an irrigated area of 6.8 million hectares over 35 years. Moreover, the production of rice and wheat in the Bhakra command area in 1996-97 was eight times as much as 1960-61 figures. Moreover, after the treaty, entire Indian part of the Indus Basin, large and small projects, led to the growth of irrigated area that was estimated 22 million hectares in 1947 to 55 million hectares in 2000.[26] Of late, a third major storage project—the Thein dam—was built on the Ravi River, which has a potential to provide eight million acre feet of water to Rajahstan and Thar Desert. This project has transformed desert with a swathe of greenery running north- south along the Pakistan border.

While as the treaty permits India to increase her power potentialities from the Ravi, Beas and Sutlej River, the development of hydropower potential in the Indus Basin has become a priority for the Indian Government over the past few decades. From 1960 onward, India has achieved steady growth in power potential on three eastern rivers. The total estimated power potential of the Indian side basin is measured as 19988 MW at 60 per cent load factor. Out of total 190 schemes in the Indus Basin, 35 schemes are in operation with installed capacity of 3715 MW and 14 schemes with 5626 MW potential is likely to be commissioned in the near future. Furthermore, 32 schemes that remain to be developed, account for nearly 28 per cent of the assessed potential of the basin.

Taking advantage of the various sections of the treaty India has earnestly initiated well designed futuristic planes for the Indus basin. India has developed many hydro-power projects in Jammu & Kashmir State like Salal, Dulhasti, Uri, Baglihar etc. India is also entitled to develop irrigation schemes in its territory to enhance the regional development in terms of agricultural areas through western rivers.

DEVELOPMENT OF INDUS BASIN IN PAKISTAN

The treaty granted independent share of water to Pakistan from western rivers and assured permanent water supply because its large canals used to get water from eastern rivers before 1947. In 1961, with the ratification of the treaty, the Indus Basin Development Fund (IBDF) became effective and Pakistan was able to develop world's largest hydraulic works in the country. In fact, the IBDF caused the green light in Pakistan.

After the treaty was signed, Pakistan secured her water supply through the diversion of three western rivers to meet requirements of irrigation canals that were dependent on eastern rivers before partition. Several immense link canals were built after the treaty. The biggest link canals are the Chashma-Jhelum link canal, the Haveli canal, and the Sindhani-Mailsi-Bahawalpur canals. The other link canals are the Rasul-Qadirabad link canal, the Qadirabad-Balloki canal, the Balloki-Sulemanki canal, Trimmu-Sindhani, Sindhani-Mailsi canal and the Taunsa-Panjnad canal.

Financial aid through World Bank helped Pakistan to build massive storage projects to ensure her electricity needs and water availability for irrigation during critical sowing seasons. The mega projects include Mangla dam on Jhelum River, Tarbela dam and Jinnah dam on Indus River along with various canals and tube wells.

These projects provide cheap and clean hydroelectricity to boost up the industrial and irrigation requirements for the country.

In the post-treaty period, Pakistan has constructed other 19 barrages or head-works and 43 major canals with a total conveyance length of 57 000 km on western rivers. These various projects meet the irrigation requirements of 40 million acres irrigated land and provide the fresh water supply to the population of 172 million besides sharing aggregate energy at 33.07 percent. Over all, the irrigation system which is lies in the Indus Basin of Pakistan serve an area of 8.88 hectares, and it is continuously increasing with significant agriculture out puts.

In 1947, at the time of independence, the total installed power potential of the country was only 60 MW for its 31.5 million people, which in 1958, increased to 119 MW. Power infrastructure gained momentum immediately after the treaty. The 1000 MW Mangla and 3478 MW Tarbela dams were completed to meet the increasing demands of the growing population, and Pakistan's installed power potential is continuously increasing. Presently 35 major and medium hydropower projects are in operation in Punjab, Khyber-Pakhtunkhawa (KPK) and 84 small hydel projects are in operation with less than 2 MW installed capacity on the Indus River and its tributaries at Gilgit Baltistan.

In Pakistan, the massive development in water infrastructure subsequent to the treaty has resulted in economic growth and green revolution. Even the treaty has provided employment opportunities in different sectors. For instance, Water and Power Development Authority (WAPADA), which is the largest civilian employer, was set up as a direct consequence of the treaty with international financial and technical assistance. The foreign technical assistance proved helpful for introducing water management know-how, irrigation development and construction of dams to Pakistani engineers.

India and Pakistan are agro based countries; growth of irrigated areas in the Indus Basin provided a boost to the agricultural economies of the two countries. Though the political relations between the two countries are strained, the signing of the treaty has removed some basic related obstructions in the economic development in the countries concerned. They are now pursuing their own interests independently, which has made the

Indus Basin a highly developed river basin of the regions serving the largest section of humanity. Development of gigantic projects across the Indus and its historical tributaries enabled both the countries to revolutionise their economies.

NEGATIVE IMPLICATIONS OF THE INDUS WATER TREATY

Despite being appreciated in different quarters, the treaty has drawn flaks from different sections of society as well. The common opinion shared in both the countries is that the distribution of water under the treaty is unfair. Most of the Indians are of the view that the allocation of 80 per cent of the Indus water to Pakistan and 20 percent to India is unjustifiable and unfair. There are also some opinions that the treaty imposed a heavy financial burden on the country, as it does not permit to utilise the full potentialities of the three western rivers to India. Number of Indian scholars such as S.K. Grag, K. Warikoo, B.R. Chauhan40 and M.S. Menon41 is of the view that on the basis of population, drainage area and cultivated lands, India should have been given a 42.8 percent share of the Indus Basin but the treaty was generous 80 percent in Pakistan and 20 percent in India. Hence, the treaty gives a false impression of the water distribution of the Indus Basin.

The Indus Water Treaty was neither envisaged nor implemented to help in equitable distribution of water. It was based on the de-facto possession of the rivers. India was immediately left with independent possession of so called eastern rivers—Beas, Ravi and Sutlej, while Pakistan though in sovereign position to exploit and manage amount of water (Jhelum, Chenab and Indus) flowing through its portion of land had share a meagre amount of water with India (in Kashmir) as it upper riparian right. It was compromise which India was itself campaigning for. Indus Water Treaty also ignores the water rights of a region on the basis of any historical usage of water it is, the absence of any plausible, possible and acceptable alternative a just and pragmatic solution. Furthermore, it needs be understood that Pakistan has to negotiate its position on the water given to it by the treaty (geography in fact) with two upper riparian countries, Afghanistan and China (Tibet). Had India to share its three eastern rivers with Pakistan it would have been deprived of the progress it has made in agriculture sector in Punjab.

In this particular case, neither the quality nor quantity of land under the usage of the waters, nor the number of people living in that region, and nor any consideration for any future demands on water was made basis for the division of the basin. Raising these questions now is to play to the psyche of certain sections of the society—who thrive on the hatred of the opposed country—; it is to play to respective vote bank.

On the other hand, large sections of the Pakistani society opined, the territories that went to India during partition were historically used less than 10 percent of the Indus waters, and the treaty was generous to India in giving it 20 per cent of the water of Indus Basin. Secondly, Pakistan's worry was that India's hold in Kashmir enables it to deprive of the water flow of the Jhelum and Chenab rivers which are the major sources of Pakistan's water supply. But the treaty in a major way gave some satisfaction and security to its water supply as long as India is in possession of Kashmir.

The treaty under study was not intended to solve and by its very formulation could not have had solved all the issues for all the times. It was an arrangement to bring two countries together, enter a compromise and work for better future and developmental avenues. Now the treaty has come under strain from various quarters for various reasons. While as demographic changes and decreasing water availability, demand more judicious approach to treaty. Some new parties (China, Jammu and Kashmir and Afghanistan) claiming their rights as upper riparian or mid riparian countries have entered into the space till now exclusively claimed by India and Pakistan.

Apart from Indian and Pakistani perspectives, one of the major issues attached to the treaty is that it has led to a regional disparity and discontent. In Jammu and Kashmir State, the treaty is perceived as discriminatory. Common view of Kashmiris about the treaty is that while signing the treaty both the countries overlooked the water rights of Kashmir. There are also a lot of current discussions on the treaty at political fronts in the state of J&K. Even on 2 March, 2003, the state legislature passed a resolution against the treaty and demanded an instant review of the treaty.

CONFRONTATION OVER THE USE OF INDUS RIVERS WATER

In 1960, the Indus Water Treaty was signed with the spirit of cooperation which ended a decade-long water dispute between the two countries. To resolve the dispute permanently, conflicting demands and claims was put aside, the rivers were divided, financial arrangements were made and technical assistances were provided. In fact, the division of the rivers provides substantial development to both the countries. The large scales of works in the Indus Basin have been taken place without any interference. But now, with the increasing rate population and accelerating demands for water in both the countries, the water dispute again occurring with new perspectives. The treaty which took a decade of intensive hard work to resolve the dispute is now in the clutch and controversies due to a different set of challenges.

Existing Disputes over the Share of Indus Basin after the Treaty

The Article III (2) (d) of the Indus Water Treaty allows India to utilise the water of western rivers for (i) domestic use, (ii) non-consumptive use, (iii) agriculture use (iv) generation of hydroelectric power from run-of-the river projects. On the hand it is also subjected in the treaty that such utilisation should not cause of damage for lower riparian Pakistan.

For the generation of hydroelectric power on western rivers of India, the treaty has different provisions. Any hydroelectric power project constructed on western rivers by India after the signing of the treaty shall be a run-of- the river project that develops power without live storage as an integral part of the plant except for pondage and surcharge storage. The maximum pondage in the operating pool is allowed to reach a level that is twice as much as the pondage required for firm power. To utilise the permitted water from western rivers, India has planned to construct some projects on the western rivers which are often opposed by Pakistan as the violation of the treaty. Pakistan feels that the Indian projects do not follow the technicalities laid down in the treaty, while India uses permissive clause of the treaty to justify its rights over projects.

The first controversy that aroused in the aftermath of the treaty was in 1970 over Salal Project on Chenab River. Pakistan objected to the design as well as the storage capacity of the project. The issue was formally taken up in 1975 when the two countries stated their negotiation over the project. In 1975, Pakistan's Minister for Foreign affairs visited India and discussed the issue with his counterpart. Therefore, India provided the required information to Pakistan that bridged the gap of many aspects related to the project, but certain fundamental issues remained unresolved.

When several subsequent meetings failed to produce any outcome, Pakistan moved to appoint the neutral expert to settle the issue. But India tried to settle the issue by mutual understanding rather than by third party involvement. Discussion again started at the political level between the two countries and after prolonged discussions by both the Commissioners, and later on at governmental level, the dispute was resolved with some alterations. Following an agreement was signed on 14 April 1978.

Salal Project dispute was not the last in the series. The other projects including the Tulbul Navigation Project (Wullar Barrage), Baglihar, Kishanganga Nemo-Bazgo, Chutak, Dumkhar and Bursar, are also under controversy mainly due to conflicting approaches from the both sides.

The Tulbul Navigation Project (Wullar Barrage) Dispute

The Wullar Project was proposed to be built at the mouth of Wullar Lake in Baramulla district of Kashmir Valley. The original Indian plan was to construct a barrage of 139 meters long and 12 meters wide with maximum storage capacity of 300,000 acre feet (AF). The basic objective of the project was to increase the flow of water in the Jhelum River during the lean season to make it navigable. The project was envisaged in 1980 and the work began in 1984, but Pakistan raised the objection on the ground objected that the project allegedly violates the provisions of the treaty.

Pakistani Perspective on Wullar Project: Pakistan objected that the project's storage capacity violates the Article I (15) [b] of the treaty, which barred both parties to create man-made obstruction that may cause changes in the daily flow of the rivers. Further, Pakistan claimed that the Article III (4)50 of the treaty specifically prohibits India from creating any storage or constructing any storage works on western rivers. Indus Water Treaty, India is entitled to construct an 'incidental storage work' on western rivers on its side, but storage capacity should not exceed more than 10,000 acre feet. Tulbul project's storage is more than 300,000 acre feet, which is more than thirty times as the permitted capacity. 52 Some more apprehensions of Pakistan over the project are:

- The project would adversely affect the triple canal project, Upper Chenab Canal, Upper Jhelum Canal and Lower Bari Doab Canal;
- Construction of the project would enable India to control Jhelum River during the winter season;
- Mangla Dam would be adversely affected by construction of Wullar Project;
- The project seems to be a security threat to Pakistan's sovereignty.

The Indian perspective over Wullar Project: India, on the other hand, claims that the project would neither increase the permitted storage capacity nor will interfere with downstream flows. Its purpose is only to improve the navigation over the Jhelum River during lean period (winter months); to connect Baramulla with Srinagar, as it does not violate the norms of the treaty. India also argues that 90 per cent of this project would be beneficial to Pakistan, i.e. it would increase the power generation capacity of Mangla Dam and would increase the efficiency of irrigation network in Pakistan during critical period as well.

On-going discussion over Wullar Project: In 1986 Pakistan referred the Wullar Project dispute to Indus Water Commission, but after one year the Commission recorded its failure to resolve it. Subsequently, India stopped the construction and Pakistan did not take the case in the International Court of Arbitration. From 1986-91, the two sides have held 13 rounds of talks to settle the dispute, but dispute remained unresolved. At 1991, both the parties reached to sign an agreement but the differences could not be resolved due to Pakistan's apprehensions. During the subsequent data exchange process, India agreed to keep 6.2 meters of the barrage ungated with a crest level of 1574.90m (5167 feet), and would forego the storage capacity of 300,000 acre feet. In return, the water level in the Barrage would be allowed to attain the full operational level of 5177.90 acre feet. However, in February 1992, Pakistan added another condition that India should not construct the 390 MW Kishanganga hydropower project, but India refused to accept this condition. Following 18 years of stalemates did not produce any results and the differences in the project persisted. As disputes dominated Indo-Pak talks and discussions at political forefronts in 1999 at Lahore, the Agra Summit of 2001, secretary-level talks of 2011, but not much development has been achieved yet.

The present status of talks over the project manifests that it has been politicized. Though the Indus Water Commission has authority to settle the disputes but assorted political understandings along with political distrust, security issues and growing demand for water and increasing energy needs in two countries are hindrances to reach any consensus.

The Baglihar Project Dispute

The Baglihar project was the major issue between the two countries that went to neutral experts for determining on technical "questions" raised by Pakistan. The dispute over the Baglihar project emerged in 1999, when Pakistan challenged the design of the project under the Article IX (1)54 of the treaty. Pakistan's objections were related to pondage level, gate spillway, under-sluices, level of intake tunnels, and height of gates and elevation of tunnels. Pakistan's main concerns were that the project is the violation of the treaty. The gated structure of the project would result in a loss of 7000 to 8000 cusecs of water a day. Further, the project gives India a strategic leverage to manipulate the flow of river during any critical situation.

The project has incurred Pakistan's concerns from economic, strategic and political perspectives. Discussions and the deliberations started only after India provided the required information in 2002, and thereafter, it started the construction of the project which was opposed by Pakistan. Hence, the issue has stirred intense political debates from both sides. During the discussion, the design of the project remained a major concern between the parties. Pakistan insisted that India should stop working on the project, but India refused to accept it. Consequently, Pakistan sent its "questions" over the project to India under Article IX (1) of the treaty as:

- The project appeared to be capable of raising the water level artificially beyond the full pondage level specified in the design and would contravene the provisions of Paragraph 8 (a) of the treaty;
- The pondage in the operating pool being 37.722 million cubic metres exceeds twice the pondage of water level;
- The site was suitable for an ungated spillway, and therefore, a gated spillway should not have been provided. This was in contravention of Paragraph 8 (e) ;
- The intake for the turbine had not been located at the highest level as required, as referred to in Paragraph 8 (f) to the treaty.

Indian reply to Pakistan's Objections

- the Baglihar was not a violation of the treaty;
- the project was a run-of-the river project;
- the storage called poundage was necessary to meet the fluctuations in the discharge of the turbines;

- the project will not disrupt the flow of the Chenab River and the water will ultimately go to Pakistan;
- India stated that the removal of gates would mean the end of the project.

The "questions" and "differences" over the project imply that one party deemed the project as the violation of the treaty, while the other party assessed the project within the parameters of the treaty. Since Commissioners level talks over the project remained unsuccessful, the World Bank intervened eventually and appointed a neutral expert to resolve the dispute.

The neutral expert, Professor Raymond Lafitte of Switzerland, classified Pakistan's objections while delivering the verdict for minor design changes including the reduction of the dam's height of 1.5 meters. The neutral expert did not question the right of India to construct the project and did not even call the project a "dispute" between the two countries, but considered it as "differences". The neutral expert required India to make some changes but Pakistan was not satisfied with the verdict, as the expert did not consider much of Pakistan's objections.

It is important to note that the neutral expert set a precedence to be followed in future if the need for interpretation of the treaty arises. The expert applied the Vienna Convention on the laws of treaties (1969) and referred to the latest bulletin of the International Commission on Large Dams (ICOLD) rules of science and the state of the art practices. The need to incorporate state of the art knowledge of science in the interpretation of the treaty was emphasized by Raymond Lafitte. The decision of the court on Baglihar Project was made while using emerging knowledge of hydraulic, environment science, climate change and contemporary research on dams. The judgment of the court, which is set as precedence and an integral part of the treaty, stated that the rights and obligations of both the parties should be read in light of technical norms and noble standards.

The Baglihar dispute was settled by the third party intervention but relations between two countries again became hostile over the project when water was to be filled in the dam. According to the provision of the treaty, a minimum flow of

55,000 cusecs has to be maintained above Merala and it should be filled during the period between June 21 and August 31. Pakistan claimed that the filling was not done in the stipulated period. Hence, the filling of the dam has made colossal damage to the country's agriculture sector in downstream areas of the Chenab River. India replied that the filling of the dam was done on time stipulated in the treaty.

Pakistan demanded compensation from India for its losses incurred at the time when the dam was filled. India insisted that it had not violated the treaty and refused Pakistan's claim. Therefore, a lot of discussions were held between the two countries, even pitching top leaderships in both countries. Finally, differences over the filling of Baglihar dam were resolved in 2010 at a meeting of the PICs in the spirit of co- operation and goodwill.

The Kishanganga Project Dispute

The Kishanganga Project is another project being constructed by India over the Kishanganga River at Gurez. The project's power generation capacity is about 330 MW and the height is about 75 meters. It is located about 160 km upstream of Muzaffarabad (Pakistan Administrated Kashmir Capital). The project involves the diversion of Kishanganga (Neelum River in Muzaffarabad) through a 23 km long tunnel into the Madumati Nala, which will empty into the Wullar Lake, through which the Jhelum River flows. Pakistan is of the view that the diversion of the Kishanganga River will reduce the flow of 140,000 million acres feet of water to the Neelum Valley in Pakistan Administrated Kashmir.

In 1992, India officially informed Pakistan about the construction of project, which later raised three objections to the project.

- The first objection raised by Pakistan was that the inter-tributary diversion is barred by the treaty, and the water drawn from a given tributary must be returned to the same river;
- The second is that the existing Pakistani usage must be protected but India's Kishanganga Project will deprive it

of 27 per cent of the river's natural flow, thereby inflicting damage to its existing 133,000 hectares of irrigation in the Neelum Valley. Also, it will affect the 900 MW Neelum-Jhelum hydro project on which construction is in progress at Muzaffarabad.

- Lastly, Pakistan criticized the design features of the project that do not meet the criterion of the Indus Water Treaty.

India replied, citing the norms of the treaty, that where a plant is located on a tributary of the Jhelum River around which Pakistan has an agricultural and hydroelectric use, the water released below the plant may be delivered, if necessary, into another tributary but only to the extent that the then existing agricultural use or hydro-electric use by Pakistan on the former tributary would not be adversely affected. To justify its claim, India stated that inter-tributary diversions in the Jhelum basin are permitted and only "the then existing" agricultural and hydroelectric uses shall be protected.

The construction of the project has created a new issue for heated discussions at different levels after the Baglihar project. The Indus Commission held a number of meetings to console the parties, but due to different approaches, interpretation of and perspectives on the treaty text, the dispute remained unresolved. Essentially, growing needs for water by both the countries and competitive behaviours have affected the discussions at every level.

Pakistani apprehensions over the project: Pakistan further objected to the project on the ground of diversion of water through the tunnel, since:

- The project will have an adverse effect on Neelum-Jhelum link project that Pakistan initiated in 1988.
- Secondly, diversion of the water of the Kishanganga River to Jhelum would ruin the Neelum Valley in Pakistan and also that the project do not confirm to design criteria (a), (c), (e), (f) and (g) mention.
- In Pakistan it is also feared that the project could reduce Pakistan's total water availability from 154 million acre

feet (MAF) to about 140 MAF, a shortage of about 8-9 per cent.

- Further, it the project would reduce the energy generation of Neelum Jhelum hydro project by about 16 per cent amounting to an annual loss of Rs. 5 billion at the current rates.
- It is also feared to reduce the flow of water in the River Jhelum by 27 per cent.

Indian perspective on the project: The response of India has always been that the water of the Kishanganga River will ultimately go to Pakistan and there would be no serious damage in lower stream areas of Pakistan administrated Kashmir. Also India's assessment is that the diversion of water through tunnel into the Jhelum would help Pakistan to generate more electricity in Mangla and Neelum Jhelum projects during winter season.

Pakistan has rejected all assessments and appraisals by India regarding the project. However, the dispute has figured on the agenda of talks even at the time and now between the Commissioners. As the Commission level discussion did not arrive at any settlement, the dispute has been referred to the International Court of Arbitration as instructed in the treaty, because the dispute involves techniques as well as legal issues. Hence, the decision of the International Court of Arbitration about the Kishanganga dispute is awaited.

On-going discussions on the dispute: A series of talks were held between the parties at various levels to resolve "differences" and "dispute" attached to the use of Kishanganga River, but talks remained unresolved and problematic. Pakistan has frequently criticised the project as the violation of the treaty, and therefore, in April 2006, India offered to modify the project and submitted a revised plan in July 2006. In the revised plan, India agreed to convert the storage and power generation project into a run-of-the-river project and construct poundage in accordance with the treaty. But again Pakistan rejected the plan mentioning that the project still has objectionable aspects. Later Pakistan communicated these objections to India in a detailed report, while the contention of India has been that the waters will ultimately go to Pakistan. Contemplating the disputes over the use of Indus Basin, it could be concluded that it is the second time in the past ten years that the dispute over the utilization of water is referred to the third party for resolution.

The Kishanganga dispute assumes a greater significance because Pakistan is also trying to construct its own project—the Neelum-Jhelum hydroelectric project—on the Pakistani side of the Neelum River (Kishanganga). The Indus Water Treaty states that the country that completes its project first will secure priority rights to the river. Hence, both countries are in contest to complete their respective projects as soon as possible without considering the objections and apprehensions of each other. There have been major delays in the construction of the projects on both sides of the border, because of the dispute and the issue of water-sharing between India and Pakistan is spiralling.

There are also some other hydroelectric projects which are seen in the light of controversy between India and Pakistan. These include Dul Hasti, Uri II, Chutak, Nimoo-Bazgo, Dumkhar, Ratle and Sawlakote Project etc. Aforementioned projects, objected to by Pakistan, have added new dimensions to the disputes attached to economic, security and strategic importance, but some are alien to the provisions of the treaty.

In the following table and figure, an attempt has been made to list out the chronology of water-related conflicts in the Indus Basin following the signing of the treaty. At the same time, the table and figure help us to understand the nature and intensity of water conflicts between the two countries and highlight how the two countries are engaged in different types of water-related conflicts.

The figure displays the conflicts over water between the two countries since the signing of the treaty. 80% is about water control, while 20% is about water allocation. Control of water from western rivers has received considerable attention from both the sides. It is because of the construction of the projects on western rivers, Pakistan fears that India is exercising "hydro hegemony" on these projects and it will use these projects as a bargaining tool with Pakistan to settle other related issues. To what extent these interpretations are valid but the growing concerns of the parties leading fierce competition over water.

The outcomes of the on-going disputes have broader implications not only for future water development but also about India-Pakistan relations. The Indus Treaty has served both the countries and stood with the test of time, but the growing economies of both countries and the energy needs are nurturing a different set of challenges. Multiplying problems related to acute water supply have also put on serious burdens on the Indus Basin Rivers. Exploitation of water with the last drops means the violation of the treaty. Under such an adverse situation, the Indus Water Commissioners are also under pressure from respective governments as they have failed to forge any final decision over certain disputes.

Reasons for Differences over Projects

It is usually easier to understand how the "questions," "differences" and "disputes" attached to these projects aroused. To be precise, they appeared on the scene from different approaches to and differing interpretations of various provisions of the main text of the treaty.

Some issues regarding the technicalities of the treaty are not acceptable to both parties. For instance, the Article III (4)75 of the treaty barred India in building any storage on the western rivers, except a limited utilisation of the treaty, and also specifies technical conditions relating to engineering structures and features, such as live storage, dead storage, limits on raising artificially, the water level in the operating pool, poundage levels, crest level of the gates, location of intakes for the turbines, and so on. One party claims to be in full conformity with the criteria laid down in the treaty on these, while the other party says that this is not the case.

The Indus Treaty is a highly technical treaty as compared to other treaties in the region. The dense technicalities allow ample opportunities for differences and have made it difficult to understand for engineers and even to Indus Water Commissioners.

Some experts are of the view that the Indus Water Treaty carried out a surgery of the Indus Basin into two as eastern and western group of rivers. Though both countries are highly dependent on each other for cooperation and development of the basin, but the division of the basin has reduced the level of cooperation between the two countries.

Environmental issues like climate change have not been covered in the treaty. Pakistan, as lower riparian has apprehensions over the projects on the western rivers and considers them as the existential threat to her inhabitants, as stored water can flush out the land and property. Secondly, Pakistan is afraid that these projects will reduce the water flow in critical times, especially during the sowing seasons. On the other hand, India's concern is to improve its energy efficiencies and economy, for which it is endeavouring to utilise the full power potentialities. Its booming economy, waves of globalization, overwhelming urbanization push India to generate more and more electricity from hydropower projects on Himalayan Rivers. Its peak power demand in the year 2007-08 was 108,886 MW, while the peak power demand met was 90,793 MW; there was a shortage of 18,093 MW or 16.6 percent of peak demand. The projects on western rivers are a crucial part of India's plan to close that gap. The hydro power sector is also an attractive revenue earner for Himalayan states, which are underdeveloped in the industrial sector as compared to other states. Therefore, the exploitation of hydro power from Himalayan Rivers is the only source to boost their industrial sector. But in reply to Pakistan's apprehensions on western rivers, Indian position is that it is not violating the spirit of the treaty. Secondly, Pakistan's security fears are misconceived as India cannot flood Pakistan without flooding it first.

KASHMIRI CONCERNS OVER PROJECTS ON THE WESTERN RIVERS

Quite apart from Indian and Pakistani questions and apprehensions, the projects on western rivers in Indian administrated Kashmir need to focus on the human security values of the people of Jammu and Kashmir, because, some projects on western rivers are being constructed by the J&K Government to boost the state's economy and for the welfare of the people. But the treaty between India and Pakistan has inflicted heavy financial loss to Kashmiris, as in the case of Baglihar Project, which has estimated that the state of J&K has to incur the loss of Rs 265 Crore annually because of the treaty and the total losses are over Rs 3325 Crore on Chenab basin.

The common view in Kashmir is that Pakistan's opposition to the development of hydropower under the Baglihar project has sidelined hopes and aspirations of the Kashmiris. With the construction of Baglihar and Kishanganga hydroelectric power projects by India, the rights of Kashmiris on these projects have been brought to the center of the Indus water issue. In case of both these power projects, pressure from the people and polity of J&K state is an important factor to look at.

While India and Pakistan have cooperated over the Indus Basin since 1960, recent disagreements over projects on the western rivers have posed serious challenges to future development of the parties. Though the treaty has the potential to resolve technical issues but these issues are so politicized with the passage of time on security and economic grounds, resulting out of political liaisons between India, Pakistan and Jammu and Kashmir. Therefore, to resolve these issues, a triangle and deeper look is crucial to take into account future aspirations of all the parties.

WATER CONFLICT AND INDIA-PAKISTAN RELATIONS

As far as India and Pakistan are concerned, no two countries in the world have so much in common as these. Both countries have similar cultural roots, linguistic similarities and shared economic system. However, since independence they have continuously been in a state of undeclared war with uncompromised issues, especially over water. The idea of sharing water is historically constructed, emotionally stimulating, and politically divisive. Though water is technically not a core issue between the two countries, differences over the use of water of the rivers is a core issue. In recent years, utilization of water has become an issue that is gaining prominence in the bilateral relationship between India and Pakistan.

In 1960, both governments agreed to sign the Indus Water Treaty, but public reaction to the treaty was very different. People in Pakistan criticised the loss of three eastern rivers to India, although Pakistan received a huge amount of financial aid in lieu of this loss even though this loss imposed heavy financial and ecological penalties upon Pakistan. In 1964, opposition parties of the countries attacked on President Ayub Khan, and used the termed as "selling" the historical rights of the country over the common rivers. While in India, the public often criticised the loss of its three western rivers to Pakistan and the treaty makes it impossible for India to utilise the full power potentialities on three western rivers.

Media, academicians, and different groups of society and agricultural communities from both sides opposed the Indus Water Treaty. Even for opposition members of both the governments, the Indus Water Treaty is suspicious and unfair. The water experts from the both countries are also not happy with the treaty. This has eventually led to the politicisation of the water issue within both countries, and thereby, creating an immense pressure on respective governments.

It is not difficult to understand the changing tone of political relations between the two countries vis-à-vis water. It can be understood by revision of recent projects being executed by India on western rivers, which are severely criticised by Pakistan. The treaty has survived various external and internal threats which were related to the two countries political relationships, but recent years have marked strained relations vis-à-vis water and therefore the Indus Water Treaty has come under the strains, mainly due to construction of hydroelectric projects, including the Salal, Baglihar, Wullar Barrage, (Tulbul Navigation) the Kishanganga, the Nemo-Bazgo. Not all of them are sans disputes and are deemed as controversial projects.

On the other hand, Indian experts have expressed frustration over long delays in approval of these projects due to Pakistani objections, and about 27 projects on the western rivers have been questioned by Pakistan. Indian analysts and media are of the view that the provision of neutral experts should be the last option and not the recourse for each and every project that India proposes. The reference does cost time, money and efforts, in terms of delaying the projects, thereby increasing the cost of not only construction but also related expenditures in not making use of the hydro potential.

Moreover, Pakistan argued that India's line of action on the riparian issue hardly warrants a high degree of trust in good neighbourliness. In addition, the political mobilization on dam construction on the western rivers has stimulated anti- Indian sentiments among farmer associations, military consortium, politicians, and fundamentalist groups in Pakistan. From a security point of view, some strategic analysts in Pakistan are of the view that the Indian intentions are directed towards flooding Pakistan during tensions and that flood waters could destroy Pakistani defenses. Pakistan has also certain economic and defensive apprehension on the construction of projects, especially on Jhelum and Chenab River.

In 2008, after filing of the Baglihar project and subsequent reduction of the water flow in Pakistan, the project has drawn serious concerns and gained critical currency among the countries' political circles. With regard to Wullar Barrage, it has also incurred political and strategic voices from Pakistan, as it fears that with the construction of the Wullar Barrage in Indian administrated Kashmir (IAK), India could close the gate of Wullar Barrage during a warlike situation, enhancing the ability of Indian troops to enter Pakistan. The project is also frequently criticized in farming communities.

The difficulties in interpretations of the treaty can be attributed to political motives rather than to differences over technical and engineering aspects of water management. Some non-state actors, especially radical extremist groups from two countries have their vested interests in the complex issue of water sharing and the treaty. Some are of the view that if the gap between water availability and requirements widens, terrorist operations and recruitment in the region will increase.

Given the present political atmosphere viz-a-viz water, it seems that water has gained a critical value within the two countries and none of the parties are ready to compromise. It seems that the temperament of the political systems, interests of non- state actors and the regional political atmosphere determine the state of affairs of India-Pakistan conflict over water. Indo-Pak water relations can be well understood taking into consideration the statement of President Asif Ali Zardari in the Washington post. According to Asif Ali Zardari, "The water crisis in Pakistan is directly linked to relations with India. Its relations with India could prevent an environmental upheaval in South Asian region, but failure to do so could fuel the fires of discontent that may lead to extremism and terrorism".

The Indus water dispute is overtly linked with Jammu and Kashmir, (a disputed territory) where the major rivers of disputed water originate. It is quite vividly expressed by the US Assistant Secretary of State, George McGhee, in his letter to David Lilienthal, in 1951. " A settlement of the canal waters question would signify those basic reversals of policy by the governments of both India and Pakistan without which there can be no political rapprochement. Thus, the canal waters question is not only a functional problem, but also a political one linked to the Kashmir dispute".

In 1960, it was hoped that the resolution of water dispute would pave the way for resolving the Kashmir dispute. At the time of signing of the treaty, Jawaharlal Nehru the Indian Prime Minister, before coming to Pakistan expressed in the Indian parliament that he was ready to resolve any issue including Kashmir. Similar views and hopes were also expressed by Pakistani President Ayub Khan. Hitherto, three wars has been fought between India and Pakistan over Kashmir, but the dispute still remains unresolved and problematic. Until and unless the Kashmir issue is settled, both countries will not be able to develop good relations in the future. If the countries came up with an agreement to settle the Kashmir dispute, nothing will prevent them from building good relationships.

INDUS WATER TREATY: NEED FOR REVIEW

Disputes between India and Pakistan over the Indus River basin began with partition in 1947. Between 1947 and 1960 the two sides addressed their differences through a number of short term agreements but the dispute could not be settled through bilateral negotiations, and international mediation had to be sought. In 1960, after nine years of negotiations, the two sides signed the Indus Water Treaty (IWT).

Under the Treaty, all the waters of the Eastern Rivers - Sutlej, Beas, and Ravi - were allocated to India for unrestricted use, except during the transition period of 1 April 1960 to 31 March 1970, during which water had to be supplied to Pakistan so that Pakistan might construct replacement works (two storage dams, eight inter-river link canals and six barrages) for water that was being received earlier from the Eastern Rivers. India agreed to make a fixed contribution of 62 million towards the cost of the replacement works. Pakistan received unrestricted use of the Western Rivers - Indus, Jhelum, and Chenab - which India is "under obligation to let flow" and "shall not permit any interference with these waters," except for irrigating existing areas and to develop a further 701,000 acres of irrigation from these rivers subject to certain specific conditions. Specific provisions were made for regular exchange of river and canal data between the two countries.

NEEDS FOR MODIFICATIONS

Despite being a long lasting successful treaty there are some limitations within the IWT that require review. Michel T Klare opines that it does not allow for the joint development of the Indus basin; nor does it eliminate the grounds for conflict over water distribution between India and Pakistan since it is a plan for the separate development of the basin (Feyyaz). It is also unusual among international water-sharing agreements because allocation is based on tributary locations; water is neither allocated on a quantitative basis between the parties nor managed by an operating rule. It is specific about which nation uses which tributary, but it does not create mechanisms to address issues specified in the treaty per se, such as groundwater use, changes in flow due to climate change, changing domestic demand due to population increases or rainfall variability.

Daanish Mustafa (2010) observes that it, by performing an amputation surgery on the basin that was much the same as the political bifurcation of the subcontinent, made matters simple and allowed the two countries to pursue their nationalist agendas without much need for more sophisticated and involved cooperation in the water field. This lack of cooperative sharing of water has considerable negative consequences for the ecology and societies of the Indus basin.

Moreover environmental and ecological changes call for re-consideration of IWT. Projections of climate change on water resources have important implications for both water scarce and flood prone regions, as many indicate dry regions becoming drier and wet regions becoming wetter. Because of climate change, the Himalayan glaciers are melting at an alarming rate. For water resources, this means an increase in water initially due to flooding. Within the next 50 years, however, experts believe there will be a 30 to 40 percent drop in glacial melt because the glaciers will have receded. A strategy to create more storage capacity for water is the only option available.

In this regard the canal withdrawals in Indus Irrigation System, more or less stagnated in 1979 after construction of Tarbela Dam, have now declined to around 103 MAF, partly due to silting of the reservoirs. This aspect has not been considered at the political level or at least has not gained prominence while it demands a common water vision by India and Pakistan that will be based on realization of the importance of the shared rivers as being a natural resource that is integral to their survival.

Pollution control is another issue that needs consideration in the review of the IWT. Given the lack of pollution controls on industry and recent reports of hazardous industrial and chemical-rich water crossing the border into Pakistan it could be inferred that water quality is deteriorating in the Indus. There are no provisions in any treaty on water between Pakistan and India for the control of pollution. Through the review of IWT the issue of the pollution can also be addressed properly.

Pakistan's Federal Minister for Kashmir Affairs and Gilgit-Baltistan, Mian Manzoor Ahmad Wattoo, pointing towards another drawback of IWT, contended that the IWT was signed by a military dictator, General Ayub Khan. He observed "Since no consultations were held or a consensus evolved, the treaty has some inherent flaws and India has been misusing it at the cost of Pakistan's interests." Fresh review of the Treaty may be helpful in dissolving more differences and is, if it ever happens, likely to produce a consensus in modern times when democratic institutions are getting progress in both states of India and Pakistan.

Thus the IWT is a product of its time and could be fruitfully modified and renegotiated to bring it more in line with contemporary international watercourse law, the Helsinki rules, and emerging concerns with water quality, environmental sustainability, climate change, and principles of equitable sharing.

INDIAN PROJECTS

More problematic is the provision in IWT relating the use of the western rivers by India. The crux of IWT is that India was given full control of Eastern rivers and Pakistan was given full control of western rivers. But the provision of usage of western rivers to India for non irrigative use of western rivers has created problems afterwards. India by virtue of the upper riparian could always use and obstruct the waters of Indus Basin. IWT was signed to protect the interests of Pakistan and not of India. Pakistan gave off the right of 3 eastern rivers for the sake of complete and unhindered use of western rivers. India got the benefit of the three eastern rivers in full but Pakistan's usage of the waters of three western rivers is yet on stake because India has started work on many projects on the cost of Pakistani concerns.

The challenge to the treaty came regarding the construction of the Wullar Barrage, as it is called by Pakistan, or Tulbul

Navigation Project as termed by India. There is controversy on the explanations of the specific provisions of the IWT. The 330 MW hydroelectric Kishanganaga project that is located about 160 kilometers upstream of Muzaffarabad and involves diversion of Kishanganga or Neelum River to a tributary, Bunar Madumati Nullah of the River Jhelum through a 22-kilomtre tunnel, is another controversial water issue between the two countries which could not have been resolved under IWT.

Located on the River Chenab in Doda district, the Baglihar hydropower project is one of the nine major hydroelectric projects identified by India on the Chenab. Pakistan protested over the design of the dam in 1992 and demanded a halt to its construction.. Taking cue from the Bagliahr verdict of the Neutral Expert that reinterpreted the Treaty in the light of "new technical norms and new standards," "state of the art" and "best and latest practices in the field of construction and operation," the risks of increased floods associated with "climate change," it appears that the Treaty has to accommodate the new realities in the Indus basin, not only in terms of technical norms but also growing pressures on the health and viability of the Indus basin rivers.

The invocation of neutral expert clause has revealed another drawback in the IWT and has damaged an impression that satisfied the doubts of many Pakistanis that the World Bank was the guarantor of the IWT. It so happened that when Pakistan approached the World Bank for mediation it clearly noted that it was "not a guarantor of the treaty," (Haq, 4) The note of World Bank, though correct legally, has raised dissatisfaction in some circles of Pakistan who always remains suspicious for Indian deception and trust only on third party that may be a guarantor in the compromises of both countries.

During 2006 to 2011 Pakistan's concerns over another controversial project Nimoo Bazgo near village Alchi in the district Leh in Indian held Kashmir could not be highlighted due to alleged negligence of its Indus Water Commissioner Jamaat Ali Shah against whom a probe on his alleged secret compliance with India has started in Pakistan. However, during a recent inspection, the Pakistani team learnt that more than 80 per cent of the work on the dam had been completed and the expected date of its inauguration is July 2012.

Notwithstanding Indian concerns over delay in the execution of the projects, Pakistan's concerns for the projects are too much serious. Though India as per the IWT is allowed to generate power from the waters of these rivers yet it did stop Chenab river flow on various occasions notable being from August 19 to September 5 wherein Pakistan was deprived of 1.2 million cusecs of water at one time alone. Moreover through IWT Pakistan does not find immediate relief. She, through a lengthy process defined in IWT, has only option just to deliver complain to India or put the case in international tribunals that definitely requires huge amount of time and money. During the whole process, India loses nothing and Pakistan gradually gets loss. India often continues to start new projects day by day and Pakistan continues to complain over them. India has planned to make 62 more dams. Therefore, there is dire need to alter the clause that allows India to use the waters of western rivers.

Whenever India takes decision to construct a dam or reservoir and the matter enters the framework of the treaty, which only provides technical specifications for building such a dam or reservoir, Islamabad invokes the jurisdiction of a neutral expert or arbitration court. During the time the case takes, the construction is completed and Pakistan in that sense 'loses' the cases. Some observers point out that Pakistan is feeling alienated from the IWT after repeated failures to get redress of its grievances and, hence, would like to replace it with a new treaty. But it is not easy to agree on a new pact. A pragmatic approach is required to amend and update the treaty to remove the lacuna it suffers from.

It looks altogether unjust that India can use all of the rivers without restrictions but Pakistan is bound to use only western rivers even with apprehension of Indian obstruction. The question remains unsolved what to do of the projects which India has already installed. Second issue may be this why the waters of western rivers should not be used before entering into Pakistan. For the sake of prosperity to both nations joint projects can be initiated on the western rivers and benefits may be shared by both nations. Already initiated projects can also be shared on these grounds. But it is necessary that the clauses of the IWT must be altered in order to give Pakistan unrestricted control of the western rivers and it will be a great benefit to energy starved nation of Pakistan.

An array of upcoming Indian projects has unfolded many challenges to the functioning of the Permanent Indus Water Commission. The institution is unable to cope with the issues which were originally not within its purview as they did not exist at that time. All above mentioned controversial projects highlight the need of mediation as well as such new mechanism and consensus under which the issues which have risen during implementation of IWT can be resolved. For this an overall review and new negotiations on the water issue are the call of the hour.

There is no provision in IWT which allows India to construct a certain number of dams. Nor is there one that prohibits India from making dams beyond a certain number. Notwithstanding prescribing restrictions on the features and operations of Indian projects on the western rivers the Treaty does not lay down any limits on the total number of projects that can be built, the height of the dams, the total power-generation capacity, etc. Ramaswamy R. Iyer (2012) thinks that the point about 'cumulative impact' needs to be considered. He however proposes a joint study by experts of both countries for this purpose.

MODIFICATIONS' POTENTIAL BENEFITS TO INDIA

India has developed disputes with three of its neighbours i.e. Pakistan, Bangladesh and Nepal. She is accused for infringing on their water rights by usurping their resources with potential to ultimately drain their respective resources during hostilities through construction of various projects on rivers whose water is flowing downstream. (Ahmad) Siddharth Varadarajan of The Hindu says: "New Delhi needs to factor in a new reality: More than Kashmir, it is the accusation that India is stealing water that is rapidly becoming the 'core issue' in the Pakistani establishment's narrative about bilateral problems."

India in pursuit of the position of regional power and on that ground desires to get the status of permanent member in the UN Security Council. In order to get international support for her case India needs an image of a cooperative country in the region. The resolution of water issues with the neighbouring states will go a long way in this regard. In past IWT has won good repute for her and for Pakistan as issue resolving countries. The review of IWT will lessen the degree of conflict in South Asia, remove the doubts of South Asian countries against India and also enhance Indian image all over the world.

India is also not satisfied with the present state of affairs and it has to bear serious economic losses because of the delays in the mechanism of IWT which have arisen due to disputes which started to arise during last decade. Indian professionals have expressed frustrations over long delays in approval of projects due to Pakistani objections. India argues that the IWT limits its ability to exploit the Indus's hydroelectric potential, representing an opportunity cost.

The waters of the Indus river system have a direct impact on the state of Jammu and Kashmir and are therefore crucial to its economic prospects. The Kashmir Valley, which is the main source of the dispute between India and Pakistan, has been affected by the IWT. In February 1951 Prime Minister Nehru invited David E. Lilienthal, virtual founder of IWT, in order to resolve the water issue since the core of the Kashmir problem stemmed from a "struggle over rivers, rivers with their headwaters in the Kashmir, flowing through Pakistan."

That is why even today the most important internal issue that strains the IWT is the view of the people in Jammu and Kashmir who see the Treaty as exploiting their rights by both India and Pakistan and they call for its annulment as an economic liability. People of the northern areas in Pakistan are also opposed to dam projects in Pakistan like the Mangla dam. Likewise Indian government is faced with the criticism over the IWT from the Kashmiris in Indian held Kashmir, who show concern over division of waters. Motions were moved in the state assembly on three different occasions by the legislators asking the Indian government to review the IWT and pay compensation to the state. (Feyyaz) According to Kashmiri Separatists, IWT has deprived state of Jammu and Kashmir to use its own water resources and became one of the reasons for the alienation of people and has severely affected the economic development in the state.

The revision of IWT and solution of water disputes can lead to the dissolution of the most important of the conflicts in the region. New ponderings on the water issue may include the concerns of the Kashmiri people an all dimensions of the water issue may be taken into consideration. This can provide India as well as Pakistan a fair chance towards longstanding solution of the Kashmir issue.

Indian government is not altogether opposed to the negotiations over the IWT. It is ready to change the IWT though under the mechanisms of the Treaty. Indian External Affairs Minister S. M. Krishna told Indian Parliament, that the Indian government "is in full compliance with the Treaty. All issues regarding implementation of the Treaty should be resolved through the existing mechanisms under the IWT" It means that India feels the need of some progress in the IWT in the wake of new realities which have appeared during last decades.

Bibliography

Akhtar, S.: *Emerging Challenges to Indus Waters Treaty: Issues of Compliance and Transboundary Impacts of Indian hydroprojects On the Western Rivers.* Institute of Regional Studies, Islamabad, Pakistan, 2010.

Ali, S. H.: *Water Politics in South Asia: Technocratic Cooperation and Lasting Security in the Indus Basin and Beyond.* Journal of International Affairs, 2008.

Allouche, J.: *Water Nationalism: An Explanation of the Past and Present Conflicts in Central Asia, the Middle East and Indian Subcontinent?* University of Geneve, 2005.

Asaithambi S. : *Economics of Ground Water Management in India,* Abhijeet, Delhi, 2008.

Ashok Jaitly: *Troubled Waters: Climate Change, Hydropolitics, and Transboundary Resources.* Stimson Centre, Washington, DC, 2009.

Asit K. Biswas and Cecilia Tortajada: *Appraising Sustainable Development: Water Management and Environmental Challenges,* Oxford University Press, Delhi, 2005.

Bagis, Ali Ihsan: *Water as an Element of Cooperation and Development in the Middle East,* Ankara, Ayna Publications, 1994.

Bhakar S.R. : *Ground Water Hydrology : Theory and Practice,* Agrotech, Delhi, 2009.

Bhave, P.R. and R. Gupta: *Analysis of Water Distribution Networks,* Narosa, Delhi, 2011.

Biswas Asit K. : *Integrated Water Resources Management in South and South-East Asia,,* Oxford University Press, Delhi, 2001.

Charles E. Faupel: *Water Treaty and Civil Rights in Sumter County,* Colorado, Westview Press, 1992.

Erik Nissen-Peterson : *Rainwater Catchment Systems,* UK: Intermediate Technology Publications, 1999.

Ferentinos L.: *Proceeding of the Sustainable Taro Culture for the Pacific Conference*, Honolulu, HITAHR, 1993.

Gideon Fishelson: *Water and Peace: Water Resources and the Arab-Israeli Peace Process*, Westport, CT, Praeger, 1993.

Gleick, Peter H. : *Water "Crisis: A Guide to the World's Fresh Water Resources"*, New York: Oxford University Press, 1933.

Gupta K.R. : *Water Crisis in India*, Atlantic Pub, Delhi, 2008.

Gurjar, Ram Kumar : *Geography of Water Resources*, Rawat, Delhi, 2008.

Kruvant, W.J.: *People, Energy, and Pollution*, Cambridge, Ballinger Publishing, 1975.

Mahajan Gautam : *Evaluation and Development of Ground Water*, APH, Delhi, 2008.

Mishra Archana : *Water Harvesting : Ecological and Economic Appraisal*, Authors Press, Delhi, 2006.

Postel, Sandra : *Last Oasis: Facing Water Scarcity*, World Water Institute, New York, 1992.

Ranjan, A.: *Water Conflicts between India and Pakistan*. Daily Times, Pakistan, 2010.

Rao K. Nageswara : *Water Resources Management : Realities and Challenges*, New Century Publication, Delhi, 2006.

Sindhu, Abid Latif: *The Pakistan-India Water War*. Terminal X, Pakistan Observer. 2008.

Swain, A.: *Managing water conflict: Asia, Africa and the Middle East*. London and New York: Routledge, 2004.

Vallette, J.: *The International Trade in Wastes: A Greenpeace Inventory*, Washington, Greenpeace, 1989.

Index

❑❑❑